Developing an ISO 13485–Certified Quality Management System

Developing an ISO 13485–Certified Quality Management System

An Implementation Guide for the Medical-Device Industry

Ilkka Juuso

Routledge
Taylor & Francis Group

A PRODUCTIVITY PRESS BOOK

First published 2022
by Routledge
605 Third Avenue, New York, NY 10158

and by Routledge
2 Park Square, Milton Park, Abingdon, Oxon, OX14 4RN

Routledge is an imprint of the Taylor & Francis Group, an informa business

Library of Congress Cataloging-in-Publication Data
A catalog record for this book has been requested

ISBN: 978-1-032-06574-8 (hbk)
ISBN: 978-1-032-06573-1 (pbk)
ISBN: 978-1-003-20286-8 (ebk)

DOI: 10.4324/9781003202868

Typeset in Garamond
by Apex CoVantage, LLC

Dedicated to the stellar team working with me on
Quality Management every day

Contents

Acknowledgments

There are 1,500-plus people I could thank for the impetus to write this book. That is the number of people that build my LinkedIn feed every day. Their likes, as well as my own, inform how the algorithm constructs my feed of industry news, product releases, regulatory announcements, and the occasional quiz in between. They all deserve my thanks as I have come to value this daily feed as one of the most incredible information superhighways in existence. This social network of professionals is a fantastically powerful vigilance system that helps comb through the many sources, bubbles up relevant news in a matter of minutes, and points in the right direction for more information on almost any given topic. Some of you are also involved in the standardization committees and industry forums I frequent, and that interaction, too, is a significant part of the fabric that has informed this book.

Next, I want to thank the people who directly made this book possible by pushing the planets into alignment for its birth. First and foremost, this means Tim Damgaard Christensen, who not only rocks as the tour manager of the transatlantic MedTech Bridge program with its Nordic cohort of medtech companies but also happened to ask me for the talk on my experiences with QMS that got this show on the road. In the same vein, I also want to extend my heartfelt thanks to my publisher, Michael Sinocchi, at Taylor & Francis who made this book project enjoyably smooth despite the COVID-19 pandemic and the approximately 6,000 kilometers (4,000 miles) of the Atlantic between Oulu, Finland, and New York City.

I would be severely remiss without thanking Dr. Nina Vartiainen and the rest of the team of quality and regulatory experts at Kasve Ltd., with whom my team and I started work on our QMS in the spring of 2018 and with whom I later joined as an external advisor in the spring of 2021. It has been a fantastic journey, and I am delighted to continue improving quality management with you all. At the same time, I want to thank our notified body,

SGS Fimko, who have never behaved as anything except the courteous professionals and genuine quality enthusiasts they are. From all my encounters with all the big notified bodies in Europe—and a few certification bodies, too—I am happy to say that none of these gatekeepers, or lighthouse custodians, is as scary or as hard to talk to as you may fear and as my apprehensions perhaps once pointed to.

I want to express my deep gratitude to Valtteri Suorsa, who, in addition to Tim and Nina, provided thoughtful remarks on my unfinished manuscript for this book. All these comments made the discussion here flow more naturally and perhaps take a few more points of view into consideration. I also want to thank Professor Anthony Johnson and Professor William A. Kretzschmar for their words of encouragement at various stages during this book project. Any mistakes remaining in the text are naturally my own.

My final thanks must and, by right, ought to go to my colleagues at Cerenion Ltd., who dove into developing the smartest medtech startup out there and saw ISO 13485, IEC 62304, and both the European and the US regulations as worthwhile challenges to tackle. Most of all, I want to thank Jussi Ala-Kurikka, who—age not withstanding—as our veteran of medical software development, was part of the team from even before there really was a team. Dr. Eero Väyrynen, too, played an inestimable part in this work and continues to act as a welcome sounding board to my thinking. My two other esteemed cofounders, Dr. Jukka Kortelainen and Dr. Timo Koskela, have also had a steady hand in shaping our company and quality management within it. The rest of our team at the company also all deserve thanks here. Their willingness to adapt and their smart suggestions on adopting the QMS continue to be one of the biggest joys in my work—and the one thing I have no qualms bragging over. Over this joint venture, we have all learned a great deal and found our victories on the path to improving brain monitoring of hospitalized patients.

I am grateful to you all. I hope you all take some measure of pleasure from this book. The pursuit of perfection in quality is certainly a big enough goal for all contributions, big and small. This book is my small contribution to achieving this goal.

All the illustrations are created by author.

About the Author

Dr. Ilkka Juuso, DSc, has a doctorate in technology from the University of Oulu, Finland, and 20-plus years of experience working on multidisciplinary R&D projects in both the industry and academia. He is one of the founders of the medical device startup Cerenion Ltd. and its chief operations officer, quality manager, and longtime board member. He is also a senior advisor with the medical device quality consultancy Kasve Oy, a postdoctoral researcher with the University of Oulu, and one of the founders of MetaVisual Ltd.

Ilkka's main interests today are international regulatory affairs (including EU MDD/MDR and US FDA), ISO 13485 quality management, and medical-grade software development. Marketing and business strategy are also always close to his heart.

At Cerenion, Ilkka has led the development of an ISO 13485–, ISO 14971–, and IEC 62304–compliant quality management system (QMS) from the ground up; its subsequent day-to-day operation; and its certification by a notified body. He has also had a key role in the development and launch of a CE-marked Class IIb medical device under the Medical Device Directive (93/42/EEC) of the European Union using that QMS.

Ilkka has a deep involvement in quality and regulatory affairs, including participation in international standardization activities concerning, for example, quality management, healthcare software, and both life cycle and agile methods in software development. He is a member of several standardization committees under the International Organization for Standardization (ISO) and its national organizations in Finland.

Figures and Tables

Figures

Tables

Chapter 1

About This Book

Four years ago, I met with a team of quality consultants engaged to help us build the quality management system for our young medical device startup from scratch. I had been deeply involved in the tendering process and had, for the previous three years, among other tasks, been looking into quality management with an increasingly attentive eye as our startup had been nearing the day it would spin off from under the wing of the university where it had been born.

On this day, I was seated at the table with three quality consultants, who had traveled in that morning, and our whole team from the company. We had just, a month or two earlier, announced that our startup had secured a 500,000-euro seed investment from two venture capital firms, so we now had the funds to really roll up our sleeves and get to work doing the things we had spent the previous year pitching to investors. Job number one, although it at times seemed there were more than one of those, was the development of a quality management system, or QMS, for short, so that we could then build a medical device product under that QMS and ship it to healthcare customers worldwide.

At the meeting, I was looking forward to a relaxed discussion on how the quality consultants saw the process going forward and figuring out for myself what supporting role I could play in the process. But things were to unfold differently. No sooner had we sat down at the table than I heard our CEO say to me, "I guess you will handle the development of the QMS from here on out, right?" I had not expected this at all, I definitely had not planned for it, but since all voiced opinions seemed to confer, I felt myself nod, and that was it. All of a sudden, I was to become our quality manager, and the meeting took on a new meaning for me.

DOI: 10.4324/9781003202868-1

This book tells the story of the following months that led to the launch of our QMS some seven months later and its audit and certification by a big notified body long thereafter. More on that "long thereafter" a little bit later.

The idea for this book came out of countless encounters with other start-ups, industry giants, quality consultants, standardization experts, notified bodies, and even representatives of the European Commission and their HAS harmonization consultants, who I thought for sure were unicorns. Since the very beginning of the process, I had wanted to get as many points of view from all the connected parties as possible in order to best shape our QMS. The words of the old Tom Brokaw ad echoed in the back of my mind as I was doing this: "In order to form an opinion you need information. To form a balanced opinion, you need all the information". The trick, I thought, would be to meet all the requirements for a QMS but do so as leanly as possible. Otherwise, the weight of the system would pull us down and keep us from achieving what we wanted—to push the science and improve patient outcomes. All during the process, I had been testing out my ideas on others and sharing my ideas on best practice when I could. Since finishing work on writing up my doctoral thesis, toward the end of the first two years of the same four-year period, I had also been itching for a new book project. The dots of a QMS and a book project connected for me when I was recently asked to prepare a presentation on my experiences for a Danish medtech incubator. In going through my notes and preparing that short intro, I started to think that there might be wider interest for this in book form, especially for something based on current information and real-world experiences, both of which I have attempted to fuse into the discussion here.

This book is not intended as a substitute for reading the ISO 13485 standard, but it will make the process of acquainting yourself with the standard easier and, hopefully, also save you from a number of misunderstandings and extra hurdles in implementing the standard. I have included checklists and tips where I thought they would be helpful and infused real experiences from both my own QMS development process and those relayed to me by my peers throughout the book. I hope all this will be useful to you as you develop your QMS, either from scratch or through an iterative process of improvement from where you are now.

It took us a little over seven months to build our QMS from scratch while also developing our startup company, our R&D pipeline, and our first medical device product at the same time. It then took us 14 months to pass our multisite audits and a further 7 months to finish product documentation and get the certificate in the middle of the COVID-19 pandemic and the uncertainty surrounding the MDR transition in Europe. It was an extraordinary experience from start to finish, and yet this, too, is just the start of the next phase for us. In this process, we got to learn a lot, innovate, and experiment with a great number of new ideas. The lessons we learned were all positive, but some more so than others. This book is written to relay some of those lessons, concentrating on the ones I feel might help you the most on your path to developing, improving, and working with your QMS.

The international ISO 13485 standard this book addresses has become a cornerstone of medical device business the world over. In Europe, the standard will now, in effect, be required of all classes of medical devices; and except for Class I devices, the quality management systems are also required to be certified according to the standard. In the US, the FDA is working on aligning its Quality System Regulation (QSR) with the standard; and the international Medical Device Single Audit Program (MDSAP), in which the FDA is also very active, already makes it possible to use the standard in auditing quality management systems for the US market. The standard already has an integral role in quality management for medical device manufacturers, but recent steps, including the transition to the MDR regulation in Europe, mean that the standard is still new to many actors, many of whom haven't yet had to work with the standard. Also, the recent incremental steps taken toward enabling artificial intelligence in medical devices, and other emerging technologies, look set to heighten the role of the standard as a gatekeeper solution. The rest of the world, too, appears to have a keen eye on the standard.

In other words, the ISO 13485 standard has no competition in medical devices, it is stable itself, there is great interest in it worldwide, and the audience for the standard is rapidly expanding. This book is written to serve all these audiences, in making sense and making the most out of the standard.

This book is intended to do the following:

■ **Be the guerrilla guide to ISO 13485 quality management**
    The book reveals the meanings and intentions of the standard to help you design a QMS that meets the requirements but, crucially, will also give you the tools you need to fashion a lean enough QMS so that you will actually like running it every day.

■ **Provide a thought-out workflow for the person creating their first QMS**
    This book is based on a tried and tested approach to developing and successfully certifying a QMS. The book walks you through the

necessary steps of creating a full QMS by first starting with things you know and then moving to writing your quality manual and standard operating procedures, providing you with insight and information all along the way. Unlike other books, the discussion here is built around tasks to accomplish and not the complex clause numbers of the standard.

■ **Teach you the necessary vocabulary to converse with your quality consultants and regulatory authorities**

This book attempts to distill a wealth of information to its core and give you a real jump start to understanding QMS and building your own QMS. This book is not intended to gloss over the benefit you will get from talking with a quality professional face-to-face about your organization's particular circumstances and tailoring a QMS to meet your needs. This book will, however, give you the necessary vocabulary and the essential concepts you will need to make that dialogue effective.

■ **Provide insight and real-world experience on developing and maintaining a QMS that even experts will appreciate**

This book is based on a real-world project set out to develop the best and the leanest possible QMS for a new medical device startup. The project is viewed through the lens of 20-plus years of experience in both the industry and academia, leading to to-the-point analysis and advice that has resonated well among industry peers and regulatory authorities.

■ **Provide the "API" for QMS to grasp QMS from afar**

The insights in the discussion let employees and managers alike get a handle on QMS and why it is affecting their work, even if they themselves are not QA/RA professionals.

■ **Be the ideal entry point for the new audiences needing to grapple with ISO 13485**

The audience for ISO 13485 is far greater than just the current QA/RA professionals of existing medical device companies. New employees will benefit from this guide, but so, too, will new startups and the countless organizations, from distributors to authorized representatives who have not been faced with the standard until now.

My ultimate intention for this book is that it contributes to the discussion of what QMS is and what it should be, and that it opens a dialogue between you and me on these matters. If reading this book provokes feedback in the form of comments or questions, I would sincerely like to hear from you. Networking and exchanging of ideas, both learning and teaching at the same time, have, for me, been the best part of my work over the past seven-plus years in medical devices and their quality management. I hope this book is just the next phase of this exchange. But most of all, I will admit, I hope you will find this book down-to-earth, easy-to-read, and blisteringly insightful.

Yours sincerely,
Dr. Ilkka Juuso, DSc

Chapter 2

Introduction

So you want to build up quality management from scratch or you want to fig-ure out how you could improve or work with an existing QMS? You may have read the ISO 13485 standard, or you may have been reluctant to jump into the standard yourself. This book will hopefully ease you into building or refin-ing your QMS and lower the bar to browse the standard when you need to.

If you are not the one tasked with the hands-on development of your organization's QMS but are looking to understand it, perhaps as your organi-zation's management representative or an employee expected to work with it at some point, this book will provide you with practical insights into devel-oping, running, and working with a QMS. For the management, this book will act as the API for QMS that provides a practical handle on the work and allows you to understand why something is done or should be done in a certain way. For the employee expected to work with QMS, this book will place your work within the larger quality framework and give you perspec-tive on why the thing you are asked to do actually matters a great deal.

This book is based on my personal experience from developing, running, and certifying an ISO 13485:2016 Quality Management System for my young medical device startup. I am one of the founders of the company and the one tasked with figuring out our QMS as our quality manager. I am also the chief operations officer and a longtime board member of our company, so I have had the privilege of seeing all our operations mature and finding out how quality management can fit in on several levels of the organization. I have not done this alone. In addition to a great Quality Management Team and our generally stellar staff at the startup, I have also had quality con-sultants available for consultation on those occasions I have wanted some

DOI: 10.4324/9781003202868-2

expert feedback. On top of this, I have had the fantastic network of peers I have been lucky enough to build over the years.

One more thing I should mention before I get into timelines is that our startup life began as a commercialization project at the University of Oulu, Finland. We had a certain innovation coming out of our research at the university, and with the aid of a two-year grant from Business Finland, we started to test the waters for building a business around it. Over the two years, we went about formulating our concept and business model, oftentimes by talking with potential users, customers, distributors, and funders. Our aim was to secure funding for our company once we spun off from under the university and to have the best possible plan to execute when we did get funding. Toward the end of the two-year grant, we had a clear idea of what our product should be and we even had a working demonstration of the product. Once we had secured our seed investment round, it was time to run with our plan. The plan called for us to build an ISO 13485–certified QMS with a standards-based R&D process, develop our first medical device according to the QMS, and launch a CE-marked medical device in Europe. It was clear that we needed the QMS in place before we could use it to develop our product, but due to real-world constraints, we needed to work on both at the same. Thus, our QMS development was tied to developing our standards-based R&D process, and our QMS certification to the certification of our product. This was not quite a chicken-and-egg problem, but we were definitely trying to forge the frying pan at the same time as cooking an omelet. If we were successful, we would have a process that perfectly matched our needs and was tuned to our way of doing R&D. But if we were unsuccessful, we could have a royal mess on our hands with so many variables to fix in an already partially operational process that it might be easier to just start over. As it turned out, we were successful. The joint development of the QMS and product did have an effect on the overall QMS certification schedule, and it did cause a delay with the QMS certification compared to what it could have been when it was the only goal, but since the end goal was to develop and release a CE-marked product through a certified process, the delay was immaterial.

The work on building our QMS began in late February of 2018, with a first meeting with the quality consultants we hired to help us in building our QMS. The spring of 2018 was an intensive period of going through one aspect of QMS after the other, usually in two-week sprints more or less according to the schedule suggested by the consultants. Seven months after starting work, we were ready to launch our QMS in October of 2018, and our first-ever internal audit was arranged a month later. The following spring, we had secured quotes from a number of notified bodies and certification bodies, and after having selected our notified body, we had our first site inspection in the late spring of 2019. After this, it took us a further eight months to achieve a status where we were ready for the second and final certification audit at our second site in December 2019. At the beginning of 2020, the worldwide COVID-19 pandemic hit and we still had some product documents in progress which we needed to finish to obtain the certificate. We received the official ISO 13485 certificate after months of delays caused by the pandemic at the end of June 2020 and the EC conformity assessment needed for the CE mark at the beginning of November 2020. It thus took us 7 months to have a launch-ready QMS, 22 months to have our multisite audits done, and approximately 28 months to get the QMS certified. This was slow but fast enough considering we also had a company to build and a product to develop at the same time— and a global pandemic to contend with too.

If you are looking to get your certified QMS faster, that, too, is doable. The fact that we had two sites and simultaneous product development in Class IIb were major factors in slowing our progress with just the QMS. Using a certification provider other than a notified body would have also greatly sped things up, as the notified bodies in Europe were involved in the massive shift from the EU's Medical Device Directives to the Medical Device Regulation and a barrage of urgent issues surrounding the COVID-19 pandemic. The choice to go with a notified body was a conscious decision, one made primarily in the interest of removing differences of opinion between the operators we would be relying on, and it remains a decision with which we are very happy today.

The remainder of this book is set up so that one section leads to the next in a logical progression; after which, you will have a complete QMS up and running or, if you are not going to be developing a QMS yourself, a comprehensive view of what a QMS is and what it does. The next section, Section 3, introduces you to the top 25 lessons I have learned from our development project. This section is, to me, the heart of the book; reading it will hopefully give you both insight and new ideas. Section 4 then sets you up with an overview of ISO 13485 quality management and all the essential pieces of that puzzle. Section 5 takes a practical approach to writing your quality manual and, in a departure from other guides written on the standard, restructures all the key information by topics where you need it, instead of the disparate clauses that each topic may be discussed in the standard. Similarly, Sections 6 through 19 will go through the base set of standard operating procedures (SOPs) you will need to have in place for a QMS that covers the standard. Sections 20 and 21 round out the discussion of the documents you will want in your QMS by introducing forms and templates, and meeting agendas and minutes, respectively. Section 22 addresses the validation of your QMS software to have you ready for Section 23, where you will launch your QMS at the point you are comfortable saying you have version 1.0 ready. Section 24 then looks at the important topic of personnel training, and Section 25 addresses the document review cycle. Section 26 introduces the various types of audits you will come across in running your QMS, and Section 27 is dedicated to the critical topic of management reviews. Finally, Section 28 addresses certification, Section 29 the day-to-day after certification, and Sections 30 and 31 provide a few last tips for running your QMS and conclusions from this book. So let's jump in.

Chapter 3

What to Know Before Getting Started

Looking back at the development of our QMS, there is a good number of lessons that we learned quickly or wished we had known from the start. This section will share these fundamental lessons to give you a practical handle on what QMS is and, hopefully, inform the QMS you will want to develop.

In this section, I present the lessons I have valued the most and the ones that seem to have resonated the best with the countless others I have discussed QMS development with over the past years. A good number of these lessons have also saved my company from getting unnecessary nonconformities in various audits. I hope the lessons will provide you with some insight over the process that will unfold over the coming sections of this book and, hopefully, allow you to get a better grip on the QMS development or improvement process you are perhaps embarking on.

I have organized the following lessons in a more or less chronological order, from how to plan the development process to what to do after the development phase is complete. Many of the lessons will be elaborated on in the coming sections of this book, but the overview here will help in setting you on the right course and in a good state of mind for what is to come. Section 30 at the end of this book will present a few more lessons to know once you are up and running.

For the reader looking to build their own QMS, this section will lay a solid foundation for the work to come and give the right mindset to start thinking about the many choices needing to be made in the following sections of this book.

DOI: 10.4324/9781003202868-3

For the reader in management, this section also spells out the top-level API for QMS; in other words, the characteristic properties and the practical handles of developing and running a QMS. To dive to the next level, next, I recommend reading the "What Is Expected" subsections under the "Writing the Quality Manual", "Writing the Standard Operating Procedures", "Audits", and "Management Review" sections.

For the reader looking to find out how their own work within some area under the QMS is affected by the wider context, this section will offer some insights on the principles that the whole operates on. I would also recommend that you take a look at the process-specific section relevant to you (Sections 7 through 18).

And for the casual reader, I hope this section provides an entertaining overview of what this thing called "quality management" means in the context of medical devices, and what to do and what not to do in quality management.

3.1 It's Not One-Size-Fits-All

The very first thing to understand is that a QMS is not something you just buy to tick a box. Apparently, you could buy a QMS from Amazon for 500 euros, but even if that wasn't suspect, would it work for you? What works for a manufacturer of a cotton swab will not be the right choice for a manufacturer of an AI-based imaging product, as Figure 3.1 illustrates. The QMS you want to set up is not one thing you can buy, it's the way of life you want to build for your organization.

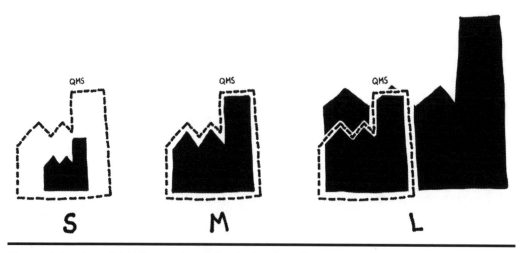

Figure 3.1   One QMS is not the right choice for all manufacturers.

ISO 13485 is a standard—you could even argue that it is *the* standard—for quality management in the context of medical devices. It is a standard, but it does not mean that quality management in medical device companies unfolds in any strictly uniform way.

In the companies I have talked with, I have seen countless approaches to quality management, ranging from truly paper-based graveyards of documents and binders to Dropbox to expensive digital document management systems. For a startup investing in a 50,000-euro (or about that in dollars) document management system is a tough proposition with an uncertain outcome. For a large medical device company, paper-based records may be a way of life at least in terms of some records, particularly legacy records—and those may even be stored off-site in a storage facility. At a recent event I took part in, the FDA representative was asked how long it could take for a company to retrieve a record the auditor asks for during a live audit. The answer was a few days in some cases. A small startup could retrieve the same document in a matter of seconds using an electronic system. This is a good example of the breadth of different approaches to QMS. It is also hopefully a good argument for not feeling like you need to emulate the big guys to succeed, if you are a startup. You shouldn't—you should learn from them but make your own choices as fits you best.

The previous example only talked of the system where documents are archived. In addition to where documents are stored, there is also the question of how documents are archived. The approval chain from writing to reviewing to issuing often involves the same number of steps, namely, those three; but the number of people involved at each step can differ greatly. Two signatures may suffice for many documents, but for some others, the dotted lines may include dozens of signatories. In the example of the 500-euro QMS from Amazon that apparently involved a good 30 or so different roles for people in the company, it could have been fine for a large company, but for a startup of only a handful of people, it was less than believable.

The previous figure made the point that a one-size-fits-all QMS is not realistic. A small manufacturer with a limited scope of operations does not need the same QMS as a large manufacturer with diverse operations. The average QMS, if there is such a thing, would only fit an average manufacturer: the QMS would introduce unnecessary overhead for a small manufacturer and be insufficient for a large manufacturer.

The size of the manufacturer and the geographical dispersion of its operations matter, but the true differentiator between organizations is not necessarily size but the scope and type of operations. Thus, the situation of

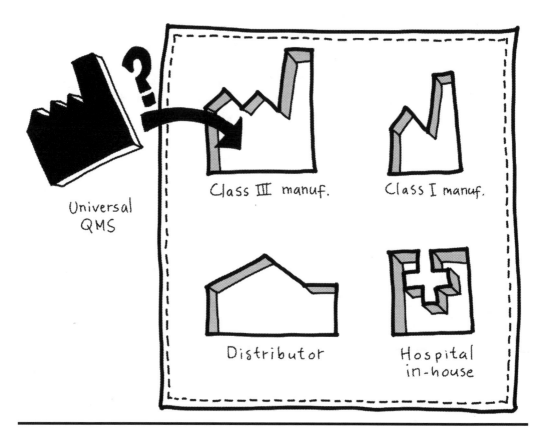

Figure 3.2   The type and scope of activities also affect what the QMS needs to be.

fitting a universal QMS to any given organization becomes more like trying to fit a round peg through a square hole, only much more complex as illustrated in Figure 3.2.

To further complicate the prospect of a universal QMS, the FDA and the European notified bodies have slightly different expectations of what a QMS is. The ISO 13485 standard looks set to become a universal standard, and the FDA has been hard at work on aligning its Quality System Regulation with the standard or at least showing how QSR and QMS differ. The medical device world appears largely happy with the ISO 13485 standard and how it could be applied globally. The standard is even a key component in the Medical Device Single Audit Program (MDSAP), but this does not mean that geographic and regulatory differences would not exist. Ultimately, the products and type of business the organization itself does will dictate what its QMS needs to achieve, and the processes it wants to use will inform how that QMS should be set up.

A QMS may be standardized, but it is not, by any stretch of the imagination, box-standard. Neither is it static, as the next lesson will illustrate.

3.2 It's Not a Turnkey Service

Unless you want to outsource your quality manager and quality manage-ment, in general, for the long term, don't think that you should outsource the development of your QMS. Consultants will help you, but they should not be the drivers. Some consultants may advertise a turnkey project to set up your QMS, but realize that it will not be—it should not be—an outsourced project where you walk to a ready-made meal (see Figure 3.3). After all, do you want to go to a restaurant, sit down for a meal, and only then discover you are allergic to it all? And it's worse than that: you will have to have the same meal every day for the next N years.

Right off the bat, let me confess that we were willing to accept a turn-key offer from the consultants we talked to at the start. We did so knowing full well that it would not be a turnkey delivery, but at that point, we didn't know yet any of the consultants and we didn't want them to ever say that the answer to a question we had was not covered by the agreement we had. So a turnkey offer may have the added benefit of a bigger commitment from the consultants to see you through the process, but we did not have to test this theory out. As it turned out, we made the right choice in choosing our consultants and could not be happier about working with them.

In general, though, a turnkey service implies that after buying something, a product or a service, all you have to do is to turn the key and walk in to find the thing you wanted to buy. This is not the way a QMS should be built. At the very least, your consultants should ask you a massive amount

Figure 3.3   You will need to at least answer a battery of questions before the key fits.

of incredibly smart questions and then, if that was the limit of your involvement, perform some sorcery and arrive at a magical QMS that you will intuitively know how to use. In the real world, you would at least have to be trained on the resulting QMS, take it for a real test-drive, and then come back to your consultant with notes. At the very least, the QMS is a complicated race car, and you are the test-driver giving notes. Most likely, though, you will want to take ownership over the whole process and the end product very early on.

You will want to be involved in the process all along. The consultants will know what questions to ask you, have an idea of what has worked for others previously, and be able to shape the QMS to your preferences. The differences between consultants in tailoring the QMS to your needs will probably be similar to buying a tailor-made and a bulk-produced suit, or making one yourself, but it will depend on your circumstances what makes sense. Also, you should be clear and concise about your wishes, but you should not drown out the very wisdom you are buying when hiring a consultant.

A further caution I would add is that since the development process will include and depend on a lot of input from you, if you squeeze the consultant on the schedule, you are actually squeezing yourself. The quality of the consultant's work may suffer if the schedule is too tight, but even more worryingly, you will have less time to analyze the material the consultant gives you and less time to react on it. The only place you will ever have all the time in the world is in that song, but rushing through QMS development will set you up for even more rushing later as you are running the QMS in the real world and trying to fix it at the same time.

3.3 It's Not Something Someone Else Does for You Even When It's Up and Running

The previous two lessons were about driving home the fact that QMS is not something you buy off the shelf and it isn't really something created for you by others either. This lesson emphasizes that a QMS is not about something someone else runs for you either. A QMS should not be a black box, as Figure 3.4 illustrates.

No quality manager worth their salt would make the mistake of thinking that a QMS is something that runs by itself in the organization. When reading the process descriptions in a QMS, individual staff members may,

Figure 3.4 It would be a crime to think a QMS is a black box attended to by someone else.

however, think that it doesn't affect them or that someone else will take care of it. Particularly, the quality manager may seem like someone who magically carries the QMS by themselves. This is a complete fallacy. The quality manager will do a lot, and many things are on their plate or under their responsibility to get done, but the most dangerous thing in a QMS is to think that the quality manager, the quality management in general, or just "someone else" sees everything and keeps everything shipshape. A QMS should describe the way of life in the organization and not be a stack of documents rolled out for the auditors to marvel at. Nor should it be a 24/7 life sentence for the quality manager.

When organizing staff training on QMS, I have been careful to emphasize that quality management is something affecting everything at the company. It is not something that only the quality manager or the Quality Management Team take care of. It is about how we do everything we do at the company. It is about planning and following those plans, measuring and controlling the output, reacting to and predicting change, and improving all this via a controlled process. Outsourcing may be a part of this, but responsibility is never something you should try to outsource—in fact, you are not allowed to do so by the standard.

When developing our QMS, I accepted a lot of responsibilities in the role of the quality manager, thinking that I wanted to make sure these functions get off to a good start and I could then gradually transfer some of the responsibilities off to other roles in the company—particularly, as new people would be recruited. This made a lot of sense during the development phase and was perhaps the only way of getting our QMS off the ground as quickly and safely as we did, but it might have also played toward increased feeling among staff that many things were handled for them. In a way, this is the reverse of the problem with the Amazon QMS discussed earlier: instead of too many roles, you may end up with too many responsibilities on too few shoulders. In our case, this has never been a problem, but the transfer of powers and responsibilities continues to be something on my mind for the foreseeable future. So think about what roles and responsibilities you want to take on and what others should take on and when. It is a good idea to pay attention to workloads for individuals when writing the processes and to have some overall division of areas of responsibilities from the start. But again, be careful not to equate area responsibility with the misguided notion that no one else would have to pitch in or take responsibility on such matters on some other level.

Once the QMS is up and running, the quality manager should be the point person for maintaining it and improving it, together with the Quality Management Team. At the beginning, you will want to be involved closely in just about everything to make sure your processes work and everyone knows what is expected of them. Over time, you should be able to take a little bit of a more hands-off approach and move from directing things to helping as needed, solving problems, and monitoring processes for improvement. You may even want to start running internal audits in-house, which you can't do if you are also running the activities to be audited. That said, don't swing the pendulum to the other extreme and start thinking that your staff will do it all for you, even if that jokingly could be a sign of a perfect zero-friction QMS.

3.4 Think About What Other Standards, besides ISO 13485, and Regulations Apply to Your Business and Product

Risk management, software life cycle, clinical investigation, and so forth all have their own standards. What else should you consider? How soon should you be thinking about other regions besides the EU or the US? Will ISO 13485 help you in these regions? A QMS needs to negotiate several worlds together, as Figure 3.5 illustrates.

The first thing I will say here is that you should consider buying ISO's guidebook on the ISO 13485:2016 standard. Most standards don't have guidebooks, but this one does, and the book also includes the standard (although importantly, not its term definitions or appendices). That book is worth its weight in gold, especially as a PDF. The book is a great reference to have at hand when you are mulling over some specific aspect of the standard and you would like the ISO to say more about what they meant in the standard, but as your first introduction into the standard, it can be quite heavy and bewildering. Note also that the guidebook is not part of

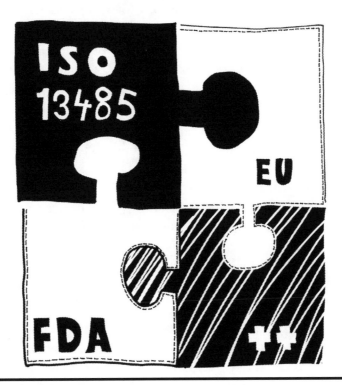

Figure 3.5 **The QMS puzzle is not just about ISO 13485.**

the standard, and the commentary it adds may or may not be in agreement with how individual regulators around the world interpret the standard. This book aims to give you a soft-landing into the standard in Section 4.

The ISO 13485 is the backbone of all your operations, and it is worth your while to understand this standard as fully and intimately as is humanly possible. The standard is essentially a global gateway standard that is, among other regulatory approaches, used by the international Medical Device Single Audit Program (MDSAP). As we will discuss later in Section 4, the standard is very well-written and appears to be very stable so that you can rely on it when developing your organization's overall quality operations. You will probably want to fit other standards into the framework given by the ISO 13485 standard and adjust your interpretations of individual requirements based on the regulations that apply in your circumstances, but no other standard will be as crucial to you going forward as this quality management system.

In terms of other standards, you may, for example, want to look at IEC 62304 for software development, IEC 62366 for usability, ISO 14155 for clinical research, and ISO 14971 for risk management. In fitting standards together, you should look at what your peers have done, what guidance is available in your jurisdiction on any related topic (especially guidance from the FDA, even if you are not on the US market, as they are quite open in providing their opinion), how well the standard fits together with the ISO 13485, and how stable the particular standard is. The stability of a standard is a complex issue and one where you will benefit from talking with your regulatory experts, but the first step in assessing the stability is to look the standard up on the ISO website and see where it is in its life cycle. Using the time-stamped status information available there, you will see advance progress information before a new standard is released and you will be able to tell when it is due for its five-year maintenance review.

In reading the standards and the regulations, you will come across the concept of "state of the art", and when you do, realize that this does not mean the same thing as in science: instead of something futuristic and cutting-edge, it refers to commonly accepted good practice. In science, state-of-the-art would refer to something novel, new, and unique; but in standards and particularly in regulations, this is almost reversed to something that the industry and society-at-large can agree on as being good. Good practice. The difference sounds more profound than it is, but it is worth knowing about this disconnect and not going overboard in trying to reach beyond the current best practice and your means.

All the standards are available to buy from the local standardization organizations and the International Standardization Organization (ISO) itself.

The standards will cost you a pretty penny on a startup budget, usually about 200 euros each (about the same in dollars), but getting the essential standards is required. There is no way around that. The price is not that bad when you consider that the standards were not written by a single person but instead by teams of experts and industry representatives who work continuously on keeping the standards both working as they should and also up-to-date following a set maintenance schedule.

Also, think about getting yourself involved in standardization in the long run. It takes effort and is a commitment, but it is the shotgun seat, if not the driver's seat, in the car. I can highly recommend it from my personal experience.

3.5 You Can't Do Everything Equally

Risk-based approach should be on your mind always: focus most on what truly matters. After all, focusing on everything necessarily means you do not focus on anything. And not focusing correctly and not prioritizing means you are wasting your resources. Think about the big picture and what truly makes a difference for the risks related to the use of your product and the benefit to be gained by using it. Focus on that and then expand your horizons as resources permit, as Figure 3.6 illustrates.

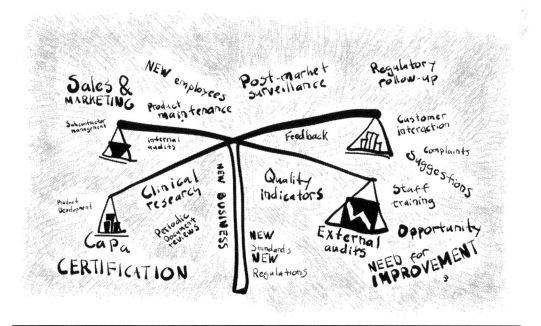

Figure 3.6   Risk-based approach gives one set of binoculars to survey the landscape.

When you write in your QMS that something will be done, realize that it will probably be you doing it or at least making sure it is done. This is especially important when you are writing the standard operating procedures (SOPs) that make up a large portion of your QMS: in writing procedures for seemingly separate activities, it is easy to overcomplicate or micromanage things so that task A and B have to be performed in process 1, while you forget that you will also be busy doing tasks C and D in process 2 at the same time.

In organizing staff training on our standard operating procedures (SOPs), I have a habit of telling my staff that they should think of the quality manager as a rubber stamp in the sense that they will not do many of the tasks entrusted to them by themself but instead will ensure that those tasks are done to their satisfaction by someone else. I feel somewhat guilty for saying this, but my intention is to avoid complacency in the thought that when it is written, the quality manager will take care of it. I have been, however, careful to avoid the notion that the quality manager is just a rubber stamp that will appear without any assessment or judgment.

The idea of placing something under someone's responsibility but not instructing that they themselves do it in practice is a key technique to use in preserving your sanity when writing the SOPs and when later working by them. The responsibility for seeing several things done can rest on a single pair of shoulders, but the back carrying those shoulders would break if it had to be personally responsible for doing all the work involved. This concept also works well for the management representative.

Even with the earlier tip, it is still not possible to focus on absolutely everything. You must still decide on priorities and resources. My advice is that you always first consider the risk and the benefit as it comes to the patients and the users of your device. Note that here, I am not yet talking about the risks associated with using a product that you might still be developing and, thus, you might not fully know the risk classification and risk matrix of. Instead, I am suggesting that all the various activities required by your QMS (e.g., staff training, supplier handling, customer communication, complaint handling, document review, and CAPA handling) will have vastly different risks associated with them depending on your overall phase of operations. Should any of these processes or any of their subprocesses go awry, they will have different impact on the users of your devices. I would suggest that you use a risk-based approach to prioritize your activities and apply resources accordingly. From there, you can work backward from high-priority processes into connected processes inside your organization, and how doing or not doing those tasks correctly could affect the end experience.

Your priorities will also evolve over time, but they should absolutely not be fleeting. A good example is the quality policy and quality indicators you will set for your organization in the quality manual. The policy is something that you should have a very good idea of from the start, and that probably should not change much over the first few years. The quality indicators are based on the policy, and you should measure those over meaningful time spans to have time series data you can base decisions on, but those will evolve as your operations mature. I found that setting up indicators to track the QMS development process was helpful, but although those indicators served their purpose very well during the development phase, some of them began to lose their value as the QMS matured. For this reason, you should revise your quality goals to match your needs over time, thereby possibly also changing your overall focus from initial development to the refinement of some aspect of your QMS. The same story applies to all your QMS improvement efforts over time: instead of churning the same QMS wheel day in and day out, identify needs and work to meet them one at a time.

3.6 Don't Invent a New Hoop to Jump Through for Every New Requirement You Encounter in the Standard

If you can't see a reason for doing something, the odds may be that you don't need to do it. Doing something just because you are told it is required is a bad excuse for not figuring out if or why it is needed. Not doing something because you don't understand it is, of course, even worse, as Figure 3.7 illustrates.

It is easy to create a QMS that meets all the requirements, but if you are not careful, running that system will be a nightmare. You will want to create a system that is as lightweight as possible so that you can focus on what matters and work on improvements to your QMS and not just the idea of improvement. To me, this is the most fascinating part of developing a QMS and later optimizing it. The following are strong indications that you might be in the process of creating a bottleneck:

▪ **You want to do something extra because you think it can be achieved at the same time as something else without any extra cost**. Now, you could be right here, and you could be on to a good improvement idea that leads to accomplishing two things at once, thereby creating a more lightweight system; but more than likely, you

Figure 3.7   QMS should not be an Olympic sport.

are just being unrealistic and lengthening the worksheet. Be mindful here. Nothing ever really comes without a cost.

■ **You want to add a review step just to be safe and because it doesn't cost anything and probably won't take that long anyway.** Nope. If a review step reduces the risk of something going very wrong, add it. But don't add the step if it just means that some other already busy folks will have to familiarize themselves with the subject matter, go over the underlying data, understand how that data led to a conclusion, understand why and how the present review should be conducted, and so forth. Many times, something extra really is just extra, and it may distract and detract from overall quality instead of adding to it.

■ **You think some document is important and it should, therefore, be revised on some periodic schedule, and you think that a year or more could be a good interval.** Revising something for the sake of revising or getting new time stamps is not the way to go. If you write that a certain document is only valid for a period X, you will have to revise the document in that time frame. Again, if it is important a certain document is revisited after a certain period, give it a use-by date, but don't do so on a whim. All the documents running with an expiration timer will be an issue for you later, particularly if you run into forced delays that are to be expected when building your QMS for the first time, or during a worldwide pandemic.

■ **You want to add a person to a review just because they were somehow involved in the process leading to the review, and this person is now expected to record that they have nothing to comment on the outcome.** Fair enough. You should make sure all the necessary people are consulted, and when revising a new version of a previously approved document, this may include names from the earlier version. But be economical here. Don't let doubt creep in, but don't accept bloating lists of names, most of whom have no relationship with the work the document is on anymore.

■ **You want to add a signature to a document just because you want someone to be informed of the creation of the document.** This is a classic issue in QMS. In some cases, this may be the most economical way of documenting that a person stands by the document, but often, there are other more practical ways of informing the person and recording their read receipt. Remember that by adding that person's signature, you are also implying that they should be involved in future revisions of the document. Instead, you could use read receipts in your document archival software, record the document in some meeting minutes, introduce the document in some tracked bulletin or a newsletter, or come up with one of a great many other ways of communicating the creation of the document.

3.7 Quality Is a Competitive Advantage as well as a Virtue

QMS is about quality. It is about safety and performance. But it is also about efficiency of operations, and as such, designing your QMS is one of the most important choices you will ever make about creating a competitive advantage for your organization. In other words, don't create unnecessary operational bottlenecks for yourself. Achieving high quality with high performance is equally a competitive advantage: a well-oiled machine is not just a high-quality machine to pin ribbons on, it performs its task with speed and reliability, as Figure 3.8 illustrates.

Understand that if you specify something in developing your QMS that goes beyond the requirements of the regulations and the standard, you will still have to do it. Don't specify unnecessary checks or reviews. Do what is needed, but don't go overboard with "just in case". Every review you specify will need to be documented and will be time away from something else. Don't have unnecessary people sign documents, as getting those signatures will become a hurdle and a burden to the people too. Don't write in unnecessary periodic checks. These will keep you very busy when you are up and running and may not be productive.

Some bottlenecks, such as waiting for regulatory approvals, are unavoidable, but others are just unplanned or poorly planned hindrances. Bottlenecks slow you down and are prone to cutting corners in the interest of catching up as things become hectic in the day-to-day operations. Identifying and analyzing possible bottlenecks, therefore, becomes a business consideration and a topic of joint interest between quality management and the overall management of the organization. This is a good area to promote quality activities to management and engage with management to improve overall quality and operations at the organization.

Hunting for bottlenecks is something the annual external audits may help you with indirectly, but mostly, it is a topic for internal audits, management reviews, and vigilant day-to-day quality management. Identifying a bottleneck and investigating its cause will let you fashion a faster, easier, and more reliable path through some process. It is not a cop-out from quality—done right, it is the exact opposite and a prime example of choosing the easier path and still improving quality. The hunt can also be like hunting for the mole in all those Cold War spy thrillers, but here, the emphasis is not on finding people

Figure 3.8   Unnecessary bottlenecks represent clear areas for improvement in the QMS.

but underperforming processes and subprocesses that are perhaps poorly conceived or instructed. Who ever said quality management couldn't be exciting? I may have once thought it, but I definitely don't anymore.

3.8 The Standard Requires Interpretation

The standard has been carefully written, and as you would expect, you can't interpret it just any way you like. But it does need to be interpreted, and therein lies the root of many an issue to be raised at one audit or another, as Figure 3.9 illustrates.

The standard works well for an idealized standard process of design first, then manufacture through a production line, package in cardboard, and ship to customers. If you are trying to emulate Henry Ford, then the standard should be ready to go out-of-the-box, but if your product is something that wasn't around in the early 1900s, then you might have to do some soul-searching to apply the standard. This is particularly true if your business is not a box-standard type of an affair. In that case, you will need to think about how the requirements translate to your situation. For example, you may think that cleaning and contamination requirements don't apply to software, but your auditor may rightly draw a line from these to cybersecurity.

The good news is that it is not about foreseeing every possible interpretation but instead earnestly trying to understand the standard and using it to understand your business and your product. The standard will raise up questions, and it is up to you to figure out if and how these apply to your situation.

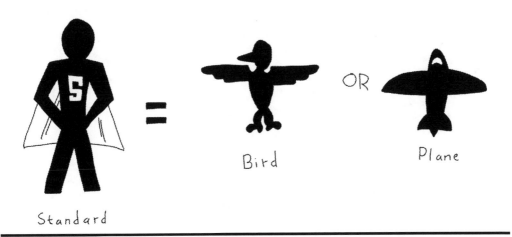

Standard = Bird OR Plane

Figure 3.9   The standard requires a fair bit of interpretation, but stay within reason so as not to overcomplicate matters.

Writing a process to comply with the standard is fairly straightforward, but it can feel like writing historical fiction: you are constrained by the larger framework just as you might be constrained by the recorded history surrounding your creation. You are free to innovate within that space, but you must hit your markers in the end. For QMS, this means you are working within a relative template given by the standard that may dictate inputs, outputs, and some processing in between.

3.9 Don't Just Claim "It Doesn't Apply to Us"

With the previous lesson in mind, it is worthwhile to consider how you approach a new question the clauses of the standard have raised. Some clauses will immediately seem like they don't apply to your business or product, but dismissing them too soon may prevent you from considering some poignant new angle that might have an impact on your operations, as Figure 3.10 illustrates.

Instead of claiming that some requirement does not apply flat out, explain to yourself why it doesn't apply or with what restrictions it could apply. This thought process may lead to the discovery of new aspects of your product and process as you consider each requirement carefully, and it will also help keep your auditors happy. This is somewhat antithetical to focusing on key issues, but it is an important way of considering all required aspects to your products and processes. The most important goal here is to find and answer the clauses that are relevant to your operations, but knowing why some

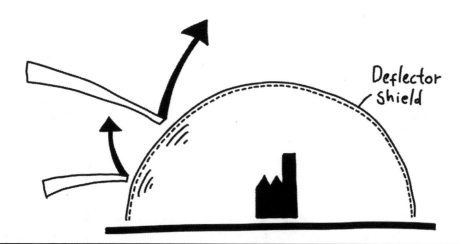

Figure 3.10   Smart interpretation is necessary to adapt the standard to your circumstances.

clauses don't affect your operations may be equally insightful. In the process of doing this, you will also discover some clauses that could be construed to affect your operations, and those, too, offer you new insight—especially about possible future expansions to your products or processes.

This lesson is also important when you define the scope of your QMS as you are writing your quality manual (see Section 5) and, later, when you are perhaps going through the lists of essential requirements (ER); general, safety, and performance requirements (GSPR); or similar for your product. Don't be arrogant in dismissing clauses and requirements, but instead, use them to look at your business and product from a new angle. You should, of course, exclude those clauses and regulations that really don't apply; otherwise you will bloat your documentation and spread your attention thin, but in the first place, it is about learning and only then limiting with a good reason.

Discussing interpretations of the different clauses with your peers and consultants is a good way of gaining perspective on any topic. Discussing clauses is also much easier than trying to describe some larger aspect of your QMS and hoping the conversation partner not only understands your setup but also has insight to offer. Talking about clauses is, by comparison, easier on you and on the other person, as both of you should be quite familiar with the clauses and topics even if you aren't acquainted with each other's QMS setups and even if you don't remember the clause numbers by heart.

3.10 Develop First, Then Consolidate

That's the ideal, right? First develop then test. Then reiterate. This applies to everything but is particularly useful in an industry where you must plan, do as you planned, and then report on what you did as a norm. This is perhaps hard to do when you are a startup and you should have finished your QMS yesterday so that you could start selling the product that you should develop under the QMS and that should also have been ready yesterday, as Figure 3.11 illustrates.

As I remarked in Section 3.2, the only place you will ever have all the time in the world is in that song, but regardless, rushing through QMS development will set you up for even more rushing later as you are running the QMS in the real world and trying to fix it at the same time. It is hard to take enough time when you are developing your QMS from scratch, and it can also be hard to take enough time during the subsequent document review cycles when you are revising processes while they are already running. You will never have enough time to make the processes perfect, but you may get pretty close, and you will get close enough if you keep your wits about you.

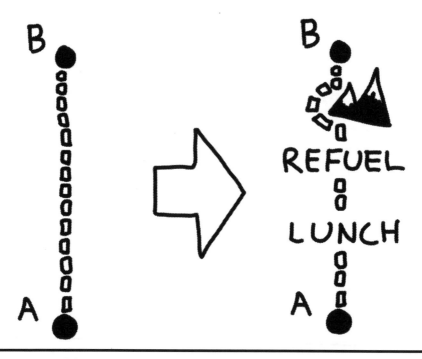

Figure 3.11   Test-drive your theories regarding processes and documents before locking them in place for the QMS.

Design the process, test it before use, and then issue it. This is particularly important when you will be using software tools to accomplish tasks: you need to know your tools will let you do what you wanted. During initial development, first concentrate on the SOPs; then once you know they work, write working instructions to support the implementation of the SOPs. In other words, use the SOPs to define what needs to happen and then let the working instructions fill in some lower-level details on how to accomplish something with the tools available.

Similarly, worry about plan or report templates only after you have experience with writing those documents. I personally would consider it a waste of resources to lock down an elaborate template before knowing the contents that need to go in it. The way I have approached templates is to write in the essential elements but allow for more information to be put in when using those templates. Once we know the resulting documents work for our needs, we can then revise the templates, but we will have saved effort in always requiring some additional information that we had thought might be beneficial but was not. At the same time, because of the flexibility in adding more information than the template required, we would not have missed out on any key details. This will, of course, vary case by case, but I would not put the cart before the horse and try to lock down complex templates before I had tested them for real in one way or another.

3.11 If You Haven't Documented It, It Didn't Happen

This is really the first rule of QMS. Everyone will tell you so. This does, of course, not mean that something bad didn't happen if you close your eyes to it, as Figure 3.12 illustrates.

It is perhaps easy to either overdo or underdo documentation. If you don't appreciate documentation, you will only document end points, obtain signatures for those, and be content with yourself. If you are a natural-born bureaucrat, you will document too much and detract from the work you are actually documenting. Worse still, you may extrapolate to the future and prescribe next steps on an exaggerated level of detail and confidence that will serve to disseminate false certainty on scheduling and will hurt you when you later must go back and correct the documents. Finding the right balance in between will let you make convincing arguments that your processes are followed in your organization but, even more importantly, will let you rewind information to investigate nonconformities and other suspected issues or points of improvement in your operations. End-to-end traceability is a requirement in the

Figure 3.12   Document because memory is not twenty-twenty.

standard (see Clause 7.5.9, for example), and maintaining this is a priority when you develop your processes or consider changes to them.

The good news is that there are many ways to document work and thinking. It doesn't always have to be about a chisel and triplicate stone tablets for recording every possible item. Think about what makes sense for the particular instance. For example, meeting minutes, plans, reports, and reviews all have different characteristics and uses. Minutes are great for recording thinking as it happens; while plans, reports, and reviews all often have predefined expectations. In my work, I have often wanted to have a captain's log of some sort that would contain all the events of note for a given stardate and let me easily rewind the tape to answer some question I am asked, for example, by the auditor. I have found that meeting minutes may serve this purpose quite nicely if your document archival system only lets you do the queries you want.

In deciding what to document and how you will naturally think about audits. After a while, you will realize that audits only happen once or twice a year, yet you need to access and refer to some existing documentation every day. The choice of how to document something should, therefore, be based on what works for you, and in general, it is not discarding information when it is readily available. The good news if you are a startup and new to documentation is that you may have many things to learn about documentation, but you won't have too many things to unlearn about it first. And you won't have masses of legacy documents—the weight of which shoots down all your fancy ideas of improvement.

After a while, the stack of documentation you have accumulated will only be as good as the tools you have to search and access it. Binders and papers have worked for centuries, but an electronic document management system will offer you distinct advantages. Whatever system you use, make sure you can work with it and that the structure in it and the document metadata work for you.

It may be worthwhile thinking about how likely it is you will need to migrate your documentation to another system later and how this migration might be affected by the fancy metadata features you have used in your system. This may be particularly topical for a startup that may be acquired after a few years and have a new parent organization that has their own established QMS they want to use over everything. It may also be topical for organizing the backups of your documents. In cases like these, it is beneficial if the documentation is well-organized, cohesive, and as a result, exportable. I, too, thought about these issues when developing our QMS, primarily because I wasn't yet convinced that the new piece of software we would be running our QMS on would still be our choice years later. As a result, I fashioned some of our documents to also work fully as printouts or documents with one additional metadata page printed out from the system. It is not worth going overboard with planning for something that is future-proof, as that does not exist, but it is good to think about a few what-ifs when developing your QMS. What future disruptions are likely, and could we plan for them in some simple way?

The last point I would make here is that some QMS documentation is subject to document retention times that need to meet not only the standard but also the applicable regulations. The documents you create should not just be available for a few days or months but years after the creation. A rule of thumb I have come to live by is to promise X years and aim at forever. In a previous life, I was involved in the digitization of archival materials from decaying videotapes and archaic reel-to-reel audiotapes to stacks of boxes with printed and/or handwritten sheets of paper inside. I would not be happy emulating those with my QMS. Luckily, with born-digital archives and backups, the classic issues facing the old legacy archives seem like a distant nightmare, as long as you beware of proprietary formats and take care of backups.

3.12 If You Write It, Follow It

Fiction has no place in the QMS. Dreaming up a perfect process description without respect for the reality of implementing that process is a recipe for disaster. Similarly, improvisation in implementing your own instructed processes is a breakdown of the system. Both will only lead to confusion and sweating, as Figure 3.13 illustrates.

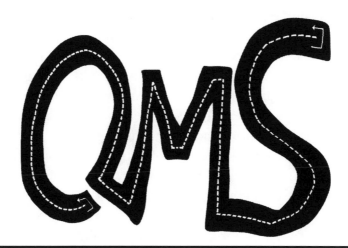

Figure 3.13   Use the road you built; don't just go off-road.

I always say to my staff that if something in the instructed processes feels stupid or cumbersome, come talk to me and we will figure out how to fix it. The fix may be implemented quickly or over time, but it will be made through a controlled process. The one thing you cannot do is change it yourself. It is up to the document review process, among other mechanisms, to make sure your documented processes are in shape. Change is welcome but not at random. Change should not be chaos or a free-for-all.

On a related note, I would also caution against writing stringent forward-looking descriptions of what you think you will do and when. There are certain things that need to go into plans, sure, but going overboard with description of future activities is best left to novels and not the QMS. The examples I could quote on this are countless. Particularly, working with engineers—of which I am one of, even though I would consider myself a pretty humane engineer—you are likely to see a lot of exact prescriptive documents that plan ahead and think out loud on what is going to happen when and in which order. This is good in itself, but oftentimes, the real world will throw wrenches into the works and change the exact duration, sequence, or grouping of activities in some minor way that does not affect the outcome but may require some micromanaging statement to be revised in some earlier document. In writing plans, you will do better focusing on what needs to happen instead of how.

The difference between what you thought you might do and what you end up doing is interesting and may lead to some insight, enabling you to fine-tune your processes, but it will also lead to unnecessary bureaucracy in revising old documents when you will also have other things to do. So documenting more may not always be a good choice.

For the previous reasons, writing your QMS and your various plans in an aspirational mindset can be dangerous. Asking more things out of your processes and staff will almost assuredly mean you are getting less of each thing. Asking everyone to follow plans by the numbers and including more numbers along that path will detract from attention to detail within those numbered tasks and will increase the likelihood that if your process happens to miss some key number in between, it won't be noticed. From the point of view of improving your processes, I would include more details in the reports; and in the plans, mostly focus on what needs to happen before the reporting stage. When writing the report, you already have the benefit of hindsight, so you can offer better insight for future improvement than you would have been able to give during the planning stage. This way, you also won't need to clean up unnecessarily micromanaging plans. This, however, is not a call for poor planning.

3.13 Once You Follow It, Make Sure You Stay on Top of It

The QMS you have given life to should have a heartbeat. In fact, it should have several vital signs for you to track. Remember to monitor these and act accordingly, as Figure 3.14 illustrates.

In many cases, it is not enough to write it and forget it until you think you need to do it. Your organization is bigger than just you, so even if you remembered to track what you do yourself, you still need to be able to monitor and measure all the processes you aren't involved in as closely every day.

Define quality indicators to monitor the health of your processes (see Section 5.2.3). Make sure these make sense as an extension of your quality policy and quality objectives—and that these are measurable. Don't worry if not all your quality indicators are numeric: if tracking some individual data items makes more sense in some other format, then do that. But realize that the standard expects these to be measurable. Also, know that it is not enough to generate the data; you also must stay on top of it by analyzing the data periodically (e.g., monthly) and then acting accordingly based on the data. Naturally, your process-specific risk management should make use

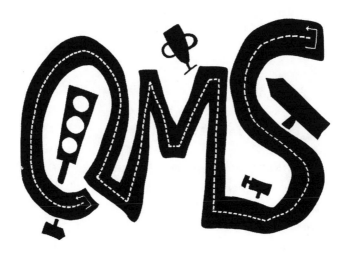

Figure 3.14   Don't neglect the road network you have created.

of this data, and your periodic management reviews (e.g., annually) should make even more use of the data.

For the masterclass solution to measuring your processes, think about how you can make the metrics rewarding to your staff so that they won't unnecessarily feel like they work in some Orwellian organization, but beware of making too tight a connection between the metrics and salaries or other incentives. You will get what you measure, and more often than not, if you make it too tempting to game the system, that is what you will get. Years ago, there was a minor scandal when government officials bought degrees online in droves just to get a raise, although these degrees didn't make them any better at their jobs. Similarly, if you tie the quality manager's bonuses to the number of nonconformities raised at an audit, you will make the audit situation more hostile and, more worryingly, perhaps usher in a culture of brushing issues under the carpet.

Years ago, I had a problem at a London hotel where they gave me a room someone else was already staying in. I went back to the reception desk expecting to quickly resolve the issue, only to find the staff strangely hesitant to work with me. After some standing around, I realized that the hotel had an advertised policy of comping stays if there were any problems. Rather than sleep on the street, I volunteered that I wasn't interested in the free night and promptly was given another room key. This, too, is an unfortunate example that you get what you design for. So think carefully before you introduce a new metric and think even harder before you tie that metric back into the system via some feedback loop, such as a salary incentive. In quality management, WYSIWYG could also be taken as "what you sow is what you get", instead of the classic "what you see is what you get".

3.14 No News Is Not Good News

In terms of new regulatory guidance and brand-new standards you need to digest, it can feel like a status quo is preferable to repeated changes in the environment. To a certain extent, this is true; but oftentimes, if you don't hear something, you can expect those in the know to be hard at work on some even bigger change. Even Jay in The Great Gatsby *had that beacon light as a sort of proof of life when he was pining over the girl—had he crossed the bay earlier to find out what the situation was, the final outcome could have been rosy, as Figure 3.15 illustrates.*

Figure 3.15 Tomorrow's front-page news may already be somewhere in today's paper.

Proof of life is what you need on your own processes, but it is also what you would like to get for some external regulatory or standardization activities while they are proceeding in stealth mode in the various committees before coming out. There are many ways you can try to build visibility into these external processes: networking and following good people and organizations on LinkedIn is a surprisingly good way of accomplishing this—often, it is only a matter of hours before a change is picked up and reported on by someone in the RA/QA community.

Also, the international standardization body, ISO (https://www.iso.org), is quite open about where each standard is in the development pipeline. To get full access to the development of a standard, you must get appointed to the group developing the standard or at least its national shadow group, but you can find out a lot by just going to the ISO website. At the website, you can, for example, check the status of each standard and the date it has reached that status. This can tell you all you need in terms of how the standard is faring, whether its review is on time, or whether it is due for a five-year checkup anytime soon.

Recently, as part of a work in a standardization ad hoc group, I wrote a simple script to process status information over a large group of standards and, thus, get an overview of how that particular landscape was evolving. The view was based on the granular information given by both the titles and the dated stage codes, which together provided a surprisingly powerful view into what was being worked on and what was either new or being revised. The view acted as a proof of concept on what can be done to build transparency into otherwise hard-to-access processes using just public resources.

The world of standards is not that hard to predict, even though you can't do it with absolute certainty, as has been shown by the tug-of-war on the IEC 62304 standard of late. There are also tools to help you track the standardization and regulation landscape (see Section 29.1).

3.15 Don't Update Documents Just to Update Time Stamps

Don't just update a document to get a new time stamp. That may seem like what the auditors want, but it will cause you and your staff headaches in knowing what has actually changed and how—and what trickle-down changes are then called for, as Figure 3.16 illustrates.

The version history of a document will help in assessing any changes, but that is still perhaps unnecessary work and work that may be repeated in your organization over and over again in different corners of the organization. I find it infinitely better to review a document, and if it does not

Figure 3.16 A document with just a new date may not be new.

need updating, say so in a review document linked to the document in your archival software. This will work for many documents, but it goes without saying that you shouldn't go this route just because you are too lazy to update a document that might need updating.

Your circumstances may vary, but I would not make the mistake of reading in the standard that a document should be kept up-to-date and interpreting that as a need to make sure we update time stamps periodically. This would be a particularly misguided interpretation in the case of some plan document that is blindly updated every once in a while—thereby also causing issues downstream where some records and reports might now be out-of-date after the plan they were made to has somehow changed—instead of just when the plan actually changes. I have seen this done and argued, but I see no merit to it whatsoever.

The ultimate example of the previous case is given by director Francis Ford Coppola, who has made some truly great films but has a habit of tweaking them for every occasion. Think about *Apocalypse Now* that has had a different cut for pretty much every release, from the cinemas to laser disc, to DVD, and to 4K. And then there is *The Godfather Part III*, which has now been reissued as a totally new cut with a different name some 30 years after the first release. I love his films, and I thoroughly enjoy each excuse to rewatch them, but you must care deeply about a document to go through all that effort in rereading and reanalyzing each new revision that closely. QMS documents, as important as they are, often may not cultivate that level of extreme commitment on the part of their users. You shouldn't expect them to.

The exception here is that if a document slips by with an incorrect date, you will want to correct that even if it causes some additional bureaucratic work for you. In that case, time stamps really matter as it may be critical to know the correct dates for some documents later. But here we are talking about two different types of time stamps, an unnecessarily updated one and an incorrectly applied one.

Some document management systems may also let you reconfirm a document with just one click and get a fresh new time stamp for it. I would be weary of this option, too, unless it came with a practical mechanism for also recording the assessment and authorities behind the reconfirmation.

3.16 Choose Your QMS Software and Remember to Validate It

I already said it in a previous lesson, and I will probably say it again: pen and paper are fine for old legacy systems and certain applications, but don't build a new QMS without a solid software behind it, as Figure 3.17 illustrates.

Don't go with a paper-based approach if you don't have to. There are many options for a QMS software out there. Choose one that you can work with, that you can trust, and that you can afford. The choices I have seen range from 0 euros a year to 50,000 euros per year (about the same in dollars).

A generic document management system may work for you just fine. Such a system may have all the access control, versioning, and digital signature functionality you want. I have even seen Dropbox used for this purpose.

A purpose-built QMS system may come with customizable modules and even crude SOPs for your tailoring. These systems may even come with expert content and tools for the medical device industry. The ability to effortlessly navigate between feedback, nonconformity records, and R&D records using some purpose-built features sounds great, but realize that your processes will then need to conform to how these features work and not the other way around. You can also achieve the same functionality using a

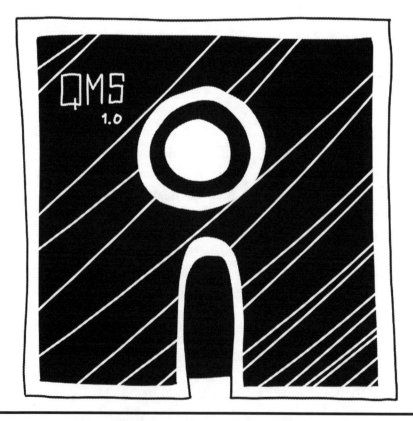

Figure 3.17 Choose a good platform for your QMS. You won't want to change it.

generic document management system, but it will mean more manual work. Hopefully, not as much as with binders of papers.

The most important question to get right when choosing a QMS software is whether it will work for you here and now. That aside, you will also want to think about how reliable that software is and how likely the software is going to be available or supported a few years down the road. This is particularly important if the software is provided on a software-as-a-service (SaaS) model in the cloud. If you want something that will run locally on your own servers, you may find that the price tags go up steeply, from a few euros a month to possibly tens of thousands of euros a year (about the same in dollars). If you are setting out on your path to creating a new QMS, it pays to dwell a little on the topic of choosing the right software platform for you. If you are working with quality consultants, as I would recommend you do, you will also want to listen to their experiences and preferences on the matter of choosing a software for the QMS. Your peers, too, will be willing to share notes.

The last point I will make here is that whatever software you choose, you must remember to validate it for your use. This, too, is a requirement (Clause 4.1.6). For some QMS software, you will be able to get prepared validation kits from the vendors, but don't think the validation is done for you. It is not. It is you who will have to think about how you use the software, how it has been intended to be used, how reliable the software is both now and in the future, and whether you are happy with it after testing and evaluation. Having to do validation may feel like something extra, but it is not. It is in your own best interest not to build your castle on sand. Section 22 will help you in your own validation of your QMS software.

3.17 Quality Improvement Is Intended to Be Continuous

You shouldn't start with something inadequate and think that you will fix it later, but don't think you have to make the QMS perfect from the beginning either. QMS is a continuous cycle, as Figure 3.18 illustrates.

Sounds easy, right? You can whip something up, and it doesn't even have to be ready at the end? This is, of course, wrong. If you try to find the minimum height of the jump so that you just about clear the bar, the odds are that you will be trying for quite some time before your jump actually clears the bar. If you need the officials there to measure your jump to know if you cleared the bar, as you will do when trying to get your QMS certified, the intervals between opportunities to jump will grow frustratingly far

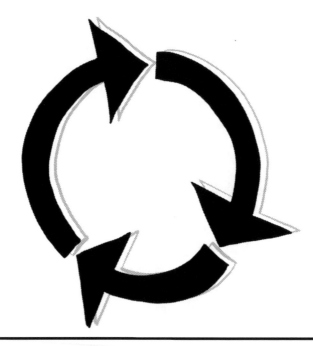

Figure 3.18   Quality improvement is never over.

in between. You will also annoy the officials who will have to watch you fail time after time. On the other hand, if you try to build something perfect that will certainly pass the bar, you may be stuck perfecting minor details of your QMS for a long time, and it may be a long time before you gain experience on running that QMS. In both cases, your investors, partners, and potential customers may grow weary and decide to vote with their feet.

The answer is again finding the right balance between not caring and caring too much. My suggestion would be to start with a good initial set of processes that cover the standard and then build on them over time to work better and accomplish more. If you are working in a startup, not all the aspects of the QMS will be as relevant to you at the early stage. If you are only now developing your product, you probably aren't shipping it off to customers, doing post-market surveillance, and overseeing product maintenance. This is even more so the case if you are at the incubator level with just an idea, looking for the right path to realization.

In any case, when you are looking to get your QMS certified, you should have processes defined to cover the whole standard as it is intended to apply to your organization. However, you should probably concentrate on better fleshing out those processes that are of immediate concern to you. You will then be in a better position to work on the other processes after you have worked out the priority processes first and gained experience with them. Later also, as you have all the processes described in detail to your liking, you will revisit and revise them to improve processes based on current and anticipated needs (see Section 25).

Continuous improvement is a part of life in any QMS. In fact, a perfect system that could not be improved upon over time would not, technically, even meet the standard. The next lesson takes this claim a step further.

3.18 There Is No Such Thing as Perfection

Don't look at mistakes through your fingers, but don't go nuts in trying to come up with the perfect system for obtaining perfect quality. Things always only look perfect from afar. The standard and real life are about adopting requirements, designing for the present day, and then moving in the right direction thereafter. This is one of the fundamental realizations I have come to appreciate in quality management. Figure 3.19 illustrates the shaky road to perfection.

If you try to create the perfect QMS that specifies actions for every single eventuality and requires the consideration of absolutely every single angle and source of information, that will never be how things unfold in reality. No human being can abide by that system, let alone learn that system in the first place. In my doctoral thesis, I quoted John von Neumann as saying, "It is very likely that on the basis of the philosophy that every error has to be caught, explained, and corrected, a system of the complexity of the living organism would not run for a millisecond". I think this quote also very much applies to QMS. No QMS is all-encompassing. No QMS is perfect. People are not perfect, and expecting people to be perfect will get any QMS into trouble. Instead, look at your stakeholders, the benefit you are trying to bring to patients and users, and the risks they may encounter while using your products. Think about what can make the biggest impact in terms of all these, and then design your processes accordingly.

Figure 3.19   Perfection is great for aspiration but poor for a goal.

My father, who traveled extensively for work before he retired, has a favorite story about airport security checks. One time, he was flying through a major airport and had in his carry-on bag a piece of nail clippers and nail scissors. At the security check, the officer at the X-ray machine noticed his clippers and decided to break off the nail file built into the clippers. He said nothing of the much sharper nail scissors in the same bag. The nail file was on his list of prohibited items, while the scissors were not. For a person looking to harm others, the scissors would surely have been a far worse item to get through the security check than the dull nail file, but as it was not on the list, it was permitted to be taken onboard. My point here, and the reason I, too, like that story, is not that lists are a bad of way of communicating banned items but that in focusing on the prescribed list too tightly, we may lose the ability or the focus on the variability that occurs in real life. Specifying too many things to focus on will not get you to perfection; it may not even get you to an acceptable state of operations.

Similarly, if during an audit you realize that you have made a mistake, forgotten to dot all the i's and cross all the t's you were meant to, be honest about it. It will make the process of arriving at the appropriate problem definition (and subsequent correction also) a lot easier, and crucially, it will also allow your auditor to retain their trust in you going forward. The audit is not about taking a victory lap through the outstanding work you have done, or even if it occasionally is that, the auditor will still find something you could do better. The observations and nonconformities discovered during audits are jokingly referred to as "golden nuggets for improvement", and that is how you should orient yourself toward them. Planning to get nonconformities is probably not a sound strategy, but expect there to always be some.

In the past few years, I have been audited repeatedly and only once did we come through with zero nonconformities. Another time, we came close. In other words, a zero-NC result does happen, it is not a unicorn, but neither is it a failure when you get nonconformities to work on. In some misguided companies, the number of NCs discovered during audits may apparently be tied directly with the bonuses the quality manager or the Quality Management Team get that year. This may lead to fierce fights over every nonconformity during the audit, but worse still, it may lead to a culture of brushing things under the carpet or closing your eyes to them. Beware of perfection as a goal—all you can ever hope to reach is an approximation of perfection, and hanging onto perfection too tightly may set your processes to fail.

I have a habit of saying that quality improvement is not about getting a nicer golden frame around your QMS certificate. Instead, it is about improving and streamlining your processes so that you capture the relevant information and perform the right operations better, more fully, more securely, and more efficiently. If you eliminate some unnecessary hoop from your processes, it is not tantamount to doing a poorer job but instead an opportunity to focus better on the other things you do. You will always have limited resources; no matter how many people you have, they will still only have a finite amount of time and interest to expend during their day. Knowing better what impact everything can have will allow you to create a lean and strong QMS that will also give you the best chance of working more on what matters. Here, "lean" should also be the kinder solution for your staff—something that leads to a safer and more reliable process that produces the outcome you want with less uncertainty and headaches.

3.19 Network with Your Peers and Get Involved in the QA/RA Community

Networking to learn more may sound lazy and superficial, but it definitely isn't either if you do it right. In my view, by far the best way to learn something new is to first read, then process what you have read, and finally, talk about it with others. Networking with your peers and stakeholders will help you strengthen your understanding of what matters and what solutions you could deploy— and as Figure 3.20 illustrates, it may lead you to meet a film star.

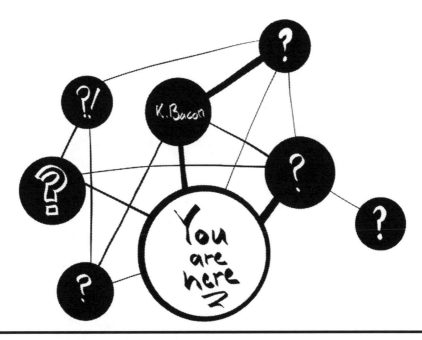

Figure 3.20   Six degrees of information exchange.

The most fascinating situations I have been in over the last few years have been ones where I have been at the same table with my quality consultants, their competitors, my startup peers, my larger industry peers, notified bodies, and the competent authority overseeing the notified bodies all at the same time. These events have been a royal opportunity to mess up in front of everyone I really should not mess up in front of, but they have also been an incredible forum for finding a common understanding on a particular topic or discovering new solutions to common problems. And occasionally, finding support for some new solution I had invented.

In this environment, I have never been afraid of asking a stupid question, although I have, of course, tried not to do that. Instead, I have asked questions and tried to provide thoughtful comments when I have been able to. In the process of doing so, I have found that I have learned at least as much about quality management as I have learned from the books and standards. So don't be afraid to ask questions and offer comments to test your understanding and ideas. This is information exchange, and it is also an invaluable way to improve your own job satisfaction; at least that's what I have found as our quality manager.

Networking is something you can first do in a small way and then expand your horizons as you gain confidence and the thirst for more. I began by networking in my own region, talking with other companies in the same field, then with regional development initiatives, and soon after, national industry consortiums and national standardization bodies. These led to discussions with international consortiums and bodies along the same lines, and recently, I have even represented my country at annual international standardization committee meetings.

Networking is not just about peers either. In addition to the previously mentioned bodies, I have also sought out opportunities to talk with potential users and distributors of my company's products to hear what they think about us and what they value. Talking with doctors, nurses, and businesspeople of all backgrounds and nationalities at scientific conferences and massive international trade fairs, like the annual Medica fair in Düsseldorf, Germany, have been a highlight of my work in the past years. I once lost my voice after running our booth for two days at Medica, but I learned something from each of the hundreds of conversations I had over the period. I can only strongly recommend the experience.

The conversations and viewpoints I have come across via networking and just discussing our QMS and our product with various interest groups have all allowed me to better understand the road we are on. Understanding where the standards and regulations are, where they are going, and what your potential users and partners think, is all key information for a QMS. I will do my best to pass on here the lessons that resonated with me the most, but there is, of course, no substitute to networking yourself.

My final advice on networking, and one which I have lived by as long as I remember, is that you should listen to everyone who you come across, but you should not believe everything you hear, and you should definitely not try to incorporate every piece of advice into your QMS. There is no one correct answer, but hearing many answers will let you compare your own answer to those and come up with a better answer.

Networking is a vital part of working on a QMS, and you should get comfortable with it in your day-to-day. Today might be a good day to add me to your network. You can find me on LinkedIn as Ilkka Juuso and via e-mail at author@theqmsbook.com. Drop me a line, and maybe tell me what you have enjoyed about this book and what more you would have liked to read.

3.20 Share the Knowledge but Not the Pain

There is a lot that goes into quality management. There are countless sources you must go to in order to get a full picture of how the medical devices business is evolving as a field. There is a lot of hearsay, vague concepts, and imperfect information of where the regulations or standards addressing the field are going. At the same time, there is a need to give a concise and consistent view of quality management to those who need to work within the framework it provides. It is your task to distill the information, formulate it into actionable processes, and help your staff appreciate it all, as Figure 3.21 illustrates.

The previous lesson really addressed tapping into the best information around and distilling it into insightful knowledge in collaboration with peers of many sorts. But as the quality expert of your organization, you will also need to keep others at your organization informed and keen to proceed in the right direction.

I have attempted to share the knowledge within my company and among my peers, too, as constant feeds of hopefully refined information. This has meant sharing information that has been relevant to the management, the Quality Management Team, or the R&D Team directly with those functions. There is little point to broadcasting everything to everyone, as the various audiences would lose interest over time. Some information may originate outside the company, while some other knowledge is built on multiple

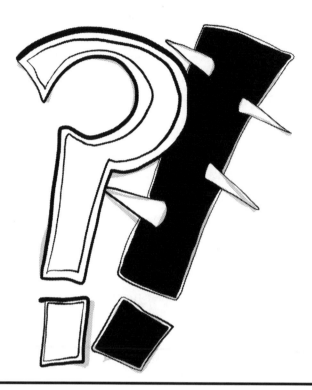

Figure 3.21   Barbarism is not speaking your audience's language—literally.

sources and assessed within some team at the company. Some information goes in to inform reports, while other information is best brought up for discussion at some meeting or as a heads-up on some online discussion board. All the information should be relevant to the other party, and there is usually no point to sharing raw undigested information or, particularly, doubts, uncertainties, and personal action points placed in the future. It may be relevant to share doubt and uncertainty in some cases, of course, but as a rule of thumb, something that you know you don't yet know is primarily an action point for you and not something to commiserate over in a group. Doubt will detract from what has been instructed, and the first duty of any manager is to provide a safe, predictable working environment for his staff to do their work in. This is also very much true for the quality manager.

There is a very good reason for sharing the knowledge with your staff beyond just the information itself: it means that they can better appreciate quality management. I hate doing something just because I am told to do it. If I am told why I must do it, I not only will oblige more easily but may also even do a better job of it. I suspect most people are the same. Spreading knowledge is, therefore, useful for completing the tasks, but it is also beneficial for job satisfaction and the ability to achieve more. My company has been incredibly fortunate in the staff we have attracted. Our staff continues to surprise us positively by taking interest in quality affairs and, frequently, by providing great feedback and suggestions for improvement. With staff like this, it is easier for the quality manager to trust that any processes accepted by the staff will also be followed and the criticism offered will be constructive and timely.

My secret objective in sharing knowledge has also been to make myself redundant. I have tried to observe this objective in just about everything I have done in the past two decades of my professional endeavors, but in quality management within a startup company, this has taken on a particular meaning. Sharing knowledge leads to a more motivated and reliable staff that is less likely to allow serious nonconformities and issues to occur. The staff will also be more open and knowledgeable to take part in quality management activities, such as internal audits, unannounced audits, and the tracing of nonconformities or other issues. It means that engineers will be more attentive to what truly matters, and it means that higher-up management is less likely to be unappreciative of quality management or be prone to abrupt changes that cause disruption to quality management.

The only downside is that if I achieve my goal of making myself redundant, I will be made redundant, but so far, that has never happened. Perhaps striving for redundancy is akin to striving for perfection—both will be lifelong pursuits. But the trick in striving for redundancy is, of course, that you are not delegating your own work to others; you are just making sure the system would cope without you, should it need to. In other words, don't be a Dennis Nedry from *Jurassic Park*, subjugating everything to your will and stature, or else the raptors will bring it all to the brink of extinction sooner or later.

The lesson remains that there is a complex flow to information, and you must try and refine the information, connect the dots, and extract the knowledge before passing it on. A mailman is probably not what your organization needs, but a good quality manager will be able to share the knowledge in an impactful way without sharing all the information as a constant barrage. People should feel like they know enough to perform their tasks and yet want to learn more. The quality manager should feel like they can both provide answers and get answers to their questions from the staff without having to resort to some form of arcane torture or the sci-fi equivalent of a Voight-Kampff test. Sharing knowledge is a cornerstone to achieving all this.

3.21 Figure on Some Things Happening Periodically, Others Sporadically, and Allow for Adjustment

The final result is hopefully not as messy as the different intercut timelines in Christopher Nolan's Dunkirk, *but even in QMS, you will have several different clocks running at the same time. It is your job to synchronize between those as is appropriate and to ensure that nothing drops between the floorboards, as Figure 3.22 illustrates.*

The document review cycle, internal audits, management reviews, and announced external audits all take place according to a predefined annual schedule. The standard is revised every five years, provided that the standardization process keeps ticking to its schedule. You can plan ahead and

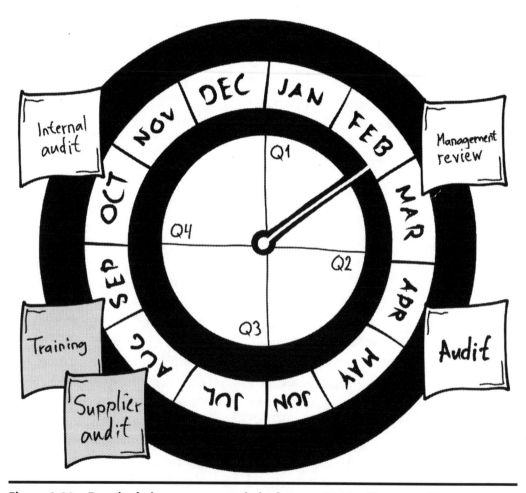

Figure 3.22   Despite being on an annual clock, your QMS will not run like clockwork.

map these all out so that the annual sequence makes sense. For example, you go through the internal document review cycle, identify areas of particular interest for improvement, arrange an internal audit to tackle these areas or the whole QMS, and arrange a management review to evaluate the status; and you do all this in time for the announced external audit by the QMS certification provider (notified body or certification body). These are the prime examples of the scheduled part of the QMS.

In addition, things will happen sporadically, at random, and generally, as the needs come up. Once, per the QMS certification cycle, the certification provider will perform a surprise audit on your organization. For a surprise audit, the auditors will just show up at your door and expect to see what they would see during an announced audit. You could be on holiday in the Amazon rainforest yourself, but it is important that your substitute or at least someone at the organization is there and doesn't try to close the door on the auditors. The fact that you accept unannounced audits and, possibly, even the process of how you handle them should be stated in your QMS processes. The certification providers will let you submit a form saying that your organization is not available for audits during some specific periods, like the Fourth of July and Christmas, so that they don't plan unannounced audits during those periods. Similarly, customer feedback may arise at any time, and you can't play hide-and-seek with that either.

As the quality manager, it will be your job to discuss with the management and agree on what planned actions will take place and when. It is also your job to plan for the unannounced audits and make sure your organization is prepared for them: staff knows that they will happen, understands that they should open the door, contacts you, and attempts to furnish access to the material the auditors seek. It is also your job to constantly observe your environment and figure out where the staff needs your help, what actions should be monitored more closely by you, and what actions beyond those scheduled should be undertaken to keep the QMS machine well-oiled.

The standard requires that you have an annual audit plan and suggests a defined document review cycle to revise your QMS documents (e.g., quality manual, SOPs, and templates). I have a habit of keeping a list of other items needing to be revised or other actions that should be performed sooner or later as resources allow. These items may include revising documents, such as annual risk management plans, that need to be revised approximately around a given date but can perhaps be completed a month or two prior or even after that date, should something more pressing coincide with that planned date. Similarly, I am deeply involved in regulatory and standardization affairs outside the company and, thus, try to build as much of a horizon as I can on such matters. Particularly, my interest in standard-ization allows me to plan ahead regarding our activities, and this, in turn, means that I usually have a list of small-scale studies we could perform to investigate some upcoming change or idea. The same also applies to react-ing to new published standards and versions of standards you already fol-low: once a standard is published, it will take some time for you to review your affected operations, perform a gap analysis, and make a plan for adopt-ing the new standard at your organization. The good news is that even the FDA allows you, as a rule of thumb, three years to adopt the new version. In the EU, the expectation is that you adopt the standard without delay, but I would strongly argue that you should not adopt something before your orga-nization really is ready to adopt it. Adopting a new version may be a much bigger task than just updating the year of the standard in your documents—you should absolutely not think of it as a search-and-replace action in Microsoft Word. Investigations into adopting new versions of various stan-dards are one of the items I have on my long list of to-do items. Other items I usually have on the list include organizing staff training on some nonur-gent topic, investigating some extra data source for possible impact into our processes, and looking at various expansions to our processes, possibly also of the geographic kind.

My point here is that QMS maintenance activity takes many forms, and while some activities happen on the clock, others happen according to a will of their own, and yet others can be performed in between as the resources are available. Trying to schedule all these activities rigidly at the start of the year will lead you to trouble. Not planning at all will set you up for certain failure.

My solution here is to plan with flexibility. It is, I am afraid to say, how I even approach family holidays: I google what I would like to do once arriv-ing at the destination, read up on the various sights on offer, and make some sort of a plan with my family, but then forget about following that plan once we get there. Instead, we improvise based on what we feel like on the day. Sometimes we follow the plan; more often, we adjust it or just do what feels best at the time. Usually, I also make a photo album of the trip after returning home, so, I suppose, that is my documentation of the activity, and my neural network is pretty much fried to follow the standard.

I have found that when scheduling ahead, not all items are equally fixed to a certain time or date, and not all items take equally long to perform or are equally important to perform. Taking note of this when preparing your schedule and allowing for flexibility where you can comfortably argue for flexibility will let you run the QMS more predictably in reality. Your staff will also appreciate the small flexibility, whether they notice it.

3.22 Plan Ahead to the Extent You Can

To evoke another Christopher Nolan film, Interstellar, *you will want to think about the future to plan for both today and tomorrow, but if you start seeing patterns in the sand or in your bookshelf, you should back off a little. The goal posts may move, but as Figure 3.23 illustrates you should still always know what it is you are working toward.*

Planning is easier said than done, but the reality is that it is dangerous to have too much of a tunnel vision, especially around surviving the present. When you are setting out to develop your QMS, there are thousands of things for you to keep your eye on and negotiate into place. It can be hard to pull up your head and look at the wider context or what you will need to do next.

There are, however, several important lines of dialogue you will need to open soon and keep alive even when you feel like the actual time for the particular discussion is months away. The prime example of this is securing a certification provider for your QMS. The provider can be an ISO 13485 certification body or, in the EU, a notified body that also performs ISO 13485 certification. In either case, the providers will be busy and securing a slot for your inspection with them may be a drawn-out process. In our case, I spent three months diplomatically engaging with all the big three-letter notified bodies, a few of their peers with longer names, and some other certification providers before even securing quotes and promises to take us on as customers.

Figure 3.23   Look up, look ahead, but don't have your head in the clouds.

The scheduling of the audits was still in the future at this point. The delay was largely caused by the bottleneck the notified bodies were experiencing because of the impending EU transition to new regulations, which meant increased work for them and a reduced number of notified bodies to share the client load. But it was also about knowing when we would be ready for the audits and planning ahead with the estimates we had.

Another example of planning ahead, in our case, was casting an eye toward FDA regulations in the US while developing our QMS for the EU market in the first place. Yet another example of planning ahead is to, resources permitting, look at how the regulations and standards are changing in the immediate future so that you can better make plans and allocate resources.

Planning ahead, or at least trying to plan ahead, has had many positive outcomes for us, so I would not say it is an optional extra to what you do; it is very much necessary to avoid just being reactionary in your business. Dwight D. Eisenhower apparently phrased a similar notion by saying, "Plans are nothing; planning is everything". He may have been right. The horizon you can create going forward by planning is a sign of a healthy QMS, provided that you don't forget the present and don't try to forget the past. It is, of course, understandable that if you are hard-pressed for resources, looking ahead is one of the activities to suffer first. All this means that from the management side, keeping an eye on future plans as well as occurred unexpected surprises may act as an indicator on the health of the QMS and its resource allocation.

If you find the future looks like too much to handle, it is a very good time for some self-reflection and prioritization. If you can expand your team to meet the challenges, consider doing that, but know why each of the potential new things is worth pursuing before that. Growth is positive, but it will come with its own pains. Hiring temporary helpers always comes with an overhead; the helpers you will need to hire in the medical device business not only cost a lot more than the holiday season helpers you might hire at a retail store, but their onboarding, too, may be a much bigger drain on your existing resources. That said, it is prudent to have a plan B and some mechanisms for coping with disruptions and added workloads.

Planning ahead is never easy or straightforward, but the first step is always the same: the willingness to look ahead. Even the best-laid plans can get abruptly laid to rest, but planning ahead means that you will still be best prepared to handle any disruptions ahead. Planning also means that once you come through that tunnel, you will be in a position to analyze whether everything went like you thought it would. Comparing the plan and the report, for example, you should be able to assess the health of your operations and make improvements where they make the most sense.

In films, all the plans laid are almost always scrapped around the mid-point of the movie, or else essential information is left out so that the viewer will be kept interested until the end of act 3. In real life, you are not plotting to rob a casino as in *Ocean's Eleven* or make a great escape as in *Escape from Alcatraz*, so a boringly predictable plan is perfectly acceptable, even preferrable. In fact, plans should probably always be boring, but the aims should be exciting.

3.23 Dare to Make Yourself Redundant

Renny Harlin's film Deep Blue Sea *has an excellent scene where Samuel L. Jackson leaves the stage just at the moment when he is starting to mobilize the troops. You should stay away from shark-infested oceans, but you should also not try to make the QMS all about you either. This way, you will go toward ensuring continuity at your organization, but you will also ensure higher quality operations during your tenure. Figure 3.24 illustrates how you can feel like a samurai and still fade into the background.*

I touched on this with a previous lesson, but the ultimate goal for the whole of quality management is to become redundant. Once the perfect process is in place and perfectly followed, all that is left for the quality management is to

Figure 3.24   A hands-off approach may give you better perspective.

marvel at your creation in action. This would be a zero-friction QMS where all the records would magically appear in the right order and at the right time, and all that the QMS would need to do is to take note of them.

This is, of course, a very tall order, akin to creating a perpetual moving machine or perhaps dabbling in alchemy, but this is exactly the right goal in my mind. Striving for your redundancy will let you develop a QMS that is not dependent on you always being there, being at your best, and making the right decisions at the right time all the time. It is the peace of mind that will let other, even more junior, staff members open the door to the auditors at the start of an unannounced audit and not have their heartrates go through the roof. Or let them pick up the phone on an angry customer.

I have a habit of saying that a QMS is the way of life for any given organization. I said that in lesson 1 previously, and I stand by it. It applies to every interest group involved in a QMS. But if you are the person responsible for running the QMS, I would say to you that a second, almost as important, lesson is that planned personal obsolescence is a further cornerstone to keep in mind when designing and revising a QMS. Do not delegate your work, ever. But making sure everyone knows what they need to know and, hopefully, a little bit more than that is your job and perhaps your best chance of preventing problems for yourself in the long run.

3.24 Be Lean but Not Mean

Actually, all the earlier lessons can be summarized by the word "lean". It's about figuring out what matters most, how to get that done, and how to get there as safely, surely, and elegantly as possible. This means using Occam's razor, common sense, old-time country wisdom, and whatever other tools you have available to cut away the excess, the frivolous, and the hierarchically inane to arrive at the most suitable, adequate, and effective processes you can obtain. In other words, the leanest way of getting it done. Figure 3.25 illustrates this with a single stroke.

Lean also applies to how you instruct the processes. Beware of copypaste and prose. It may seem tempting to quote some instruction you have already finished elsewhere; for example, reuse some process specification you have defined in another SOP. But realize that if you later want to change that specification, you will have to do so in more than one place. This will not be optimal, and you may have several add-on issues to tackle stemming from the different locations the specification was copied to and used from.

Figure 3.25   Keep It Simple Stupid (KISS).

It is better to define something once and refer to that one place for a definition elsewhere. That way, you will also retain the link between the locations
more easily (see Section 20.3.4).

Similarly, writing prose may get you into trouble by bloating the process but
also by introducing more terms for one thing than you really need. In some
cases, you may inadvertently run across a reserved term—a term defined in
the standard, for example (see Appendix 1). In other cases, you might be sitting
in an audit and wondering why the thing you know is in there is not coming up in your text search, and the reason is that you got fancy in your use of
vocabulary. I have been there and done that. It is not a novel you are writing,
so be economical with your words if it doesn't hurt the reader.

The word "lean" also has another meaning for me. A meaning, which
I have found to be a very effective tool in charting our road forward all
throughout our company's path from a university project to a spin-off to a
medical device manufacturer with CE-marked Class IIb product out in the
market. That other definition is "to lean forward", to look ahead. Not to fall
on your face, hopefully, but to look far and wide to get as much information

and as many viewpoints as is possible with some questions so as to then start building your railroad tracks in the right direction. The great news is that if you are lean in how you set up your QMS, you will also have some time available to you later when you are running that QMS and can lean ahead to face new challenges.

3.25 Find Your Passion

It sounds unforgivably corny, I know, but unless you find the angle that truly interests you in QMS, you will soon just be going through the motions. If following the same process from day to day is what you want from your job and the predictability of that gives you a sense of security, you may be immune to production line fatigue, but I know I am not, as Figure 3.26 illustrates.

Luckily, so far, no two days on the job have ever been exactly alike for me. The processes remain in slow change, like the tectonic plates of the earth's crust, and there is intrigue in navigating those and attempting to affect change in them without blowing anything up. At the same time, the processes provide ample room for optimization and detective work in their application. The CAPA process, for example, used to plan and perform

Figure 3.26   Like it or not, you have to like it to live it.

corrective and preventive actions after detecting issues, is perhaps the prime example of this as a true detective kit allowing for great exercise of those little gray brain cells Hercule Poirot always talks about. Similarly, interacting between you and your staff at your organization, hearing about their experiences from work with your QMS, and coming up with improvement ideas to investigate, as well as promoting awareness of QMS matters as opportunities arise, are all things I enjoy in my work. There is even a certain type of pleasure to be had in devising a solution to filling some external regulatory form despite its occasional shortcomings and cryptic or missing instructions.

Over my tenure as our company's quality manager and having worn COO, cofounder, and board member hats, I have come to realize that there is a lot more to QMS than just following the same recipe day after day. My advice to you is to find what your interests are in QMS and use those to fuel your QMS improvement efforts going forward. I am not saying you could forget about some less-interesting aspects of the standard or your QMS, but use your drive to really improve your QMS instead of just talking about improvement.

With that hopeful and, hopefully, helpful note, it is time to get started with sketching out what a QMS is and what it should be in your case. The next section will dive into looking at what the cogs are that make up a QMS.

Chapter 4

Getting Started

We have now discussed quite a few important topics to consider when setting out to create or overhaul your QMS. This section will introduce the basic building blocks of a QMS and the principal ducks you will need to have coached into a row to make a good go of this. Let's start with a few fundamental questions.

4.1 Why Do Quality Management?

The easy answer is because it is required by regulations if you want to do business in the medical devices sector. That, however, is a sloppy answer. You don't obey traffic laws because adherence to them is required. You obey them because you want to get from point A to point B and the traffic laws give you a reasonable expectation that you, and everyone else, too, will get to their point B with as little hassle and heartache as possible. Obeying the laws is still not enough by itself; you must also keep your wits about you in traffic, observing events and reacting to them as needed—occasionally even preemptively. This is also true for a QMS.

The better answer then is that we do quality management because we believe managing quality is the best way to ensure a good outcome with as little risk as possible. In short, quality management is about giving organizations a framework for monitoring and steering their operations in the way they see as leading to the best possible outcome and—in the unfortunate case they veer off that course in some way—to let them analyze the lead-up to the situation and make the appropriate corrections in a controlled way.

DOI: 10.4324/9781003202868-4

Quality management is not about creating records purely for an archival graveyard, say like the one at the end of the *Indiana Jones* film, but it is about what you do with those records that you do create: both when things are going smoothly and when they are not.

4.2 What Is ISO 13485 Quality Management?

ISO 13485 quality management is based on an international standard for quality management systems at medical device organizations and, more specifically, the ISO 13485 standard on "Medical devices. Quality management systems. Requirements for regulatory purposes". The standard, and a QMS based on it, offers a way of defining, performing, and recording the operations of an organization engaged in medical device business. The quality management system set up by the organization provides a framework for these tasks and incorporates a notion of continuous improvement via a process of analyzing past performance and making appropriate improvements based on the analysis.

In a way, the ISO 13485 standard is the application programming interface (API) used inside your organization's QMS to "program" the processes following a commonly accepted interface or a model. Earlier in this book, I present Section 3 as the outward-facing API for QMS. I believe this is fair, as the lessons given in that section provide a practical handle on the box that is QMS for the "outside", but within the box—and you have already taken the red pill to dive into that rabbit hole—you will do well not only to heed those lessons but also to have an eye on the nuts and the bolts the standard gives you.

Almost all activity in the standard is through a process: a path from an input to an output, whereby the input is somehow refined or used to create added value, which is then the output to the next process. Each process should be suitable, adequate, and efficient in meeting the requirements set for it; and the process should be monitored to make sure it keeps meeting these requirements and can be improved over time. A "process" is, therefore, the Lego block to building your QMS in many ways. I would not be frightened by the idea that everything is a process if the concept seems foreign to you. The opposite of a process might be a haphazard occurrence that happens to lead to some outcome; for example, a favorable roll of the dice or the act of God often cited in contracts. If there is method to the madness, if it leads from point A to point B in some determinable way, it could probably be described as a process. I, of course, say this to decrease any friction in accepting the use of the term, not as an encouragement to court chaos.

In cinematic terms, I would call the quest to melt the one ring in the *Lord of the Rings*, as Tolkien wrote it, a process (or even a sequence of a great many subprocesses), and I might call the hunt for the eighth passenger in the air ducts of *Alien* a process where each check of the radar display, each squirt of the flamethrower, and each closed pressure door might be a key step of the ultimately failed process. The iterated sequence of events that Tom Cruise goes through in *The Edge of Tomorrow* might also be good illustration of a process, and one which leads to a vastly improved process by the nth iteration. I would, however, not call what John McClane does to clear the Nakatomi building of terrorists a process. And Vincent Gallo's *The Brown Bunny* may have been a process to make, but as a film, it is certifiable madness. In the use of these lighthearted film references, I, of course, take it for granted that a script, a novel, or a plan of some sort existed for the process ahead of time and that it could be repeated over and over again as needed.

Another key concept to be aware of is the plan-do-check-act (PDCA) model, which is often used to describe work according to the standard. The model demands that you should plan how you do something, do it as you have planned (unless you can't, in which case, you update the plan), check the result, and then act accordingly. This is an elaborate way of saying that you should plan what you do and check what you got. The filmic equivalent here could be any heist film where someone gets shortchanged with a gym bag full of cut-up phonebooks instead of cash or a bag of sand instead of diamonds. The PDCA is a good concept to know, particularly for Google searches, if you want to find out more.

The standard is written from a fairly classic waterfall state of mind, but it is frequently and routinely utilized, along with more agile approaches, especially in software development. As a standard, I find the ISO 13485 very well-written and actionable. It does not give you the ready-to-use engine for your QMS, but it does give you much of the building kit you will want to flesh out into your actual QMS. This book will help you make sense out of the parts in doing just that.

ISO 13485 itself is an international standard based on the more general ISO 9001 standard, which is perhaps better known to the general public as a manufacturing standard. The lineage is often cited but seldom appears to have any great impact outside of standardization circles. Currently, there is an ongoing debate about realigning the ISO 13485 standard with the newer structure of the ISO 9001 standard published since the former was forked, but the merits of this continue to be argued. Personally, I believe that the ISO 13485 standard has become the backbone of too many organizations and too many initiatives across the globe to now be suddenly reworked in any major way.

The ISO 13485 is by now the backbone of practically all medical device manufacturing in Europe, the FDA has been working on aligning its own Quality System Regulation (QSR) with the standard, and the standard is the basis of the international Medical Device Single Audit Program (MDSAP) where the FDA has had a lead role and which is now a requirement in Canada and accepted in multiple jurisdictions across the world, including Australia, Brazil, and Japan. The long-beleaguered transition from the Medical Device Directives to the Medical Device Regulation in Europe and the simultaneous occurrence of Brexit all mean that a significant overhaul of this keystone standard would be an unwise upset to the global industry. I can't see it happening anytime soon, and neither do the senior standardization experts I have talked with.

If anything, the ISO 13485 standard may become more important in the future. As the standard is the most essential standard addressing quality management in medical device organizations and as medical devices are gradually looking to move to new technologies, such as autonomous artificial intelligence and perhaps other technologies causing products to evolve while out in the field, the standard could prove to be a critical part of the regulatory solution. At the moment, products are expected to reach a stable state, then be subject to regulatory action, and pending approval, be released into the wild. Initiatives, such as FDA's Pre-Cert, have looked to move the magnifying glass from the product to the organization making that product and, thereby, allowing the product to evolve in some at least foreseeable measures. This signifies a noteworthy moving of the envelope, perhaps ushering in the next generation of medical devices, not yet the autonomous self-learning AI that is displayed in science fiction but perhaps a step toward introducing some motion-blurred version of the old white-box and black-box models of machine learning. In an environment like this, a firm grasp of the quality management system of the manufacturer might prove to be just the right mechanism of control, which in turn could serve to further elevate the ISO 13485 standard as a gateway solution.

The growing importance placed on the QMS will, however, not decrease the importance of obtaining solid clinical evidence and running post-market surveillance over the life cycle of your devices. Post-market activities may increasingly include the systematic compilation of real-world evidence (RWE), which in turn will feed your clinical evidence processes through your QMS.

The previous discussion is a product of the countless conversations and at times philosophical ponderings I have been a part of in the forums I have been lucky enough to take part in. It is science fiction for now, for the most part, and while it is not, strictly speaking, relevant to building your first QMS or overhauling your current one, it is nonetheless good to know that the ISO 13485 standard you are building from is neither arcane nor soon to be made redundant.

4.3 The ISO 13485 Standard

The ISO 13485 standard is one of the best standards I have seen: it is easy to read and provides a level of detail that does not go into micromanagement, it does not impose the use of some archaic data structures, and it doesn't fly on some philosophical metalevel either, where you would need to construct several levels below it to translate it to this world. The standard is written on a user-friendly level of being actionable but leaving enough room for adjustment to fit the real-world needs of individual organizations. The standard does require interpretation, as discussed elsewhere in this book, but there is logic to the interpretation.

If you will be sticking your hands into the clay to build your QMS, reading the standard itself is required sooner or later. There are countless books out there that attempt to take you through the standard one clause at a time—the prime example of this is the guidebook published by the International Standardization Organization (ISO) themselves—but these books only really add commentary on the clauses of the standard. This book now in your hands hopes to restructure the clauses of the standard to serve a thought-out workflow that gives you the narrative to familiarize yourself with QMS (if that is new to you), dispel some easy misunderstandings, and get you on the right path to building or refining your QMS. The workflow will take you from the quality manual to the standard operating procedures, and to running the various activities of your QMS. At the same time, this book will walk you into the world of the standard so that once you do pick up a copy, you will already know what to expect and have all the necessary tools to make sense of its contents. At that point, you may already have the bones of your QMS in place and will be picking up the standard to fine-tune some detail in it.

With the previous case in mind, the following subsections are intended to give you an overview of the standard and how you can rely on it in your own work. The clauses of the standard will be covered in more detail, where relevant, when we put pen to paper writing our quality manual and processes a little later.

The body of the standard consists of a foreword and nine sections, each structured around a clause of the standard. In addition, there are either two (internationally) or five annexes (in Europe). Also note that while the guidebook published on the standard by ISO is excellent and it does give you the clauses of the standard, you do not get any of the annexes or term definitions with it.

The first four clauses provide introductory information (Clauses 0, 1, 2, and 3) that is relevant to understanding the standard. The main content of the standard addresses the quality management system (Clause 4); management responsibility (Clause 5); resource management (Clause 6); product realization (Clause 7); and measurement, analysis, and improvement (Clause 8). The clauses are further subdivided into numbered topics yielding the specific clause numbers often cited in discussion of the standard and during audits. Finally, the international annexes provide an overview of differences to the older 2003 version of the standard (Annex A) and the ancestral ISO 9001 standard (Annex B), while the additional European annexes ZA, ZB, and ZC instruct the use of the standard to meet the regulatory requirements defined in the European Medical Device Directives. You can get by, for now, without the annexes, but if you are heading for the European marketplace, you will want to check out the Z annexes before arrival. For Europe, pay special attention to whether the Z annexes you see in your copy are harmonized to the old European directives (MDD) or the new European regulation (MDR).

I personally have been asking the question of why the Z annexes could not be published as a separate guidance instead of increasing confusion by issuing a new dated version of the standard just for the sake of including the annexes. In response, I have received favorable remarks from harmonization consultants and standardization experts, but the status quo has not changed. In other words, there is ISO 13485, the European harmonized version of it for MDD, and a third as-of-yet unpublished version harmonizing the standard to MDR. It is also worth noting that the European standards have an "EN" prefix, but this does not necessarily indicate that the standard is harmonized to MDD or MDR. All these are the same standards; only the Z annexes are different. In my view, the standard should be international, and any regional guidance on it, separate and light. The European harmonization process appears to be in deep trouble, but the good news for the manufacturers is that ISO 13485:2016 continues to be the state-of-the-art solution you should follow, claim compliance to, and get certified to.

Note, too, that even the standard itself has a version history table of sorts in Annex A—you, too, will include such information in many of your essential QMS documents. Keeping track of changes and updating a version history will become second nature very soon.

This book will refer to the clauses of the standard by their clause numbers and offer commentary on the clauses when relevant. In case a number is included in brackets after the clause number, that refers to the sentence number within the clause.

The following discussion provides an overview of each clause. The discussion here is intended to introduce you to the standard on a high level and provide remarks useful in developing the quality manual and SOPs later in the later sections of this book.

4.3.1 Clause 0—General

Clause 0 is an often-neglected prelude to the standard that should not be missed, as it plays an important role in setting up the standard and provides necessary concepts to understand what is to follow in the other clauses. The word cloud in Figure 4.1 shows an overview of what to expect in the clause.

Clause 0 discusses the application of the standard by an organization involved in the life cycles of a medical device and the need to also observe applicable regulations, which may vary from one jurisdiction to the next. The clause refers to ISO 9001 as part of the lineage to the ISO 13485

/this international standard 17 /standard 18 / requirements 25 /requirements for 5 /quality 11 /quality management 11 /quality management system 7 /management 19 / management system 9 /system 10 /an organization 5 /organization 10 /medical 9 / medical devices 5 /devices 5 /the requirements 5 /product 5 /organizations 5 /requirements of 5 /regulatory 12 /regulatory requirements 11 /management systems 5 /systems 5 /the organization 5 /applicable 7 /applicable regulatory 5 /applicable regulatory requirements 5 /requirement 5 /organization to 5 /the term 5 /process 8 / processes 5 /iso 7

Figure 4.1   Word Cloud for Clause 0.

standard and the intention of the latter to be compatible with other quality management standards. Clause 0 is sometimes neglected or even flat-out omitted in literature covering the standard, but despite its diminutive name, it comprises roughly 9% of the text in the standard and offers some foundational requirements and definitions for the standard.

The clause states the following requirements for the QMS (for the purposes of this book, think your quality manual):

■ Should reference the standard and explain why the organization uses it. Use can also be by choice.
■ Must define the organization's role (e.g., manufacturer, distributor, and supplier) under applicable regulations (see Section 4.4.4).
■ Must show that the organization understands how the standard is to be interpreted in their regulatory context and that they realize this may be different from nation to nation.
■ Must cover the listed processes—including design and development (D&D), production, storage and distribution, installation, servicing and final decommissioning and disposal of medical devices and the D&D, or provision of associated activities (e.g., technical support)—or provide an acceptable rationale for their exclusion.

Equally importantly, the clause also clarifies the use of some essential concepts that show up repeatedly in the standard:

■ as appropriate: clarified as required unless excluded, providing an acceptable rationale. This is not something you can just ignore because it doesn't seem relevant. If the requirement is related to your ability to meet requirements or to perform corrective actions or manage risks, you should not attempt to exclude it.
■ risk: clarified as risk pertaining to the safety or performance requirements of the medical device or the meeting of regulatory requirements. In Europe, also check the Z annexes for further qualifiers. In other words, business risks are generally not addressed by the standard. Note that the term "risk" is also given a definition in Clause 3 based on ISO 14971.
■ documented: clarified as not just documented but also established, implemented, and maintained. This represents a possibly significant change in meaning for a few clauses where you might otherwise think it is enough to have some aging record on file.

- product: clarified as something that can be a product or a service. You would expect this to be the case, but it is worthwhile spelling it out here, particularly as ISO 9000 did make a distinction between a product and a service. Note that the term "product" is also given a definition in Clause 3.
- regulatory requirement: clarified as a regulatory requirement for the QMS or the safety or performance of the product. This is a good practical limitation of the concept, which could otherwise be dauntingly broad. The jurisdictions applicable to you will define what these requirements are exactly.

The section also establishes the definitions for "shall" (required), "should" (recommendation), "may" (permission), and "can" (possibility or capability). These are defined as you would expect, but if you are not accustomed to these concepts in a professional setting, make sure you use them as defined here.

Of the provided clarifications, particularly the definition for the term "documented" is worth taking note of. This simple definition changes the meaning of several clauses from merely documented (as in some record must be retained) to also being established, implemented, and maintained (as in arrangements or a process should now make a reference to the creation of the record, possibly instruct how it is created; and the record should then exist). For example, Clause 6.4.1. demands that requirements for the work environment are documented—and thus, not just recorded but also established, implemented, and maintained. In most clauses, the difference in distinction may, in practice, be small to nonexistent, but it is worth knowing about this possible distinction. Clause 0, therefore, represents a small earthquake to the standard, a little bit larger on the Richter scale than its name suggests, and something not to be missed when reading the standard.

The clause also explains that the standard considers just about all activity in a QMS to be a process: something with an input, an output, and some processing in between to create added value. The standard attaches four properties to a process-based approach in general:

- Being founded on requirements (and meeting those requirements)
- Creating added value
- Tracking performance and effectiveness
- Being improved through objective measurement

What is more, the standard considers processes to be linked together to form a network or the system in a quality management system. Thus, your QMS must explain what the processes are and how they are linked. The clause gives you several items to check off when writing your quality manual in Section 5 and helps to explain some later clauses affecting the SOPs you will be writing in Sections 6 through 19.

4.3.2 Clause 1—Scope

Clause 1 comprises approximately 3% of the standard and addresses the scope of the standard as applied by an organization to its quality management. The word cloud in Figure 4.2 shows an overview of what to expect in the clause.

The clause introduces the idea that an organization, regardless of its size or type, may adopt the standard to demonstrate its ability to consistently meet both customer and applicable regulatory requirements in delivering medical devices and related services. The clause notes that the standard may, for example, be used by manufacturers and suppliers but also other organizations if they so choose.

An important requirement made by the clause is that an organization can't outsource responsibility for processes covered by this standard even if it uses suppliers or subcontractors (both of which are now called "suppliers" in the standard's parlance). Note that the retained responsibility also extends to monitoring, maintaining, and improving such processes.

/this international standard₆ /standard₆ /requirements₇ /quality management system₇ /organization₁₀ /provide₃ /medical₄ /medical devices₂ /devices₂ / related₂ /related services₂ /services₃ /applicable₆ /applicable regulatory requirements₂ /regulatory₃ /regulatory requirements₃ /such organizations ₂ /organizations₃ /including₂ /design₄ /design and development₄ / development₄ /medical device₂ /device₂ /activities₂ /of this international standard₂ /are applicable₂ /by the organization₃ /the organization₉ /the processes₂ /the responsibility of the organization₂ /responsibility₂ /design and development controls₂ /justification₂ / exclusion₂ /requirement₂ /not applicable₂

Figure 4.2 Word Cloud for Clause 1.

The clause also states that clauses under 6, 7, and 8 may be excluded if an acceptable rationale is provided based on the organization's activities or product. Furthermore, if exclusion of design and development (D&D) controls is allowed by the regulatory requirements applicable to you, doing so may be argued, but you may then have to implement alternative approaches defined by the regulations, and it will be up to you to argue how your organization is still in conformance with this standard.

4.3.3 Clauses 2 and 3—Normative References, Terms, and Definitions

Clauses 2 and 3—which comprise 0.6% and 15% of the standard, respectively—clarify the role of the ISO 9000 standard in providing normative (i.e., binding) additional information, terms, and definitions for use in applying the ISO 13485 standard. The word clouds in Figures 4.3 and 4.4 show overviews of what to expect in the clauses.

The majority of Clause 3 consists of the definitions and notes for the 20 new or modified terms introduced by the standard. Note that some terms, such as

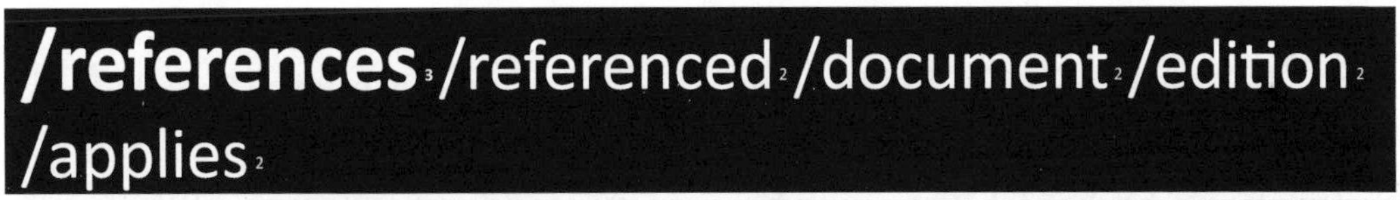

Figure 4.3 Word Cloud for Clause 2.

Figure 4.4 Word Cloud for Clause 3.

"document" and "record", are not defined in ISO 13485 and no explicit reference—beyond a general normative reference here—is made to the fact that these terms are in fact defined in ISO 9000:2015. If you find yourself wondering about the definition of some term not found in ISO 13485, you should therefore check the ISO 9000 standard. If no definition is provided in either standard, the standard dictionary definition applies. Section 4.4.8 offers further discussion on the terminology. See Appendix 1 for a quick reference to the terms defined by the two standards. Also note that the otherwise excellent ISO guidebook on the standard omits the definitions of the terms in Clause 3.

4.3.4 Clause 4—Quality Management System

Clause 4 (11% of the standard) establishes fundamental requirements for the QMS. The word cloud in Figure 4.5 shows an overview of what to expect in the clause.

The requirements set by the clause include the quality policy, quality objectives, process architecture, process control, process monitoring and improvement, document and record management, and control over changes to processes, documents, and records. The clause thus contains several key requirements affecting the design of the QMS, the quality manual, the SOPs, and even software tool validation and the technical file for a medical device. The clause gives you specific requirements for the quality manual, quality policy, quality objectives, medical device file, and the control of documents and records—other clauses will also affect these requirements, but the lists here provide an excellent starting point.

Figure 4.5   Word Cloud for Clause 4.

The control of documents and records is a major topic in this clause, and one which is fundamental to QMS. If you do happen to go into the ISO 9000 standard referenced in the previous clause, look up the terms "document", "documented information", and "record"; and after you have collected your jaw from the floor, think about how you want to make sense out of these in your QMS. For most readers, this will not matter, but some of you may find an interesting nut to crack here. Section 4.4 gives you the definitions that I would recommend, and that should be sufficient for building a modern ISO 13485 QMS.

Worth highlighting here is Clause 4.1.5, which echoes Clause 1 to state that the company retains responsibility for any process it outsources if that process may affect product conformity to requirements, and this includes the responsibility to monitor, maintain, and control the process. The definition here may thus be broader than in Clause 1, where the requirement only spoke of processes expected by this standard. Note also that Clause 1 does not give you the right to exclude subclauses from Clause 4. Clause 4 will be examined in more detail in Sections 5 and 6.

4.3.5 Clause 5—Management Responsibility

Clause 5 (6% of the standard) requires that the organization's top management take quality seriously, ensure adequate resources and reviews for it, and ensure the whole organization knows this to be the case. Despite its relative short length, this clause is the foundation of any successful QMS, as the commitment, involvement, and resources given by your management

Figure 4.6 Word Cloud for Clause 5.

will, in nautical terms, set the course and speed for your QMS. The word cloud in Figure 4.6 shows an overview of what to expect in the clause.

The clause includes requirements for establishing the quality policy, quality objectives, QMS planning, organization's internal communications, and management review. The management review and the role of the management representative is covered in some detail in this clause. Note also that Clause 1 does not give you the right to exclude subclauses from Clause 5. Clause 5 will be examined in more detail in Sections 5 and 6.

4.3.6 Clause 6—Resource Management

Clause 6 (5% of the standard) requires that the organization provides resources to implement and maintain its QMS (i.e., to continually meet QMS, regulatory, and customer needs). Remember that you may have a valid rationale for excluding some parts of the clause here (see Clause 1). The word cloud in Figure 4.7 shows an overview of what to expect in the clause.

For human resources, this means ensuring staff education, skills, experience, awareness, and motivation are appropriate for any work affecting product quality. Documented processes for improving these factors, assessing the effectiveness of any training organized, and keeping records of all these is required.

For infrastructure, this entails establishing requirements for infrastructure used in production, environment control, and monitoring or measurement. This applies to both hardware and software, and it includes the determination of the related maintenance activities and their intervals. The work environment is discussed in more detail in Clause 6.4.1, where it is elaborated that establishing requirements for the work environment and processes for monitoring and controlling the work environment may also be needed. Here, you must consider health, cleanliness, and clothing, and also employees temporarily working in the environments.

Finally, if contamination control is needed (remember to provide a rationale in your quality manual if it doesn't apply), documented arrangements are

/the organization₁₀/quality₆/requirements₁₀/ personnel₈/work₁₄/product₁₁/training₅/the organization shall document₆/document₈/the work ₈/requirements for₆/control₆/work environment₁₀/ environment₁₀

Figure 4.7 Word Cloud for Clause 6.

needed (note that the standard does not say that a process is needed here) for the control of possibly contaminated product to protect the work environment, personnel, and product. Special requirements apply to sterile medical devices.

4.3.7 Clause 7—Product Realization

Clause 7 is almost a standard within the standard as it represents about 34% of the content of the whole standard. Remember that you may have a valid rationale for excluding some parts of the clause here (see Clause 1). The word cloud in Figure 4.8 shows an overview of what to expect in the clause.

The clause gives you the high-level framework for all your product realization activities and instructs subprocesses, such as planning of product realization, customer-related processes, design and development (including planning, inputs, outputs, reviews, verification, validation, transfer, control of changes, and the file set), purchasing, and production and service provision. It represents a substantial part of the standard and a part that goes to the core of your organization's operations—unless you have a valid rationale to exclude parts of it.

In many cases, you will want to bring in another standard, or a set of standards, to fit into Clause 7 and help you manage your product realization activities. A common example here might be IEC 62304 for software life cycle

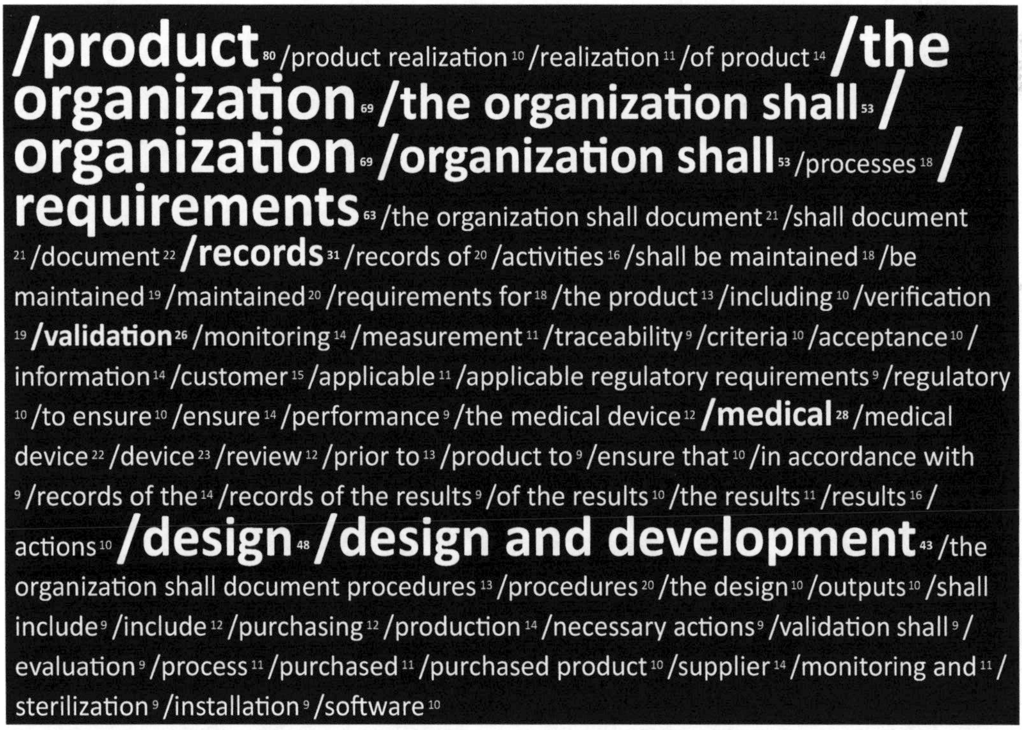

Figure 4.8   Word Cloud for Clause 7.

management and IEC 60601 for hardware devices. These are only two examples; depending on your operations, you may have other standards you either want to use or are forced to use here. The discussion of these standards is beyond our focus here, but the concept of utilizing other specific standards within Clause 7 is something you should be aware of and discuss with your quality experts.

4.3.8 Clause 8—Measurement, Analysis, and Improvement

Clause 8 (16% of the standard) concerns itself with monitoring, measuring, analyzing, and improving your operations. Remember that you may have a valid rationale for excluding some parts of the clause here (see Clause 1). The word cloud in Figure 4.9 shows an overview of what to expect in the clause.

A key topic here is the measurement of your product and the control of nonconforming product (including both products detected before and after delivery). Improvement activities also pack a punch, as they address your CAPA activities: the corrective actions you take to remove issues and the preventive actions you take to prevent their reoccurrence also elsewhere in your QMS. Similarly, the monitoring here builds on the customer processes defined in Clause 7 to address feedback, complaint handling, reporting to authorities, and conducting internal audits.

4.4 The Pieces of the Puzzle

Looking back on our own deep dive into QMS, one thing we were wrestling with at the start of our own development process was knowing what the pieces of the puzzle were and how each piece fits together to make the whole.

Figure 4.9 Word Cloud for Clause 8.

At first, we were hesitant to make changes in any particular process template we were shown by the consultants as we weren't sure how those changes would affect later processes. Then once we saw more of the processes come together, we were willing to make larger and larger modifications to tweak the processes to our preferences and even write a few processes from scratch. In the end, we made several passes over the full set of processes to tweak them all. It would have been preferable to have a fuller grasp of the whole from the start before beginning work on any individual processes. That is what this section attempts to provide you: to let you see the forest before the trees.

It is, of course, a cliché of the highest order to say after a project that we would have liked to have known the end result better at the start so that we could have been quicker, better, and smarter in reaching that result. Hindsight is always twenty-twenty. But it is worth knowing what the overall pieces are that you will be working with in your QMS and what interest groups you may be interacting with and how. This section is dedicated to answering the questions of what the big pieces are that make up a QMS and how they fit together. After this section, it will be time to start drafting your QMS.

Now that we have the necessary general introduction out of the way, let's start to look at what the actual building blocks of a QMS are and who the stakeholders are that have an interest in your QMS or need to work with some of those building blocks. This section will introduce you to the documents, records, registries, external stakeholders, people at your organization, tools, activities, and terminology you will be relying on in your QMS. Let's look at these one by one.

4.4.1 Documents

One way of looking at a QMS is that it consists of documents that instruct processes and the records created from following those processes. The layman's term "document" (and interestingly enough, also the definition given in ISO 9000) thus refers to both "documents" and "records", but when a distinction is made in a QMS, it is between a document instructing action and a record being made of the completed action. To muddy the waters, the layman's definition, too, is frequently used. It is worthwhile noting that stricter requirements often apply to documents than to records, although both should be retained in a safe, reliably accessible, and—unless otherwise successfully argued—version-controlled way. Maintaining a version history may also be required as not only must the changes be made in a controlled manner, but they must also either be identified (for documents) or remain identifiable (for records).

The fundamental types of documents involved in a QMS are introduced in the following. In the standard, these matters are mostly covered in Clause 4. In this book, we will begin by writing the quality manual in Section 5 and then go deeper into documentation management with SOP-1 in Section 7.

Quality Manual

The quality manual is your first port of call for the QMS. It is the master document in your QMS—the one place where all answers originate from. The manual may be long or short, it may contain all your processes or simply refer to them, but it is the root of your QMS and the one document you will hand to new employees and auditors when you first encounter them. It may also be read by your customers if these are business entities looking to understand how you work.

The manual will be revised through the document review cycle (see Section 25) or sooner, if needed, but always through a controlled mechanism. Having a quality manual is required by Clause 4.2.2 of the standard. In this book, writing the manual is addressed in Section 5.

Standard Operating Procedures

The standard operating procedures, or SOPs, are the real meat of your QMS documents. Each SOP is a document that instructs a particular process or perhaps a bundle of related processes within your organization. The SOPs should cover each process with an adequate level of detail and act as the first place to look for any specifics regarding a process after the quality manual.

The SOPs should align with the requirements set by the standard and any applicable regulations. It is not required to follow the clause structure of the standard when writing the SOPs, but having an understanding of how the two map together will be beneficial in audits, as your auditor will be approaching your processes from the point of view of the clauses of the standard. The same will also be true of many other quality professionals looking to understand your QMS from the outside or new employees coming in with previous experience of the standard.

The SOPs will be revised through the document review cycle (see Section 25) or sooner, if needed, but always through a controlled mechanism. In the standard, processes are covered in just about every clause. In this book, the general layout of SOPs is discussed in Section 6; after which, the individual SOPs are addressed in Sections 7 through 18, and then finalized in Section 19.

Working Instructions

Working instructions are an extension of your SOPs that are written to help the performance of some individual tasks. The instructions can thus contain more detailed, grassroots-level information on a process than the higher-level SOPs. An example of an SOP might be your organization's overall approach to personnel training (see SOP-4), and a working instruction you might write as an extension of that might be how an employee can use your online learning environment.

The working instructions aim to provide the exact information at the point where it is needed and, thus, enable a task to be completed with less friction and more certainty. Without the instructions, an employee might have to, for example, go through the entire SOP and translate it to some settings on a piece of machinery they need to use for the task. Having this translation ready in the working instruction eliminates unnecessary points of error.

Somewhat surprisingly, the term "working instruction" or "work instruction" does not feature in the standard at all. The term "work instruction" does come up in the guidebook published as a companion to the standard by the ISO. In the guidebook, working instructions are mentioned as an example of an action that your organization can take to address risks. This, of course, makes sense, as a more straightforward instruction is more likely to be followed when performing a task, but it also means that you should approach the maintenance of working instructions with the necessary level of care. The guidebook suggests that working instructions tag along with your processes and that, in addition to requirements set in your policies and procedures, any requirements set in the instructions are to be implemented and maintained.

Working instructions can thus be a part of the arrangements, as the standard says, you have made to fulfill the requirements set by the standard, the applicable regulations, and your customer. A working instruction may apply to one or more SOPs, but you should ensure that all these connections are reviewed and kept up-to-date. A good idea might be to reference the instructions from the relevant SOP and then make sure they are reviewed as part of the document review cycle.

If you are developing your first QMS, I would not worry too much about creating working instructions. If you think they are beneficial to work in your organization, or even a must, then definitely go ahead writing the necessary working instructions. More likely, though, you should focus on writing the process descriptions in the SOPs first, and only then see what additional grassroots-level information is needed—and why this should not be updated to the SOP itself.

The question of when you want to augment the information in your SOPs with working instructions is a choice left to you. No working instructions are specifically required by the standard. No template for working instructions is imposed on you either, but I would recommend using your general document template with the appropriate document ID and document version identification. Remember to retain all issued versions of your working instructions for later reference, unless you have a good, documented rationale for doing otherwise. Also consider using a version history table or otherwise pointing out any changes to the users of your working instructions. Pay attention to also ensuring that the correct versions of working instructions are used even when these are printed and sticker-taped to some piece of machinery or stored in a binder in the working environment.

Templates and Forms

Templates and forms are not, strictly speaking, mentioned by the standard, but you would be hard-pressed to explain why your documents look different for every employee evaluation, nonconformity, or SOP in your QMS. In practice, you must have templates and forms, but the way you go about creating them is what makes the difference. Also note that if the templates or forms are relied on by SOPs, they should be considered a part of your core set of QMS documents.

When you are creating your QMS from scratch, you have a great opportunity to think about what you want every document or every document of a specific kind to include. You may start with a generic document template that has a header and a footer and the fonts you want to use. You may then start thinking about what information you should have in all your SOPs and start building a rough idea of the table of contents you will use for SOPs. The same template should also be applicable to your quality manual, with a few small differences (see Section 20). You will be scratching your head more if you try to come up with a template for a risk management plan or a subcontractor evaluation before you have had a chance to work on the SOPs covering the use of those documents. Appendices 2 and 3 will give you example templates for the manual and the SOPs, respectively.

The way I have generally approached templates is to design templates with what I considered the essential elements but then allow for more information to be put in when using those templates. I have tried to test-drive templates and forms during the development, of course, but I have wanted to leave in some mechanism for not losing other information that I had over-looked during design. This way, once we know the resulting records work for our needs in practice, we can then revise the templates, but we will have saved effort in not always requiring some additional information that we had thought might be beneficial but was not. We also won't have missed out on some information that would have been left out without the flexibility in the use of the templates. The amount of flexibility possible will vary case by case, but I would not put the cart before the horse and try to lock down complex templates before I had used them for real. At least once.

Beware also of inheriting templates from somewhere and using those in your QMS without a proper test-drive. The templates may have worked for someone else in their circumstances, but this is not a guarantee you will like using them in your setup. The inherited templates may be missing some information you should include, and they may call for information to be entered that is not relevant or useful for you. This also applies to ready-made document templates you can buy online: they will probably be more complex and bloated than they need to be just so that they look to you like worth spending money on.

Finally, please note that while templates and forms are perhaps there for convenience, they may be QMS documents and should be controlled as such. You can't just change a form whose use is instructed by an SOP half-way through applying that form without going through the necessary work to revise the SOP and notify your staff. What you can do, though, is be smart about what kind of templates and forms you create, and allow for flex-ibility in additional information.

Section 20 goes into more detail on creating forms and templates.

4.4.2 Records

Records hold a special, reserved place in the standard, and in a QMS, they are the recordings that something instructed in your QMS documents (e.g., quality manual and SOPs) has been done. Records hold the answers to what was done, who did it, when, and to what effect. You will create records for just about everything in your QMS. There will be meeting minutes, plans, reports, and filled-in forms of every which kind. It is your job to orga-nize these records in some practical way so that they can be searched and accessed as it is appropriate.

Records are needed to comfortably proceed to the next step or process in your QMS and perhaps to convince your customers and auditors that they can rely on you. The records, the ease to which they can be accessed, and the ability to analyze them and make decisions based on them are crucial to improving your QMS over time too. The place where you will be fretting the most about records is probably the audit, where it's not enough that you have a documented process, you must also show that it has been followed as instructed and followed to a good outcome. That said, the audit is only an isolated event of short duration, so you should not be recording things just for the sake of the audits but for all the other uses you envisage.

A consideration with records may also be whether they are intended primarily for internal use within your organization or if they need to be distributed outside of your organization. For example, the declaration of conformity (DoC) is a record that is mostly intended to be distributed with your product and to provide necessary information about it to your customers. It thus makes little sense to display internal IDs on this record, and indeed, such records may be confusing to the reader—certainly they can't use any IDs displayed on the record to read more on the topics covered. You do, of course, have to be able to link such records distributed externally to your internal copies of the same records, but this is perhaps better accomplished through product IDs, product version IDs and dates.

My mugshot was once displayed full page in half a dozen regional newspapers just because I supplied a number of photos to use with a story and happened to write "main photo" on one of the files. The file name was interpreted to be significant while laying out the article even though it was not intended so by me or by the journalist responsible for the story. This is, of course, a far cry from including extra identifiers on a DoC, but it maybe goes to show that providing unexpected or additional information may not always be as safe as you think.

A further important consideration to note here is that if your records deal with personal information, they may be subject to legislation, such as the General Data Protection Regulation (GDPR) in Europe, and if the records contain medical or patient information, that is a whole other thing to take seriously. Even the standard makes a mention of the latter type of data.

The discussion in this book will refer to records as relevant to each process.

Official Copies

Clause 4.2.4f of the standard requires you to ensure that those documents of external origin that your organization has determined to be necessary for planning and operation of your QMS are identified and distributed in a controlled fashion. The standard uses the layman's term "document" instead of "record", although you could argue for the use of either term. As these documents arrive on your doorstep without any freedom to reformat or edit them, I might call them records and have introduced them here for that reason. Concrete examples of such external documents are standards, regulations, and the manuals of some tools you use.

Medical Device Files

The standard makes a point of requiring that you establish and maintain a medical device file for each medical device type or medical device family (Clause 4.2.3). This file is, in essence, a master record containing or referencing the documents and records demonstrating conformity of the device to the requirements of the standard and any applicable regulatory requirements. This file is, therefore, your technical file, the collection of the necessary technical records for your medical device. The medical device file will be covered in more detail in Section 17.9, but for now, it is enough to know that it is an important set of records.

4.4.3 Registries

Sometimes it does not make sense to rely on a stack of individual records when a register is much more practical for entering the information and keeping it in one place for easy searching and monitoring. For such use, registers, think Excel spreadsheet or databases, make more sense than individual document-like files.

Registers or databases are not featured in the standard, but both are taken for granted as probably being a part of your organization's overall setup. Neither is required, though, strictly speaking. You could accomplish the same with folders of records, but this might not be the most practical way of keeping track of the information in the records and their status. On the other hand, if your database is not sophisticated enough, you may run into issues proving issuance dates and authorities for any entry or line in your database. Remember that you will probably want to, or even be required to, validate the database tools you use.

If you have a powerful database engine at your service and the necessary know-how to validate that, that is probably the best and most efficient solution for you. If, however, you are starting from scratch, I would suggest using registers as living records, providing an overview over some particular type of records that you have created and issued in your QMS elsewhere. This way, registers can perform the function you really want from them: pool together relevant information from records and provide you with a practical overview of several records at once. And you don't have to stress about issuing rows in registers and proving when it was done and by whom. You must still take care over updating registers, but mostly, it is now about remembering to update the registers after the underlying records have been appropriately issued. I would still advocate for letting one named person (or their substitute) update each register to avoid duplicate work and omissions by misunderstanding. The discussion in this book will refer to registers as relevant to each process, but ultimately, the choice of when to use registers is up to you.

4.4.4 Stakeholders

In addition to people at your organization, who we will look at shortly, there is also a diverse group of other actors who may have an interest in your QMS or may be required to work with it. In addition to the four organizational roles named in Clause 4.4.1 of the standard—manufacturer, authorized representative, importer, and distributor—a number of other roles may come up in your QMS. The key stakeholder roles are discussed in the following. A word of caution, though, be careful about trying to assign responsibilities with the following roles in your QMS, as in most cases, that will not be possible. In a few cases (e.g., suppliers and distributors) you can place burdens of responsibility if you are then willing to pay for the privilege and maybe limit your pool of options. Instead, you may show your understanding of some requirement placed on you in relation with the subsequent roles (e.g., notified body and competent authority).

Manufacturer

The standard defines a manufacturer as the entity who makes a medical device available for use under his name. The standard also talks of responsibility for design and/or manufacture of a medical device but, in practice, assigns this responsibility with the act of making the device available and not with the organization who may be conducting design and/or manufacturing activities on behalf of someone else. The definition wishes to say that the manufacturer is the entity who makes something available for use as a medical device. This is where the buck stops or all the information streams from R&D, post-market, and everywhere else cross. All the responsibility for anything belongs here unless you can convincingly argue otherwise, and even then, you will be sitting up front in the courtroom, should it come to that.

In all likelihood, the "manufacturer" means "your organization"—unless you really are a casual reader looking to understand QMS without the need to implement it, in which case, good on you for making it this deep into the book. We will make a QMS aficionado out of you yet. The term "manufacturer" is one of the four organization roles mentioned by Clause 4.1.1.

Suppliers and Subcontractors

Suppliers and subcontractors (both of which are called "suppliers" in the standard's parlance and may have been called "providers" in ISO 9000) are external parties who provide product or services to your organization in the form of, for example, raw materials, components, medical devices, sterilization services, distribution services, and maintenance services (see Clause 0.1). In other words, suppliers undertake to perform some part of adding value in your processes. It is important to remember that the responsibility of the outcome will rest with you almost regardless of what kind of agreements you draw up with the supplier. Even if you will likely sue the supplier for damages if something goes wrong, you can't say, "It wasn't me, talk to my supplier", if something does go wrong. In the eyes of the standard, you can't outsource responsibility.

The term "supplier" occurs 27 times in the standard, and it is safe to say a lot of importance is placed on how you interact and control your suppliers. It is even expected that your suppliers, too, may voluntarily want to use the standard in their own operations. You may also want to contractually oblige them to do so. Section 11 will go into subcontractor management in more detail.

Authorized Representative

This is one of the four organization roles mentioned by Clause 4.1.1 in the standard, where it is also given a definition as an entity given a mandate to act on behalf of the manufacturer for specified tasks. The role is not given any special responsibilities in the standard, but instead, it is expected that the whole standard (or part thereof) may be adopted by the authorized representative. Remember that your applicable regulations may set requirements here.

Importer

This is one of the four organization roles mentioned by Clause 4.1.1 in the standard, where it is given a definition as the first entity in a supply chain to make the imported medical device available in the specific country or jurisdiction. The role is not given any special responsibilities in the standard, but instead, it is expected that the whole standard (or part thereof) may be adopted by the importer. Remember that your applicable regulations may set requirements here.

Distributors

A "distributor" is one simple term, but that term has widely different meanings across the world. In Europe, distributors are facing new expectations of responsibility following the transition to the new Medical Device Regulation and, as a result, may expect to have duties in, for example, traceability and post-market surveillance. In the US, distributors can be little more than warehouses or purchase order processors who may even actually rely on your organization's warehouses. It all greatly depends on the type of product you have and what types of marketplaces and sales models exist for it.

The simple way of looking at distributors is as an extension to your organization, a go-between for you and the customer. The standard defines a "distributor" as an entity in the supply chain who, on his own behalf, furthers the availability of a medical device to the end user. This broad description applies to all the cases previously discussed, although the standard adds a note saying that mere logistics on behalf of the manufacturer or a distributor are exempt from being considered "distribution". The definition also leaves the question of responsibilities wide open and leaves you to figure it out in negotiating distribution agreements.

The term "distributor" is one of the four organization roles mentioned by Clause 4.1.1 of the standard. The role is not given any special responsibilities in the standard, but instead, it is expected that the whole standard (or part thereof) may be adopted by the distributor. The one exception is in the case of implantable medical devices, where the manufacturer is obligated to require its distributors to maintain records for traceability and to keep these records available for inspection. Similar expectations may conceivably arise in the case of other types of devices too.

Customers and End Users

Customers feature heavily in the standard. Customers are often mentioned together with applicable regulatory requirements and even on the same level. In some cases, your customer may also be another organization who, for example, purchases your product for use in their own product or service.

In such cases, your customer and end user may be different, and it is important to consider both to the extent you can.

You can begin addressing your relationship to your customers and users in your quality manual, where they will likely feature in both the description of your organization and product, and the quality policy your management sets for your organization. This will be discussed in Section 5.

Patients and Their Families

The standard itself does not mention patients at all, but expect your risk management for a medical device to be thinking about the patient constantly. Many of your risks will need to be translated into harm that may come to the patient, as will also the benefit you want to create. For this reason, patients will feature in the quality policy and SOPs you are writing.

In addition to patients, you will also probably want to address the healthcare staff and the environment somehow. I would also recommend thinking about other possible interest groups, such as the families of the patients your device will treat.

Certification Body or Notified Body

If you want to obtain a certificate for your QMS, you have two options: a certification body and, in Europe, a notified body.

Certification bodies are providers who are accredited to perform inspections of your QMS according to standards, such as ISO 13485, and provide corresponding certificates. Note that not all certification bodies may be accredited to the same version of the standard, and thus, to obtain the certificate you want, your choices may be limited. This will be particularly true when a new version of the standard has just been published and the body accreditations have not yet been updated.

A notified body, on the other hand, is the body entrusted by the European Union and the regional competent authorities to oversee the medical device market in the EU. This involves performing EC conformity assessments and post-market oversight of medical devices on the market but also of the manufacturers behind the devices. The latter includes performing surveillance inspections of the manufacturer's quality management system and providing certificates on these.

Your certification body or your notified body will feature in the SOPs you write, although neither features in the standard itself. Both will have requirements for you to fill in later communication with them, and both will expect to be notified of significant events and planned actions. Your SOPs should state this clearly. My last piece of advice here, and one that should be quite obvious, is that you should not think of either provider as your supplier or consultant but instead as a go-between serving a higher purpose.

Authorities

The competent authorities in the EU are the official national institutions who oversee the notified bodies and—should it come to that—manufacturers working in their jurisdictions. They are also the ones who will inspect manufacturers of Class I devices that do not need to go through notified bodies to enter the market but are subject to ISO 13485 quality management (although this does not have to be certified).

In the US, the authority you would most likely be addressing in your SOPs is the Food and Drug Administration (FDA). The FDA may be compared to a European competent authority, but it, of course, serves a larger geographic market area than a national competent authority in Europe and also has many functions associated with a notified body (e.g., post-market surveillance) and has some that notified bodies are not as readily allowed (e.g., industry assistance and training).

4.4.5 People at Your Organization

The standard speaks of the top management, the management representative, the personnel, and the whole of your organization. It also talks of personnel performing work affecting product quality, supplier personnel, and specialist personnel. All these are concepts that you will likely want to use in your quality manual and SOPs. In addition, the quality manager, the Quality Management Team, the Management Team, and the individual C-level officer roles are concepts that you may want to use in instructing your processes. Each of these roles is subsequently introduced.

Top Management (Management Team)

The role of the top management is inherited from ISO 9000, where it is defined as a single person or a group who directs and controls an organization at the highest level and, thus, has the power to delegate authority and provide resources within that organization. The ISO 13485 standard does not alter the definition but instead attaches several big responsibilities to top management. The term "top management" only appears 13 times in the standard and its appendices, but this low count does not accurately reflect the weight placed on the role by the standard. In fact, the whole of Clause 5 is dedicated to management responsibility and that refers squarely to the top management of the organization.

Top management may, in practice, be synonymous with the Management Team of the company. The Management Team usually consists of the C-level officers in charge of running the company day-to-day. The chairman of the Management Team is usually the CEO.

Management Representative

The management representative (MR) is a member of the Management Team and appointed by them to be their main contact point with the QMS. In hierarchy, the MR is thus above the quality manager or quality managers, if there are several. The standard defines the following duties for the MR irrespective of any other responsibilities they may have:

- Ensures QMS processes are documented (thus also established, implemented, and maintained; see Section 4.3.1)
- Ensures the promotion of awareness of applicable regulatory requirements and QMS requirements throughout the organization
- Reports to the management on QMS effectiveness, including any need for improvement

In essence, the MR oversees the QMS at the organization and, for example, is often the person in charge of organizing the periodic management review (see Section 4.4.7). Note that the MR must have a deputy. The MR may also be the person responsible for regulatory compliance (PRRC) as defined by the EU MDR. The requirements for the MR are in Clause 5.5.2 of the standard.

Quality Manager

This may come as a bit of a surprise, but the term "quality manager" does not feature in the standard or its accompanying guidebook at all. In practice, most, if not all, organizations implementing ISO 13485 quality management do have one or more quality managers. If there is just one quality manager, they are often in charge of running the QMS and a natural choice for the chairperson of the Quality Management Team. If there are several quality managers, you should be careful in defining their relative roles.

The power and responsibility of the quality manager depends on how you define that role in your QMS. The standard does not place requirements on the role. You may have heard that a quality manager needs X years of experience and some applicable education, and this is true in case the quality manager is also the person responsible for regulatory compliance (PRRC) at your organization, as defined by the EU MDR. Otherwise, the qualifications, role, and responsibility of a quality manager are essentially up to you, but if you are going to use the role in your QMS, you should make sure you also define those characteristics and qualifications adequately in your QMS. The quality manager should also have a deputy.

Quality Management Team (Quality Team)

The Quality Management Team (or Quality Team for short) is the team of personnel entrusted with ensuring your organization's QMS is running smoothly. Your Quality Management Team should be the operational unit that has the necessary qualifications, responsibilities, and authorities to run your QMS. This includes running the document review and CAPA, and ensuring all other QMS processes also run as instructed. The team may, for example, have high-level representatives from your organization's clinical evidence gathering and product realization activities. The standard does not define a Quality Management Team, but for running your QMS effectively, you should have something in place that meets your needs and gives your management representative or quality manager the necessary core team to run the day-to-day.

C-Level Officers and Others

In addition to the roles stated earlier, you may also want to define various other C-level officers as roles you can attach responsibilities and authorities to. Common examples include the chief executive officer, chief operational officer, chief financial officer, chief technology officer, chief medical officer, and chief marketing officer (note that a CMO may confusingly refer to either a medical or a marketing sphere). You should also define deputies for C-level officers.

If you do not wish to tie down the definitions in your processes to a single person filling that role, you may also use more communal roles, such as a technical expert and a medical expert, but beware of tying responsibilities to perform some activities on such shared hats. In general, C-level officers are safer options for ensuring something is done, and more generic roles are good options for ensuring that some viewpoint is heard while doing that.

As a final note, remember to define the roles used within your organization somewhere in your QMS documentation. This definition should include responsibilities and qualifications, and it can also include deputy arrangements. In this book, I suggest writing these definitions as part of your overall organization description in the quality manual, preferably as an appendix to the manual itself (see Section 5). You can also later use such definitions as you are preparing new job announcements or revising the qualification requirements for some position.

4.4.6 Tools

You will know what tools and machinery you need to have at hand to produce your product, but also remember to think about what software you will need in that. The standard requires you to carefully consider your infrastructure and maintain it adequately. This also applies to your software, which will need some form of validation and maintenance over time. This includes the software you use in your QMS. In this book, we will address tools and resources with SOP-3 in Section 9.

4.4.7 Specific Activities

The following list is a brief introduction into the main activities just about all QMS setups have in common. In this book, we will be addressing each of these activities in more detail when writing the SOPs in Sections 6 through 19.

Document Review

The term "document review" does not appear in the standard, but the standard does require that the organization documents a QMS and maintains its effectiveness (see Clause 4 in Section 4.3.4, for example). This includes establishing, implementing, and maintaining any requirement, procedure, activity, or arrangement required by the standard. The effect of this demand is that your organization needs some mechanism for maintaining your QMS, including its quality manual and SOPs. The term used in this book for such long-term oversight and periodic revision of your process instructions is "document review", but you could call your mechanism something else if you wanted to. Clause 4 makes several requirements you must fulfill in creating the mechanism, which we will discuss in detail in Section 8 (SOP-2) and, from the point of view of running the activity, also in Section 25.

Internal Audit

The internal audit is your internal mechanism for checking that you are working as you have said you are in your QMS. It can be run by your organization internally or with the assistance of a consultant or other supplier, but it is important that no auditor inspects their own work. Internal audits can lead to observations, nonconformities, and actions to take by your organization in fixing some discovered issue or enacting improvements. Internal audit reports are frequently used in your internal management reviews and in your external audits.

The agenda for your internal audits may vary, but it is expected that you cover your whole QMS over a predefined period of time and that you organize some internal audits annually. An individual internal audit may cover the whole QMS or only a part of it. Internal audits are addressed in SOP-6, which we will be writing in Section 12 of this book. Section 26.3 also offers practical advice on audits.

Management Review

The management review is the periodic activity where your top management reviews your entire QMS at documented planned intervals to ensure its continuing suitability, adequacy, and effectiveness. Typically, the review takes place once a year. Management review reports are often then reviewed in external audits. The management review is addressed in SOP-6, which we will write in Section 12 of this book. Additionally, Section 27 offers practical advice on performing the review.

External Audit

External audits are run by your certification body or your notified body to review whether your instructed processes meet the requirements and whether you are in fact meeting your instructed processes. Such audits will often request access to your QMS documents, including the quality manual and SOPs, and the reports from your most recent internal audit and management review.

External audits are not mentioned by the standard, but they are a required part of obtaining and maintaining a certified ISO 13485 quality management system. Section 26.3.2 of this book covers the topic in more detail, and external audits will also feature in SOP-6, which we will be writing in Section 12 of this book.

4.4.8 Key Terminology

As discussed earlier, the terminology to use in your ISO 13485 QMS consists of terms defined by the ISO 13485 standard and the ISO 9000 standard, as well as commonly accepted dictionary terms. The three sources take precedence in this descending order.

Inherited Terminology from ISO 9000

There is a very long list of terms defined in ISO 9000, which are inherited by the ISO 13485 standard in a normative (binding) manner. Many of these terms do not feature in the ISO 13485 standard at all, but some are still used in the context of QMS just the same. See Appendix 1 for a list of the terms and whether they are expressly used in the text of the newer standard.

New Terminology Defined by ISO 13485

The ISO 13485 standard updates ISO 9000 terminology with 17 new terms. These terms are all up-to-date and are widely used in the context of medical devices. The terms introduced by the newer standard are "advisory notice", "authorized representative", "clinical evaluation", "distributor", "implantable medical device", "importer", "labelling", "life-cycle", "manufacturer", "medical device", "medical device family", "performance evaluation", "post-market surveillance", "purchased product", "risk management", "sterile barrier system", and "sterile medical device".

If you need to refer to the definition of any of these terms, you will find them in the ISO 13485 standard itself. Note that the otherwise great guidebook on the standard published by ISO unfortunately does not give you these definitions.

Terminology with Changed Meanings

In addition to the new terms introduced by the ISO 13485 standard, the definition of a few terms originally introduced in the ISO 9000 standard also changed. These terms are as follows:

■ **Product**
The new definition emphasizes "product" as the result of a process. The definition moves away from the old definition of a product being something the organization produces without any transaction taking place

between it and the customer. Instead, ISO 13485 considers the customer as part of the requirements elicitation process and addresses purchasing information and postdelivery activities, which assuredly increase the level of interaction required between the manufacturer and the customer. The term "product" now appears a whopping 254 times in the standard.

■ Risk

The old definition almost brushed away "risk" as the effect of uncertainty. The new definition moves toward managing risks in a more concrete way by defining "risk" as the combination of a) the probability of occurrence of harm and b) the severity of that harm. This definition is compatible with ISO 14971 risk management and IEC 62304 software development. The term "risk" now appears 46 times in the standard, but it is in fact present throughout the standard (e.g., consider the use of the term "as appropriate" discussed in Section 4.3.1).

■ Complaint

The old definition positioned "complaint" as an expression of dissatisfaction made to the manufacturer on its product, service, or complaints handling process. The new definition changes the focus to the product and any related service, and the alleged deficiencies in their identity, quality, durability, reliability, usability, safety, or performance. The term "complaint" now appears 20 times in the standard.

Expect there to be variation on how different organizations and their QMS setups define these concepts, and therefore, expect the definitions to also likely be addressed during any initial certification audit of your QMS.

The previously stated three changes in meaning are flagged up by the ISO 13485 standard. In addition to these three, I would argue there are other subtle changes not flagged up. One example is the term "provider", which has now effectively been replaced by the term "supplier". Another more groundbreaking silent change is the term "document", which has stealthily evolved from a generic concept of any document-like object to what was perhaps better captured by "documented information" in the ISO 9000 standard. The term "document" as defined in ISO 9000 and as still supposedly in use by the ISO 13485 refers to any document, record, or other piece of information on any medium. The term "documented information", in essence, refers to documents that answer some requirement of the standard and, as such, is closer to what the ISO 13485 now considers a "document". The difference may seem like semantics, but the difference is quite marked as it is the difference between observing requirements for document control (Clause 4.2.4) or requirements for record control (Clause 4.2.5). The principal difference in the two types of controls is that in the former, all changes must be identified (thus itemized and explained), while in the latter, the changes only must remain identifiable. The term "document" appears a whopping 243 times in different meanings in the standard.

Expect there to be some further differences between ISO 9000 and ISO 13485, both apparent and subtle ones. Expect there to be further small differences in expectations between these standards and any later revisions of them, including also in the context of the Medical Device Single Audit Program (MDSAP) across the globe. Standards are our best guarantee of achieving interoperability across the global landscape, but even a standard does not give you the right to an expectation of plug-and-play uniformity in the real world.

In cinematic terms, the ISO 13485 standard is like the 4K standard in films that ensures that the content will play in any 4K-compatible device, but it does not give any guarantees on what is done with the millions of pixels by the filmmakers. The 4K standard does, of course, raise expectations that the content will be professionally made, look great, and entertain you; but none of these things can be taken for granted. Likewise, the ISO 13485 standard promotes interoperability and raises expectations, but ultimately, it only acts as a framework for performing activities in your organization and for getting a grasp of those activities from the outside.

4.5 The Stage Is Yours

Phew, we made it! Now you know enough of everything you will need to slot into place to start building your QMS. In the next section, we will break ground by first looking at what the quality manual is and then how to write it. Before then, it may be a good time to take inventory of your circumstances for developing the QMS.

If you are heading into the development project alone, you are in for a pretty big task, but it is doable if you have an entrepreneurial background and know enough of each field of operations. Even in this case, you should have a deep soul-searching conversation with your organization to make sure they know what the whole organization is embarking on—after all, you will not be running the QMS for your organization by yourself. If after the discussion, your top management thinks that you will be taking care of the QMS for them, and in the long term, too, my advice for you is to run. Your organization is not ready for QMS, and you won't want the ulcers, gray hairs, and handcuffs that you would be in store for. If on the other hand, your top management wants you to draft the QMS and walk them into it, that is probably not suspicious and not too different from what I did either.

Hopefully, you are not alone. Your QMS stands the best chance of meeting its goals and becoming something that is not just a burden to run but something that enhances quality if you have a team of willing and knowledgeable people to work on the QMS from the start. Personally, I would also be weary of people who are too eager to jump into QMS development, as that could mean you are in for some royal bureaucracy and micromanagement, but I hope that is just me.

In developing your QMS, you will want to think long and hard about why some individual thing is done so that you can design a good way of incorporating it in with all the rest. I have never built a space station, but I'd imagine that it is not unlike building a QMS: it takes enormous resources to jet up some piece of the station from the Earth, so you will want to make sure you want the piece up there and that it will fit together nicely with whatever else is up there before you burn the rocket fuel to actually get it up in place. In space, there might be less friction involved in the maintenance of the station than is perhaps involved in the maintenance of a QMS, but the expense of having something replaced is comparable in both. So think carefully about each process and how you want it to slot in with the rest of your QMS. To loosely misquote JFK's famous speech, "don't take a decade, don't go for the easy way or the hard way, but find the smart path in between". This book will give you the signposts based on the standard to do just that.

If you have a team, you should all work on the fundamental questions together in drafting the quality manual. You could then fan out into smaller task groups for the individual SOPs you will be creating. Some members of your team could be involved in only a single SOP, while others may be contributing to more or even all the processes. The involvement of your top management is most important when writing your quality manual, especially the quality policy I would have you include there (and the standard requires you to include somewhere in your QMS). If you get the quality manual more or less done first, you will have an excellent launch pad for starting work on your SOPs.

If possible, I would engage a quality consultant who has experience with ISO 13485 quality management, preferably in your target jurisdiction. Having their wealth of information and steady hand to guide you as needed will make the whole process of developing your QMS more predictable and even enjoyable. You will get all the necessary information to build your QMS from this book, the standard, and the host of guidance documents that may be relevant to you, but having a good consultant pick up your call or even guide you through the process will be money well spent. But do not make the mistake of thinking that a consultant will give you a free ride—it will not be free, and it will not even be a ride, as you must be driving or at least helping with the navigation constantly to get where you want to go. Unless, of course, that cliff Thelma and Louise had their eyes on appeals to you as a final destination.

Also plot a schedule for your work. It will be all too easy to get bogged down in the minutiae of this process or that, and while it could be time well spent fleshing out some important design choices, you are most likely just adding details that you will end up cutting sooner or later anyway.

I would recommend working on the quality manual and the first SOP together with your team and then splitting the group up to prepare additional SOPs based on skills and experience. Then once new SOPs are available as drafts, you can share those with the group, give feedback, and agree on the next steps. Scheduling one to two weeks per SOP from conception to a finished version 1.0 would be my goal, but I would expect to perform a second pass after all or most of the SOPs have been prepared to that stage. You may want to use some project management tools here, but you don't have to. If you are a WYSIWYG kind of a guy and your team is small, you will probably do well just focusing on the content.

Don't plan on a constant burn over several months as that probably won't happen. It is worth taking a little bit of breather every once in a while; for example, as you have a first pass ready for a group of related processes and think about what you have done. For us, the summer holiday (yes, we sort of had one) came at a good time so that we all could put down the pen for a short while and let the thoughts brew a little on the background. In most cases, not that much changed after the pause, but occasionally, some important observation was made, and importantly, I feel like the pause prepared us better for thinking about the connection with the next processes. Weekends will also work the same so that even if I personally burned through weekends working on several occasions, my team and I still got a chance to reflect a little before picking up work full steam on Monday.

During writing, I recommend keeping a list of the roles you have used in the text and a plot of the various periodical events, such as reviews and audits, you have penciled in. You will hopefully notice how you can combine several needs in one event to achieve more at once and, thus, avoid specifying multiple similar events in parallel and duplicating your bureaucracy. Don't go overboard with this as you might drown under the weight of an overgrown event, but do consider what tasks you could group under monthly Quality Management Team or Management Team meetings, and what reviews you could group into the annual management review, for example.

Now in retrospect, I would perhaps also place more effort on mapping the connections between SOPs from the start. I might keep more systematic lists of the inputs and outputs of the processes, and where deliverables are expected to go after the process. A map of these would be a fantastic tool while writing the SOPs.

Each organization will be slightly different in how they need the pieces of their QMS to interact, but the pieces themselves are uniform on a top level. The previous sections of this book will have introduced you to all the hats you will need to place on your QMS board to start figuring out the moves involved. The next section will get you planning the opening moves.

Once you are happy with your quality manual and SOPs, it would be a good time to still share the documents with representatives of the rest of your organization, picking people who should be able to comment on the subject matter in each SOP. The top management should have been in the loop already when you were drafting the quality policy and the quality manual around it (in Section 5), but now I would be particularly interested in subject matter experts from inside or maybe even outside of your organization.

Once you are well and truly happy with your QMS documents—the quality manual, the SOPs, and any associated initial forms, templates, and registers—you are actually getting close to being ready to launch your QMS. More on that in Section 23. But first, let's get cracking on the quality manual.

Chapter 5

Writing the Quality Manual

The quality manual is the first point of entry into to your QMS. It should set the context, the scope, and the goals of your QMS as well as introduce your processes on a high level. I also like to define constants affecting several of the other processes in the quality manual; for example, principles for document retention periods and device lifetimes—that way, these are available for all your SOPs in one convenient and predictable location.

This section will take you through what is expected of a quality manual, provide you with a template for creating it, and then walk you through the requirements of the standard to create a manual that meets the expectations in a smart, concise, and readily maintainable way.

5.1 What Is Expected

The quality manual is the gateway, or the airlock, to your QMS. It is both the foundation stone of your QMS when you are adding new processes or figuring out any conflicts between them and the best bird's-eye view of the lay of the land for an outsider, such as an auditor, a discerning B2B customer, or a new employee. It sets the scene for all activities inside your organization and describes your relationship to the world around you. It even sets the overarching quality policy your organization will aspire to. It is in many ways the backbone of the way of life you want to build for your quality management operations.

As you are writing the first sections of the manual, it will all probably seem quite aspirational, but it should not be flying off in the stratosphere

DOI: 10.4324/9781003202868-5

sprinkling stardust and hype on all that read it. Out of all your QMS documents, the manual is the one place where you can exercise a little more artistic flair to make it easier on the reader, but it should all still be very much grounded in reality. The details of your processes will be in the standard operating procedures (SOPs) we will be writing in the next sections, but here you are laying the foundation for all that is to come: the negotiation of the various SOPs together, the context of interpretation for any particular SOP, and the underlying common understanding between you and your reader—whether that reader is an employee, an auditor, or a customer.

The formal requirements for the quality manual are given in Clause 4.2.2 of the standard. The quality manual must define the scope of the QMS, explain any exclusions you have made on the clauses of the standard, describe the processes that make up your QMS, and also outline the documentation used by the QMS. Furthermore, description of the interaction between your processes is a requirement for the manual. In practice, a description of the organization, its mission, and the general overview of the type of products it works with is also expected here. Not having this description here would make it more challenging to set out the quality policy and objectives a little later. The policy and objectives need to be defined somewhere in your QMS, preferably on a level of some elevated standing as these will affect all the other parts of the QMS, so I would do that here in the manual.

Table 5.1 gives an overview of what is required of the manual by the standard and what I would recommend you consider when writing it.

Recently, there was lively discussion on one regulatory professional's forum comparing notes on how big a quality manual should be. The

Table 5.1 Requirements and Recommendations for the Quality Manual

Required	■ **The scope of the QMS**. Explain what operations your QMS covers and what clauses of the standard are not relevant and why. Remember that you can only exclude requirements from Clauses 6, 7, and 8, and even then, only with a valid reason (see Section 4.3 in this book). ■ **The processes of the QMS**. Explain what processes your QMS consists of and how these relate to each other. ■ **The structure of your QMS documentation**. Explain what documents and records make up your QMS and how they relate to each other. You might, for example, have a quality manual that is supplemented by process-specific SOPs that, in turn, make use of working instructions and defined template documents to create individual records.

Table 5.1 *(Continued)* **Requirements and Recommendations for the Quality Manual**

I would recommend	■ **An overview of your organization**. Don't go overboard here, but your readers will benefit from having a short introduction into your organization, why it was founded, where it is located, and so forth. ■ **A short overview of the kinds of products this QMS will cover**. Don't try to describe the specifics of the products you intend to work with, but it should be helpful to explain whether you, for example, work with high-risk implantable products or some basic bandages to dress wounds. ■ **Quality policy**. Clause 5.3 of the standard requires your organization to have, somewhere in your QMS, a top-level quality policy that is communicated, understood, reviewed, and—I would also add—adhered to continuously. I feel that the quality manual offers an excellent location to define this policy and that defining this policy is the logical next step after introducing your organization and products. ■ **Define global constants affecting all other processes, or several of them, in the quality manual**. Examples of such constants could be principles for calculating document retention periods, device lifetimes, and so forth. You may want to write in some latitude for refining these further down the food chain as circumstances require, but the quality manual should be a good place to set up the mechanism.
Food for thought	■ **Consider what types of periodic changes that are external to the quality manual are likely to take place and how these changes will affect the manual**. For example, if you write in a lot of detail on any given process in the quality manual, these details may change as the SOPs for the processes are revised during regular document review. If the changes made in the individual SOPs do not affect the input of any other process or SOP, it is likely that the changes should not require you to revise a well-written quality manual. Predicting this here in how you write the manual may make your life easier in the long run as you will be forced to make less trivial edits to your manual. ■ **Consider including a reference table or a few paragraphs of text mapping the clauses of the standard to your SOPs**. If your QMS is very lean, or written to use the structure of the standard, this may not add utility, but it is worthwhile considering how the clauses of the standard map to your QMS. Your auditors will approach your QMS from the point of view of the clauses and not necessarily from the delicate narrative structure you have intended.

experiences on encountered manuals ranged from a single-page document to a multitier affair resembling the file management view built into the Windows operating system or a full-blown website. On another forum, a consultant once told me that the manual is just a graphical diagram of the individual processes. In fact, there is no one correct answer, but if you go for a diagram, remember that you still need to cover the requirements of the standard, including, for example, the written quality policy, somewhere in your QMS. Each of these approaches has been successful, so the primary consideration should be how your organization wants to represent the information in question. What matters is that the quality manual works for you: it sets up your QMS, introduces it to those needing to grasp your QMS, and functions as a part of the overall documentation you have set up for your QMS.

One of the first questions to answer when setting out to write a quality manual is if you want to write one monolithic document or a set of documents. Some consultants may still advise you to think of the quality manual as a synonym for your QMS. They may advocate writing in all you want to say about any process or subprocess into the manual and thereby circumvent the need to write separate standard operating procedures. You could do this and write in all the detail of your processes in your quality manual, but in most cases, I would advise against that for the following reasons:

■ **Your quality manual serves as the primary entry point into your QMS**. You will want to share that entry point with auditors, new staff members, and possibly even B2B customers. If you wrote everything in one document, you would be sharing it all as the basis of, for example, every surveillance audit of your QMS from here on out. You would be asking all new staff members to read a monolith and figure out which sections are important to them and which are not. This is doable but probably not optimal. It therefore makes sense to write that entry point, or index if you will, as succinctly as possible so as not to waste everyone's time and possibly overwhelm them with superfluous details on processes that are not relevant to them.

■ **Maintaining a monolith may be gargantuan task**. After you have successfully launched your QMS, you will go into a continuous cycle of document reviews, where every month or so you will be asking different process owners to review and revise their process descriptions to make sure they are still accurate and effective. If all your processes were in a single document, you would have to be even more careful when handling this document review so that changes don't flow over from one process to the others, or worse still, overwrite each other.

■ **Training on a document undergoing constant change will be a hassle**. You would need to be careful with what has actually changed within the quality manual and what has not, even though the whole quality manual will have a new version number. This will have ripple effects in organizing staff training on the changes performed. The quality manual is the one document in your QMS that should really be trained to all your staff, and attempting to deviate from that—or keep track of which section of a single monolithic document is relevant to whom—may be more trouble than its worth.

■ **No other document in your QMS is superior to the quality manual**. If you write your whole QMS into your quality manual, there is no distinction here, but setting your quality manual up as the parent of other documents in your QMS may have advantages; for example, it allows you to define something, like the quality policy, once and reuse it elsewhere.

Ultimately, the choice between one document or a set of documents is, of course, yours. In this book, I have opted to go with a hierarchical set of documents and would not look back. Similarly, the choice of where to define something—in the quality manual or a specific SOP is largely up to you. For most things, the standard requires something to be defined, but it does not make many requirements on where within the QMS those are defined. This book gives you a suggested structure for what is defined in the manual and what in the individual SOPs, but in most cases, you could decide otherwise if you truly wanted to.

It is worth noting that the ISO 13485 standard gives us a great overview of the quality management system we want to build. It doesn't exactly give us a blueprint of what we want—there are still regulations, other standards, and the specific circumstances of your organization's business to consider in implementing the standard—but it does give us a practical framework to build our QMS within.

5.2 Pen to Paper

Okay, let's finally put pen to paper or fingertips to keyboard keys. This section will walk you through the writing of the manual. You will find a template for creating the manual in Appendix 2 when you need it.

The quality manual is the place to introduce your circumstances and your QMS, and perhaps get a few global matters defined too. You will begin by writing what you already know then move to topics that are increasingly new and some that you will want to revisit after working on your SOPs in Sections 6 through 19. In writing the process descriptions here in the manual, stick with a very high-level overview of each process. Most of the specifics should be left to the SOPs we will write for each process a little bit later. You may even want to treat the process descriptions here as placeholders for something you will fill in after working on the coming sections. Also note that in both the manual and the SOPs, you can make use of appendices and references to structure the content and thereby make its reuse easier when later referring to it from your other documents.

The manual itself can be as long or as short as you see fit. In practice, I would aim at 10 pages and be happy if I ended up somewhere between 5 and 30. This is also a good place to define a general document template for your organization's QMS documents. If your organization already has a generic template and you would like to dive straight into creating your quality manual, you can also use that template for now. There are some things specific to a QMS template, but for now, you can skip those and get writing as we will be working on templates a little later. If you would like to get started with the full template straight away, read Section 20 now and then return here. The template presented in Section 20.3 follows the design discussed in this section.

My suggestion for the outline of your quality manual is shown in Table 5.2. Note that the first half of the manual is intended to read like a standalone introduction into the QMS, while the second half of the list mainly consist of references to the process-specific SOPs.

I highly recommend writing the manual in the order specified in the table, from top to bottom. This way, you will progress naturally from the things you should already know (e.g., description of your organization and your product), to things you probably already know at the back of your mind (e.g., your quality policy), and to things you then need to flesh out (e.g., the individual processes). In addition to being easier for you to write, this order will also nicely set out the narrative inroad for your auditors and other interested parties getting to know you through your quality manual. Also know that you will probably be making another pass over the manual after having worked on the SOPs, so don't worry too much about getting everything perfect from the start here.

Although not shown in the outline table, your general document template will probably also introduce other practical information elements, such as a document record table (consisting of, for example, document name, document ID, version, issuer, issuance date, and signatures), and some of this

Table 5.2   Outline for the Quality Manual

A) Purpose of the document	■ What is this document? ■ What purpose does it serve?	Novel content
B) Organization overview	■ Information about the organization ■ Identified role of the organization in medical devices ■ Basic structure of the organization ■ Type of products manufactured	
C) QMS overview	■ Scope of the QMS and rationale for exclusions ■ Quality policy ■ Quality objectives (see appendix) ■ Structure of QMS documents ■ High-level principles (e.g., document retention time schemes)	
D) Key roles	■ Definition of top management ■ Definition of key roles, such as the management representative and the quality manager	
E) Products	■ Any generic definitions on device lifetime, product version numbering, and so forth	
F) Processes	■ Overview of the processes defined by the organization, including their interrelationships ■ Identification of any prioritized core processes ■ Overview of all the processes based on the clause structure of the standard	Short intro + references
G) References	■ Any references you may have used	Novel content
H) Appendices	■ Staff responsibilities and qualifications by role ■ Quality objectives ■ Inter-process relationships	
I) Version history	■ Version numbers and dates for this document, along with short description of key changes and identification of the person who made that change	

information may also be carried over to the document header or footer. Refer to Section 20 for more on templates.

Let's go over that outline in more detail, focusing on the most important and novel sections of the manual. The structure I propose here is based on several years of experience, but you are free to modify it or add to it if you like. The standard does not impose any one structure on you or any maximum set of information you may have in a manual, but it does expect to see certain information in your manual. Less is more when it will come to keeping the content current over the coming years, so be concise but not to the point of cruelty toward your readers.

5.2.1 Section A—Purpose of the Document

This is a short introduction that helps orientate the reader on why this particular document was written, what purpose it has, and what role it is given by the organization's QMS. In the case of the quality manual, this may simply be a short statement that the document is the quality manual of the organization's ISO 13485 Quality Management System, and that it introduces the organization's QMS and refers to other QMS documents for more details.

5.2.2 Section B—Organization Overview

Section B gets down to the business of your QMS. In writing each of the following subsections, you are now diving deeper into your QMS. Writing these subsections in the given order leads you down a logical path to defining your whole QMS one step at a time.

About the Organization

A general-level organization overview is, strictly speaking, not required by the standard, but it will be difficult for the reader of the manual to get a handle on your organization without some sort of a soft-landing in the form of a brief introduction of your organization and the business it is in. Think about being dropped into a Christopher Nolan film like *Memento* or *Tenet* and spinning your wheels in all directions while you try to figure out what is going on. In films, such tricks work great, but in real life, your reader will grow frustrated with you if you make them guess what the point of it all is. QMS documents really are not about intrigue and the Aristotelean dramatic arc but instead about focusing on the essential information and walking your reader into it.

Having a soft introduction of your organization here will not only ease the reader into your QMS, but it will also make it easier for you to introduce your scope and quality policy a little later in the manual. It is also something auditors have, by all accounts, come to expect from the manual. The introduction should be short and sweet. Your organization's registered name, registered address, and a brief "about us" description of where you come from and where you want to go. The important part here is to clearly state what role your organization takes under the medical device regulations applicable to you; for example, a manufacturer, an authorized representative, an importer, or a distributor (required by Clause 4.1.1). Note that the regulations applicable to you may affect your choices here.

In our case, we were just getting started as a startup company after spinning out from under the wing of the university, so we wanted to say that. We were working on our first product, so we said that. We saw ourselves as the manufacturer of a medical device product, so we said that. My advice here is that you shouldn't take things for granted but instead, be quite explicit in stating your role. This is something your reader will look for in the text, so don't make them guess or deduce how you see yourself.

It is also worth noting that while Clause 4.2.2 of the standard covering the quality manual does not require the organization's physical locations to be listed here, the guidebook on the standard published by ISO does request addresses and functions performed at these addresses to be listed here. The guidebook, of course, does not have the official standing of the standard, so the choice here is up to you. You will, in any case, have to define the addresses somewhere in your documentation, including the certification application. The manual, therefore, is a good choice. Note that any changes to these locations will be of interest to your certification provider and may trigger a new audit of the premises, so you should discuss such moves with them in advance. Similarly, the question of handling remote locations, even offshore locations, appears to be a reoccurring discussion on forums for regulatory professionals. If this applies to your situation, it, too, will be a serious conversation between you and your provider.

Organizational Structure

Your organizational structure is perhaps best represented as a chart or a tree diagram. We thought about the different functions we will have: the shareholders, board, CEO, Management Team, Communications Team, and Quality Management Team, for example. These go into a chart nicely. In addition, I would write the more detailed roles and responsibilities of personnel as an appendix of the manual that we can refer to here without the fear of bloating text or duplicating it.

The requirement to define roles and the interrelation between roles stems out of Clause 5.5.1 of the standard but is conveniently addressed on a top level here in the quality manual. You may also consider defining substitutes by roles in the same appendix. The process-specific responsibilities and authorities of the roles should, however, be defined in more detail in individual SOPs.

Figure 5.1 provides a sample organizational chart. Make sure the chart you provide makes sense to you and is true to life at your organization. Of particular interest here from the point of view of the standard is that you clearly define your top management and any chart you provide matches with that definition. Additionally, you may want to define what personnel affect quality at your organization and depict that in the chart too.

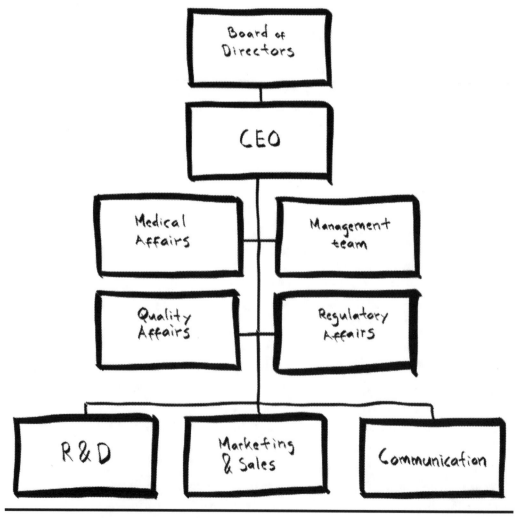

Figure 5.1 Organizational chart.

5.2.3 Section C—QMS Overview

Section C picks up speed by defining the scope of your QMS, your overarching quality policy, and the overall document hierarchy used by your QMS.

Scope

The first item to cover in the overview is the scope of the QMS and the operations you intend to fit within your QMS. For example, are you only designing medical devices or also manufacturing and possibly selling them to end users? This will affect what clauses of the standard apply to your operations.

Within the organization role you defined in Section B, you should now provide further clarification on whether you provide a product and/or service, and whether you are involved in the design, development, production, and/or sales of the product and to what kind of customers. Per Clause 0.1 of the standard, your organization may be involved in one or more stages of the life cycle of a medical device or a service. The stages may, for example, be one or more of the following: design and development, production, storage, distribution, installation, servicing, support, decommissioning, and disposal. The right answer here is the answer that describes your particular situation the best. You should use these established terms if they apply to you, or if they don't—for example you are adopting the standard by choice—explain your role here the best you can.

An example here might be that you are a medical device manufacturer engaged in the development, production, and sales of a particular kind of a medical device intended for medical professionals. Make the definition broad enough to cover the intended purpose (intended use) of all your devices but narrow enough to be of value to the reader.

The requirement for the definition of the scope is in Clauses 1 and 4.2.2a.

Exclusions

The standard allows you to exclude requirements made in Clauses 6 ("Resource management"), 7 ("Product realization"), and 8 ("Measurement, analysis and improvement") of the standard if, and only if, you can provide an acceptable rationale as to why such requirements are not applicable to you. The rationale may be based on the activities undertaken by your organization or the nature of the medical device you work with. It is, however, absolutely crucial that you include a clear, acceptable rationale for any exclusions you make here. Also, don't make further exclusions in your SOPs later, but instead, gather all your exclusions here.

Be careful here and remember what we previously discussed in Section 3: the standard requires interpretation, and nothing can be dismissed right off the bat. Also note that you are not allowed to make exclusions to requirements made in Clause 4 ("Quality management system") or Clause 5 ("Management responsibility") or Clauses 0 to 3 either.

The requirement for the definition of exclusions is in Clauses 1 and 4.2.2a.

Quality Policy and Quality Objectives

The next big thing is the quality policy—your organization's shining light in shaping quality management and making a difference in the world for the better. For example, how do you see your relationship with new science, clinical studies, and feedback from the field? What role do customer satisfaction, patient outcomes, or intellectual property rights play in your operations? The policy will be your North Star, which may evolve over time, but it should not be fleeting or in constant change.

The requirement to have a quality policy and quality objectives comes from Clause 4.2.1a. Furthermore, Clauses 5.1b, 5.1c, and 5.4.1 then require that your top management is involved and that you establish both a policy and the objectives based on it. The core requirements for both are then set out in Clauses 5.3 and 5.4.1, as described in the following. The requirements for the quality policy are written so that your top management must ensure the policy does the following:

■ is applicable to your organization's purpose
■ includes commitment to requirements
■ includes commitment to maintaining QMS effectiveness
■ provides a framework for establishing and reviewing quality objectives
■ is communicated and understood within the organization
■ is continually reviewed for suitability

Similarly, the top management must ensure that the objectives do the following:

■ are consistent with the quality policy
■ are established at relevant levels and functions with the organization

■ answer to product and regulatory requirements
■ are measurable

The general idea behind the quality policy is that it allows you and your organization to pursue your intended use and benefit while understanding and adhering to applicable requirements in an effective, safe, and sustained manner. The policy is something that you should have a very good idea of from the start and that probably should not change much over the first few years. In writing your quality policy, don't worry about fancy prose or reference to specific clauses in the standards or regulation. Make sure you address the previous items, but otherwise, be yourself and talk with your management to arrive at a description that captures the essence and the drive of your organization. The policy will inform everything else you do later in developing your QMS, so it is worth spending some time on it, but if there are small things that your organization doesn't yet know or may want to tweak later, that's okay. The quality policy will be reviewed continually—I would recommend coupling this with the management reviews as a fail-safe for periodic rereview—and the management will get to revise it as needed.

I would attempt to keep the policy to a length of half a page or a page at most. Some auditors have reportedly even asked staff members to recite the quality policy by heart, and although that is just seven kinds of stupid, you should be clear and concise on what the policy wants to say for your reader's sake. If you are the only person at your organization who can appreciate the beauty of the quality policy you have written, then you have messed up, as not many others at your organization will observe or strive for the same policy. In some companies, you may see the quality policy posted on walls of the factory floor or even distilled down to simple quotes on their business cards, so think about what you want to set as your goals here and be concise in how you word them.

Building on the policy, the quality objectives are then an extension of your policy toward measurable aims to strive toward in your operations. I would aim at a handful of objectives overall and, instead of writing them into the body of the manual, include them as an appendix to the manual for easy reference. I would approach the objectives as themes you can pick out from your overall policy, and think of these as the folders for the individual quality indicators you will end up having to measure in tracking your processes.

Your quality indicators are the third level of defining trackable quality metrics at your organization. The indicators are measurable, preferably numeric, values that you can periodically (think: monthly) collect from your organization. The indicators should provide you and your top management with adequate information on the overall status of your operations to assess how well the quality objectives are being met and your quality policy realized. Thus, when your policy discusses a drive to meet customer requirements, one of your objectives could be "high customer satisfaction" and one of the quality indicators under that objective could be the number of complaints as a simple monthly count or a factor of all feedback.

Strictly speaking, you do not have to define the quality indicators in your quality manual, but thinking about the indicators now when you are writing your manual and SOPs, and then finalizing the indicators after the SOPs are ready are good ideas. In general, you will want some indicators for each of your quality objectives while also making sure you cover all the processes in your QMS. A handful of objectives and about two dozen indicators might be a good starting point for a new QMS, but the exact figures will depend on your circumstances.

The indicators will not be set in stone as your management will have the right to modify the indicator list, as well as the responsibility to monitor the indicator data. As your operations mature, so, too, will the indicators you track, but also pay attention to the longevity of the indicators and get meaningful time series data on any of the indicators. I would suggest entering the list of quality indicators as an appendix to your manual and updating that list as you progress through the SOPs in Sections 6 through 19. Alternatively, you can focus on the policy and the objectives here, and then set the indicators and track them (e.g., via a registry) when you launch the QMS.

Once you have defined the scope of your QMS and written a policy and objectives you are happy with, you will have laid the foundations for your QMS. Get a cup of coffee, tea, or whatever it is you enjoy as your energy drink of choice. Also, make sure that your top management is happy with the policy and that, if you prepared the policy for them, any changes they want to make are observed. The checklists in Section 5.3 will help you check your bases when writing the policy and the objectives.

Structure of QMS Documentation

The third major item to outline in this section of the manual is the overall structure of your QMS documentation and whether the documents are managed as a physical collection of binders of papers or on some electronic document management system. Unless you have some hippo-sized reason for going with a paper-based approach, I would give the electronic system serious consideration.

Regardless of whether you manage your documentation electronically or physically, the structure of the documents may again be effectively represented as a diagram. Here, I would simply present a tree diagram of the top levels of my stack of documentation; for example, something like shown in Figure 5.2.

In implementing your document structure on an electronic platform, you will want to play around with the different platforms to make sure your chosen platform supports the structure you want. In all likelihood, the structure you want to define won't be all that mystical that any decent software couldn't support it, but if you get to choose your platform, you should make sure you can and want to work with it (also see Section 22 for software validation). The basic set of documentation you will be working with on the top

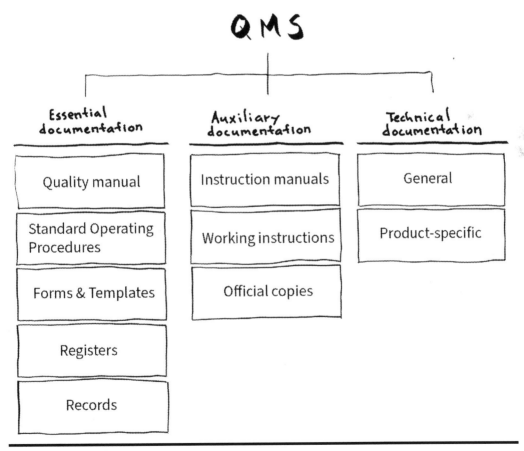

Figure 5.2   Basic document structure.

level is fairly standard, and Section 4.4.1 previously introduced you to all the key types of documents.

You can define many more documents in this hierarchy if you like, but I would just define the top levels here and then expect to find appropriate places for other documents under the tree when writing the SOP discussing each document. Logical expansion is the name of the game here, especially as you have yet to write all the SOPs.

The requirement to outline the overall QMS documentation structure comes from Clause 4.2.2 of the standard.

High-Level Principles

The body of your previous description will have quickly set out the foundations of your QMS, why it is developed, what role you undertake, and what is its scope. In doing so, you will probably have touched on aspects, such as whether you intend to keep records in an electronic versus paper-based format, whether your QMS is in English or Japanese, and whatever else was relevant to you in setting up your existence earlier. There are two further topics I would specifically address here.

Firstly, I would briefly refer to SOP-1 as the key to your document IDs. The details of this will be handled in the SOP, and thus, a mere reference will do here.

Secondly, I would set out your basic approach to both document and record retention times here. As discussed in Section 3.11, QMS documentation is subject to retention times that need to meet not only the standard but also the applicable regulations. Clauses 4.2.4 and 4.2.5 of the standard require that documents instructing records are available for at least as long as the records made based on them; records, on the other hand, are available at least X years after the devices made based on them are on the market (i.e., from the time the device is released by the organization); and none of this expires in under two years. The definition of X is up to you here, but realize that the applicable regulations probably talk of five to ten years or longer instead of the two-year minimum given by the standard. A rule of thumb I have come to live by is to promise X years and quietly aim at forever. If you know you will need to address differing requirements from the various jurisdictions that apply to you on these matters, you may begin to do that here and make allowances for subsequent adjustment in your SOPs (particularly SOP-11) and product-specific documentation.

5.2.4 Section D—Key Roles

In addition to the organizational chart that may be included in the quality manual, the QMS must define key roles and both their responsibilities and authorities. To a large extent, this is done in the individual SOPs, but introducing the key roles and their qualifications is best done in the manual. The requirement to ensure responsibilities and authorities are defined, documented, and communicated within your organization rests with top management (Clause 5.5.1).

The roles were already introduced in Section 4.4.4, but as a refresher, the central roles you will probably be dealing with in your quality manual and SOPs, are introduced here are as follows:

■ Top management
■ Management representative
■ Quality manager
■ Quality Management Team
■ Various C-level officers (e.g., chief technology officer)
■ Various subject area expert positions at your organization (e.g., medical expert and regulatory expert)

I would mention these roles here, but leave any detailed definition of them for the appendix to the manual on staff responsibilities and qualifications by role. This way, all the key responsibilities, authorities, qualifications, and arrangements for deputies are conveniently located in one place.

As a reminder, C-level officers are safer options for ensuring something is done, and more generic subject area expert roles, or communal hats, are good options for ensuring that some important viewpoint is heard while doing that. Remember to also define deputies for critical roles somewhere in your QMS; for example, in an appendix to the manual that describes staff roles.

Note also that Clause 5.5.1 requires you to document the interrelation of all personnel who may affect quality and to ensure the independence and authority of these personnel in such tasks. Defining an organizational structure and placing these roles at the appropriate locations under that structure, as well as defining substitutes for key roles, will begin to answer this requirement. That is about as much as you should aim to do in the quality manual. The rest of the details will be in the SOPs and the devil itself in how you run your organization in the day-to-day.

In Europe, you may also want to define the person responsible for regulatory compliance (PRRC) here, but as there seems to be a fair amount of confusion around the exact role, responsibilities, personal liability, and other characteristics associated with the definition and a great deal of variation across the industry, I might be wary of taking a stand in the QMS just yet. For small companies, this role can be outsourced to a consultant, and larger corporations have apparently split the role across multiple people, each taking responsibility for some specific area. If the European regulations are applicable to you and you are new to QMS, I would discuss this matter with your quality experts to make sure your definition is sound. You can also check out real examples of how companies have defined PRRCs from the online EUDAMED database run by the European Commission.

5.2.5 Section E—Products

A section on products is not required by the standard, but I would recommend it as a practical place for introducing any product-related concepts you may need elsewhere in several SOPs. For example, defining your overall approach to device lifetime, product version numbering, and product identification might go in here. Product classification under the various regulations that might be applicable to you, I might save for SOP-11, but make this reference here. Similarly, SOP-10 is your reference here for instructing the product realization process in general

Clause 7.5.8 requires you to have a documented system for assigning unique device authentication to your products if this is required by the regulations applicable to you. This requirement is a short piece of text in the standard but a profound requirement for your operations. In some cases, your basic product version numbering may be enough (e.g., in case of a truly cloneable software module this probably identifies the product beyond any doubt), but in other cases, you will want to lean on unique IDs specific to a production batch or even packaging. You may also comment on your approach to the traceability of products (Clause 7.5.9, see SOP-11) on a high level here.

The alternative to introducing these mechanisms here is that you do so solely at a lower level in your SOPs or even product-specific documentation. You will then need to always dive deeper in audits and perhaps jump through more hoops to ensure your staff and customers share and remember your definitions. The quality manual should thus be a good place to introduce at least the existence of such concepts. I would introduce my approach to product versions here and refer to SOP-11 for more details on identification and traceability.

5.2.6 Section F—Processes

The requirement for the manual to include or reference the documented procedures of the QMS is a fundamental one in the ISO 13485 standard and is stated in Clause 4.2.2b. In my view, it is impractical for maintenance reasons and for training and general readability reasons to include the whole process descriptions in the manual, although this, too, would be permissible by the standard. If you do have separate SOPs, it is unwise to repeat details here or go into too much detail while attempting to introduce the processes in the manual as any edits to the underlying SOPs would then need to be reflected in the manual as well. This would lead to frequent unnecessary editing of the manual. The consensus among quality professionals is that the process descriptions in the manual should be brief, be on a high level, and have the primary objective of referencing the actual SOPs in question.

Clause 4.2.2c further requires you to describe the interaction between the processes. You can begin to answer this requirement by providing a high-level diagram of your SOPs showing the connections between the individual SOPs and possibly pointing out critical paths as well as which SOPs act to serve other SOPs. Figure 5.3 shows an example.

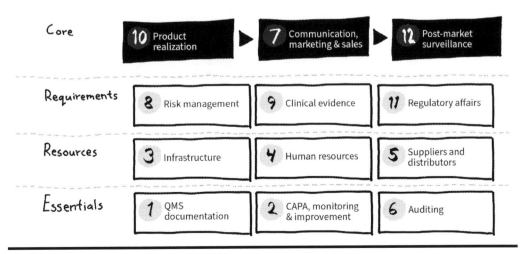

Figure 5.3 A bird's-eye view of your SOPs.

The previous diagram is a high-level sketch of what your process architecture could look like. In the diagram, the typical SOPs are divided into four groups (from bottom to top in the diagram): 1) Essentials, 2) Resources, 3) Requirements, and 4) Critical path of core SOPs you run on top of the rest. We will go through each SOP separately in the coming sections. You could decide to segment your QMS differently, but if this model makes sense for your setup, you can use it as a basis for your work here. You can always return to the diagram later as you are finishing your SOPs.

Section 5.2.8 will present another way to look at your SOPs, this time taking a true bottom-up approach building a view of the links between your SOPs as declared in the SOPs themselves. Both views offer practical aids for figuring out your QMS processes. The first diagram gives a great overview of your processes to a new reader, while the diagram presented later in Section 5.2.8 will be practical for maintaining your SOPs through the periodic document review process.

In this section, we are focusing on writing your quality manual, and the SOPs themselves will be written starting from Section 6. I therefore suggest that for the now, you leave this section somewhat open and return to it after Section 19. The checklist at the end of that section will remind you to do so. Alternatively, you can start drafting a high-level sketch of your processes here, but realize that you may want to edit that a little bit later.

After introducing the high-level network of processes, I would present the processes themselves in a way that roughly matches the clause structure of the standard. Instead of long-winded discussion of each process or clause, I would introduce the principal SOPs that answer to the processes required by each clause of the standard. The goal of this description is thus twofold:

■ Introduce all your individual SOPs as required by the standard and as may not always be achieved to the best effect by a high-level process network diagram, such as the one previously presented.
■ Give those of your readers who are already familiar with the standard, such as your auditor or B2B customer, a solid landing zone or a menu into your QMS. This section will ensure that you cover all your required bases, but it may also act as a good starting point if you experience a sudden case of brain freeze during some meeting or audit.

I would, therefore, structure this section to generally follow the clauses of the standard, but I might depart from that in a few small ways. I would thus group my processes under the following five headings.

General QMS Requirements

This section roughly matches with Clause 4 of the standard. Here, I would explain that this quality manual sets up the relationship between your QMS, the standard, and the applicable regulations. Your commitment to maintaining an effective QMS in this context, and in the context of your organization's role, is hopefully evident from the quality policy you have defined earlier, your subsequent QMS planning activities, and all your day-to-day activities since making that definition.

We already introduced the processes of your QMS and the network they make up using a chart of the overall network of processes. The essential document and process controls are instructed by SOP-1 and SOP-2, respectively. Your process-specific risk management activities (SOP-8) will address the control of these processes following a risk-based approach that places greater emphasis on the control of high-risk processes. Internal communication is instructed in SOP-7 and post-market surveillance in SOP-12. The medical device file is a special type of a document that is instructed in SOP-10. Regulatory affairs are instructed in SOP-11.

Management Responsibility

This section roughly matches with Clause 5 of the standard. Here, I would refer to the quality policy (Clause 5.3) contained in the manual as the basis of demonstrating management commitment (Clause 5.1), customer focus (Clause 5.2), and quality planning (Clause 5.4). For quality planning, I would also refer to SOP-1, which instructs QMS planning and, among other subprocesses, the document review. I would further refer to the appendix of the manual on responsibilities, authorities, and even qualifications of personnel. Finally, audits and the management review are instructed in SOP-6.

Resource Management

This section roughly matches with Clause 6 of the standard. This consists of three main topics: management of infrastructure (SOP-3), management of human resources (SOP-4), and management of the work environment (also SOP-3). In addition, the provision of these resources is a topic, but unless you have a specific process for this, I would not invoke a specific SOP here but instead leave provision to the previously mentioned SOPs and the relevant activities defined under management responsibility. I also would bring up SOP-5 as the place for instructing supplier management and SOP-3 for instruction on software validation, both of which are required by Clause 4, but more logically handled here under resource management.

Product Realization

This section matches quite neatly with the massive Clause 7 of the standard. Here, I would refer to my SOP on product realization (SOP-10), which covers most of the topics of this clause in the standard. In addition, I would link to SOP-7 for internal and customer-related communication, SOP-12 for post-market activities, SOP-8 for risk management, SOP-9 for clinical evidence, SOP-11 for regulatory affairs, and SOP-5 for purchasing and supplier management.

Measurement, Analysis, and Improvement

This section matches nicely with Clause 8 of the standard. Here, I would link to SOP-2 for monitoring, measurement, and CAPA. Customer feedback and the use of maintenance activity information is in SOP-7. In addition, I would link to SOP-10 for related product-realization activities and SOP-6 for audits and the management review.

5.2.7 Section G—References

If you have used references in your manual, include them here. The standard does not require you to have references, but if you have used some books, extra standards, or documents to advise you, it is good to include them here so that you will also remember the documents when you are later revising the manual or, indeed, using the manual. You might, for example, want to mention this book that you are holding in your hand if you follow the advice it gives.

You may also reference the ISO 13485 standard, if you like, but that should pretty much be given from the purpose of the document in Section A of the manual.

5.2.8 Section H—Appendices

The use of appendices is entirely optional and not required by the standard. You could include all the necessary information in the body of the manual itself, but I find it is better to structure some of the content as self-contained appendices. This way, maintaining the information and referring to it from elsewhere is easier.

In this book, I would have you include three appendices to the manual:

- Staff responsibilities and qualifications by role
- Quality objectives
- Inter-process relationships

Let's go through the appendices one by one. The use of appendices to cover this information is entirely optional, but the previously stated information does need to be somewhere in your QMS.

Appendix on Staff Responsibilities and Qualifications by Role

This is part of how you meet the requirement to ensure responsibilities and authorities are defined, documented, and communicated within your organization (Clause 5.5.1), and the interrelation, independence, and authority of the personnel is addressed (Clause 5.5.1). Here, you can define all the key job titles in use at your organization, the qualifications required from the title holders, and the responsibilities and authorities of each. You may also define role-level substitutes here in case of holidays and absences, as this may come in quite handy when later running your QMS. Make sure that any substitutes you define also meet adequate qualifications for the role they are substituting for.

Keep the definitions simple. A list of a few bullet points for responsibilities, authorities, qualifications, and deputy arrangements will be sufficient. You can later use this information, for example, when you need to write announcements on open job positions. Having this information here will help ensure that you won't hire someone without first defining their job adequately—something which would be frowned upon by your auditors.

Appendix on Quality Objectives

The quality objectives were discussed in Section 5.2.3. The objectives could have been inserted into the body text in that section, but as that could easily get messy after a while, I prefer to place these into an appendix so that it is easier to edit them and refer to them from across the QMS.

Placing the objectives in an appendix also gives you the option to list the relevant quality indicators under each objective. This may lead to duplication as you will in all likelihood be tracking those indicators using a registry, but having the indicators here will ease sharing information on what indicators you track should you need to do that. If you opt to use the register only for listing the indicators, make sure you can still prove their appropriate approval during assignment (e.g., via management review, Management Team minutes, or reports). See Section 5.3.2 for a checklist on objectives.

Appendix on Inter-Process Relationships

To me, this is the most interesting appendix out of the set—maybe because I was so chuffed to come up with the sneaky method for its creation. The list of associated SOPs (see Section 20.3.4) shown in each SOP will prove very handy when drawing up this diagram and, later, when keeping it up-to-date. This appendix, together with the diagram shown in Section 5.2.6, should give an excellent overview of your processes and the links between them, and thus, meet the requirements of the standard. The basic idea is that you can see which SOP refers to which SOP, and vice versa. Figure 5.4 shows a conceptual example where the SOPs referenced by each SOP are mapped out on each row.

This is basically the switchboard of your SOPs. You can use this appendix to figure out forward and backward connections between your SOPs when you are running the document review activity or when you are trying

	SOP 1	SOP 2	SOP 3	SOP 4	SOP 5	SOP 6	SOP 7	SOP 8	SOP 9	SOP 10	SOP 11	SOP 12
SOP 1	-	■	■	□								
SOP 2	■	-	■	■					□			
SOP 3	■	■	-									
SOP 4		■		-	■			■		■		
SOP 5				■	-	■	■					
SOP 6				□	■	-		■				
SOP 7				□	■	□	-	■				
SOP 8				■	□	■	■	-				
SOP 9	□			□					-			
SOP 10				■	□							
SOP 11												
SOP 12				□								

Figure 5.4   Example of SOP-to-SOP links as a two-way table.

to see dependencies between SOPs for running CAPA activities, for example. You can look at the row for any given SOP to see what processes it links to and then look at the column for that SOP to see if any other processes link to it in addition. In this diagram, one-way links are further highlighted by using a white box marker for them, and a black-box marker for two-way links.

Drawing the previous diagram will be easy after you have written the SOPs. The section for using the SOP template (Section 20.3.4) presents a handy method for creating the diagram almost as an afterthought. It is not an afterthought, of course, as you will have been thinking about process dependencies carefully in writing the SOPs and, thus, also created the information to use here. As you will be figuring out the SOP linkages during writing the SOPs yourself, note that the previous figure is only conceptual in nature. The final diagram will be born out of the links you make. For now, only worry about writing the SOPs and making the links that make sense to you. The figure will almost sort itself out in the end.

5.2.9 Section I—Version History

A version history is something you should consider as an essential part of every significant QMS document from here on out. Note that I said "document" and not "record" here, although you are, of course, free to also itemize changes in records.

The version history is a critically important part of QMS requirements. The version history may, for example, be recorded within the document itself, as an appendix, or in the metadata of the document in some document archival software. The version history information, along with who made what changes and when, must always be available. For lower-level records, it is enough that such version differences are retrievable (e.g., via comparing two archived versions of the record), but for actual key QMS documents, such as your quality manual and SOPs, these differences must be spelled out in a readily accessible way.

This section will come in handy during audits when you will need to quickly show how any one document has changed over time. Everyone else, too, at your organization who needs to work based on the changed document will appreciate the available history information to see what has changed and how it might affect their work. Having a version history may not let you off the hook on training your staff regarding the changes, but it will be a part of the overall solution to ensuring change does not go by unnoticed.

The requirement for version control is in Clauses 4.2.4 for documents and 4.2.5 for records.

5.3 Checklists for the Manual

Writing a quality manual doesn't sound too bad, does it? The type of content needed and the amount or structure of it is very manageable. The devil is, of course, in how you manage to write the manual so that it is relevant to your organization and meets all the requirements in a way that is also appropriate to your operations.

The following quick checklists look at your quality policy, your quality objectives, and finally, your complete quality manual. The checklists are intended to help you in ensuring that you have addressed all the key requirements. If you get stuck in any of the checkboxes, return to the previous discussion, in this section, for help.

5.3.1 Checklist for the Quality Policy

After finishing work on the quality policy, you can perform a quick check of your work using the following checklist (Table 5.3). The checklist contains the key items to tick for a quality policy, but it, of course, does not check the content of what you say in the policy. Once you are happy with the policy, you may move to checking your quality objectives in the next section.

5.3.2 Checklist for the Quality Objectives

After finishing work on the quality objectives, you can perform a quick check of your work using the following checklist (Table 5.4). Notice that there is some necessary crosstalk here between the policy and the objectives. Once you are happy with the objectives, you may move to checking your full manual in the next section.

5.3.3 Checklist for the Finished Manual

The following checklist (Table 5.5) is intended to meet the requirements set in Clause 4.2.2 of the standard, which is dedicated to the quality manual,

Table 5.3   Checklist for the Quality Policy

Checklist

☐ **The quality policy is appropriate to your organization's purpose**
Does the policy lead you to fulfill your purpose better?

☐ **The quality policy includes a commitment to requirements and an effective QMS**
Think about your customer, your product, your regulatory requirements, and your QMS.

☐ **The quality policy is in a language that is understandable to your personnel**
Make sure the language is appropriate and the message relatable to your audience.

☐ **The quality policy is understood to be reviewed**
Your policy must be reviewed by the management for continuing suitability.

☐ **Your quality objectives can be derived from your quality policy**
You can develop objectives that is based on this policy and that is covering the whole policy.

☐ **The quality objectives can be reviewed in relation to your quality policy**
Your QMS should provide a mechanism for reviewing the objectives and the policy.

☐ **You have top management approval for all the previous items**
Get some record of this (e.g., a signed statement or Management Team minutes).

Once you feel confident you have ticked every box, it's time to move on.

Table 5.4   Checklist for the Quality Objectives

Checklist

☐ **Your objectives are consistent with the quality policy**
The objectives can be derived from the policy, and they cover it adequately.

☐ **Your objectives are measurable**
It is possible to define measurable indicators for each of (or at least most of) the objectives, and the objectives themself are not too abstract to be useful.

☐ **Your objectives cover QMS process requirements**
For example, the handling of issues detected in the efficiency of the QMS (including CAPA).

☐ **Your objectives cover product requirements**
For example, meeting customer requirements consistently.

☐ **Your objectives cover applicable regulatory requirements**
For example, notifications to regulatory authorities are handled as required.

☐ **Your objectives address the relevant functions within your organization**
Your objectives capture relevant operations at your organization.

☐ **Your objectives are established on relevant levels within your organization**
Your objectives capture information on a relevant level within your organization.

Once you feel confident you have ticked every box, it's time to move on.

Table 5.5   Checklist for the Finished Manual

Checklist

☐ **Your organization and product are introduced**
A general-level introduction to your organization and product(s) is given.

☐ **The role of the organization is defined**
For example, a manufacturer. Pay attention to regulations and how these may affect your role.

☐ **The scope of the QMS is defined**
For example, development, manufacturing, sales, and/or maintenance.

☐ **You have made the commitment of your top management clear**
Management is understood to support quality and QMS, and is committed to meeting the requirements. This should be evident in the text and in approvals of the text.

☐ **You have defined required key roles and responsibilities**
For example, top management, management representative, and quality manager. Remember to address any deputies and the interrelation of personnel who affect quality. See Section 4.4.4.

☐ **You have defined a quality policy and quality objectives**
You cleared the previous checklists. See Section 5.3.1 and Section 5.3.2.

☐ **The processes introduced by your QMS cover the standard**
For example, D&D, production, distribution, installation, and disposal. See Section 5.2.6 for help.

☐ **Any excluded processes are given an acceptable rationale**
If a process is required by the standard, you can only exclude it with a very good reason (see Section 3.8). Also pay attention to regulatory requirements.

☐ **The application of your processes makes sense for your organization**
The application of processes makes sense throughout your organization under its defined role.

☐ **In introducing each process, you also link to the relevant SOP.**
You may not be able to do this until after writing the SOPs in Section 6, but remember to come back here then. The SOP checklists will remind you to do so.

☐ **You don't claim you aren't responsible for some process**
You can outsource a process, but you can't outsource the responsibility for it.

☐ **The processes are prioritized somehow**
You apply a risk-based approach to the control of processes.

☐ **The inter-process relationships are described in a practical way**
You describe the sequence and interaction between processes in a meaningful way.

☐ **You have outlined the structure of your documentation**
You provide a conceptual overview of your QMS documentation.

Table 5.5 *(Continued)* **Checklist for the Finished Manual**

Checklist
☐ **You have defined the document and record retainment periods** Beware of regulations that may be stricter than the two-year minimum of the standard.
☐ **You have enough resources to carry out what you have instructed** Don't fall victim of specifying here more than you can cope with. See Section 3.1.
☐ **Regulatory requirements are incorporated** You probably can't list the requirements separately, but make sure you know what the requirements are and that you are complying with them. Pay attention to different jurisdictions if this is relevant to your context.
☐ **If you use the terms "shall", "should", "may", and "can", these are used in the same sense as the standard uses them**.
Once you feel confident you have ticked every box, it's time to move on.

but it also addresses further requirements introduced in the other clauses of the standard.

5.4 That's It?

Congratulations! You have now successfully finished your almost-print-ready quality manual. This was no small feat to do. You may still have some gaps in the manual that can't be filled in before you finish writing the SOPs in the next sections, but that aside, you can now take pleasure in having completed a significant portion of your QMS. In some bygone years, this could even have been enough for you to run your QMS, but today, you have a good number of requirements to still tackle in your SOPs. Let's look at those SOP-by-SOP in a little while, but let's first start with what are the general expectations for a standard operating procedure (SOP).

Chapter 6

Writing the Standard Operating Procedures

The quality manual addressed in the previous section sets up your QMS, the motivations for it, and the grand lines you are building along. The standard operating procedures (SOPs) are where you will start putting in the concrete processes within those master strokes of the brush. We will now take a small step away from the relative aspirational freedom involved in a quality manual and land more squarely in the domain of process engineering as we start to craft the individual processes for your QMS. A human touch is very much needed though to keep your processes both practical and on point.

The next few sections will take you through what is expected of SOPs, provide you with a template for creating them, and then walk you through the key requirements of the standard to create a set of SOPs covering and complying with the standard.

The discussion here will give you the necessary framework to write your SOPs, but you will have to put in the detail within that based on your organization and its relationship to medical devices. As we discussed in Section 3.1, there is no one-size-fits-all QMS, and subsequently, there is no plug-and-play set of already-written SOPs you should adopt. Instead, the discussion here will let you see the important pieces, flesh out your approach to negotiating the pieces together, and write smart, concise, and readily applicable SOPs as a result.

At the end of each section on a specific SOP, you will find a checklist to help you make sure you have covered the basics, and Section 19 will provide you with a final checklist for ensuring you consider all the last polishes involved.

6.1 What Is Expected

It is up to you to define how you want to structure the processes of your QMS. The standard gives you a base set of markers to hit with the processes, but it does not impose any structure or limit to how you define the standard operating procedures (SOPs) comprising your set of instructed QMS processes.

If you are starting from scratch, it makes sense to begin by looking at the list of clauses described in the standard and then taking note of their structure in dividing your entire QMS into the individual SOPs. For some processes, the requirements are quite clear; for example, you must have a process for the management review, and even the expected minimum inputs and outputs for that activity are given by the standard in Clause 5.6. For some other processes, like your risk management process, you will have to compile requirements from all throughout the standard and may still need to apply another standard, the ISO 14971 risk management standard, to come up with a solid process that complies with the expectations. This book will walk you through the creation of your full set of processes in the following sections. The discussion ahead will point out key questions to ask yourself and provide you with many answers I have found to work, but it can't hand you a ready-made solution to everything.

In addition to identifying which processes you will need to instruct; you will also want to think about how the various processes then link together and if there are any relative prioritizations to be made based on the type of operations you have. This will inform the construction of your network of processes but also your risk-based approach to keeping a closer eye on some of the more critical processes where issues have a higher chance of affecting your products and their users. These core processes are some-thing you will then want to monitor more closely, address carefully in your process-specific risk management, and handle most carefully when making changes to as part of your document review cycle.

The fundamental expectation for any system of SOPs and the SOPs themselves is that it all complies with the standard: you have a procedure, an activity, or an arrangement for every required activity in the standard (although you may have been able to make some exclusions in Section 5 of this book), and what you instruct complies with what the standard expects. It thus makes sense to follow the structure defined by the clauses of the standard for the overall architecture of processes in your QMS, but know that this is not required by the standard.

To comply with the standard, each process should conform to the general model of processes as having an input and an output, with some value-adding processing in between. Your processes may have several subprocesses and, thus, several inputs and outputs for different needs. If you are used to object-oriented programming, this is not much of a stretch for you: each SOP is basically an object that specifies inputs and outputs, and instructs several different (sub)activities you can run as needed. If this sounds foreign to you, don't worry; no programming experience is, in fact, required in QMS.

It is also practical to adopt the PDCA model (see Section 4.2) of plan, do, check, and act, with appropriate records kept at each stage—and do not forget about traceability from one step or process to the next.

Remember also that you must describe the processes and their interrelationships in the quality manual, so after finishing work on your SOPs, go back to your quality manual to update Section F. The checklist at the end in Section 19 will remind you to do so.

6.2 Planning Your Network of Processes

The most fundamental question to ask yourself when setting out to write SOPs is how you want to slice the standard into manageable processes. The number of slices to create and the way you slice the standard with each of the SOPs is up to you. If you took the top-level clauses of the standard as your guide, you might only have five SOPs. As we looked at previously in Section 4.3, these could be as follows:

- **SOP-1: Quality management system essentials** (Clause 4)
  including general requirements, control of documents, control of records, the medical device file, and software validation.
- **SOP-2: Management responsibility** (Clause 5)
  including QMS planning, responsibility and authority, management representative, management review, and internal communication.
- **SOP-3: Resource management** (Clause 6)
  including provision of resources, human resources, infrastructure, work environment, and contamination control.
- **SOP-4: Product realization** (Clause 7)
  including customer-related processes, planning of product realization, customer-related processes, design and development, purchasing, and production and service provision.

■ **SOP-5: Measurement, analysis, and improvement** (Clause 8) including monitoring and measurement, control of nonconforming product, analysis of data, handling of feedback, and improvement (including CAPA and internal audits).

This division makes complete sense, and it might make it quite easy to approach audits: as most questions during audits are derived from the clauses of the standard, you could pull up an SOP based on the clause quoted and build your answer from there. The mapping between the standard and your QMS would be very straightforward. The trouble with this approach is, as you may already begin to see by glancing over the previous list of what is included in each clause, is that it may not be an optimal way to run your QMS: related topics are placed in separate SOPs (e.g., management of the work environment v. management of software, internal audits v. the management review, and customer communication v. feedback handling). The standard also has a habit of dropping additional requirements regarding some topic under a logical but seemingly disconnected topic—and depending on your organization's role and scope of operations, you might even find more examples of this than I have. I would also be scratching my head in writing the SOP to address the whole of Clause 5 and would, thus, have to, for example, describe all the ways your top management takes responsibility in all your SOPs. This, to me, sounds like an exercise in Greek philosophy. I would be afraid of the resulting metalevel spinning-yarn description curling up within itself and sinking to the bottom of the Mediterranean, where it would no doubt find a cozy spot for my whole QMS alongside the Atlantis buried there.

Another reason for having more than five SOPs is that periodically revising any of those SOPs would be a bigger task than necessary: you would need a longer time to review each SOP for revision needs and cover several disjointed topics at the same time, and then if you make changes to any topic, also perhaps address training needs for the other topics that happen to be covered by the same SOP. None of this would be impossible to do, but I believe it would not be practical and it would be far from optimal. For maintenance, training, and practical use reasons, I would recommend adopting a more developed set of around 9–12 SOPs.

In my model of 12 SOPs, I have opted to address a few topics as SOPs of their own when they could have been injected into some of the other SOPs in the package. These three SOPs on clinical evidence, regulatory affairs, and post-market surveillance are on topics where I see a need to adapt to evolving conditions and differing jurisdictional requirements out there in the real world. In order to best accommodate such flexibility and allow for adequate room to grow without the hassle of rerouting references later, I have engineered each as an SOP of their own.

You can compile the topics into a practical set of SOPs in several ways, but the following is the playlist I would recommend after years of working on my QMS. Table 6.1 presents my suggestion of SOPs and a rough outline of their contents. The following sections will then go into greater detail on all the SOPs presented here. If it would make more sense for your circumstances to move around some topics, you can do so. The following discussion on the SOPs is centered around the topics themselves, not the SOPs per se, to facilitate just that.

Table 6.1   Suggested Set of SOPs

SOP	Contents
SOP-1: QMS documentation	Types of documents and records, ID scheme, metadata, templates, access controls, change control for documents and records, and QMS planning
SOP-2: CAPA, monitoring, and improvement	Monitoring of processes and product (including quality indicators), handling nonconforming product, improvement (including CAPA), document review, and process change
SOP-3: Infrastructure	Work environment, contamination control, hardware and software, monitoring and measuring equipment, and property owned by others
SOP-4: Human resources	Qualifications, responsibilities, and authorities; training; evaluation of the effectiveness of training actions; and planning of personal development
SOP-5: Suppliers and distributors	Outsourcing of a process, supplier selection and evaluation, supplier personnel competence, purchasing, and verification of purchased product,
SOP-6: Auditing	Internal audits, external audits (including unannounced audits), management review, and supplier audits
SOP-7: Communication, marketing, and sales	Internal communication, customer communication (including feedback handling), communication with certification bodies (including notified body), and communication with regulatory authorities
SOP-8: Risk management	Risk assessment, risk control, risk communication, risk monitoring, and risk documentation

(Continued)

Table 6.1 *(Continued)* **Suggested Set of SOPs**

SOP	Contents
SOP-9: Clinical evidence	Clinical Evaluation Plan (CEP), Clinical Evaluation Report (CER), and Post-Market Clinical Follow-Up (PMCF)
SOP-10: Product realization	Planning of product realization, determination and review of product requirements, design and development (including planning, inputs, outputs, reviews, verification, validation, transfer, control of changes, and the file set), and production and service provision
SOP-11: Regulatory affairs	Understanding of applicable jurisdictions, monitoring of regulatory changes, monitoring of changes in standards, QMS certification, product requirements, product classification, product identification and traceability, product labeling, medical device file, product release, regulatory notifications, and contact details for regulatory authorities
SOP-12: Post-market surveillance	Information sources and Periodic Safety Update Report (PSUR)

6.3 Identifying Core Processes

The standard is big on the risk-based approach and for good reason. Things will go wrong, chores will be forgotten, corners will be cut, and amnesia will beleaguer even the best of people. For this reason, it is practical to look at what is likely to go wrong and what impact that will have on your users.

Applying the risk-based approach is not the same as identifying and mitigating the risks involved in your product; it is really about identifying the risks involved in the processes you employ in your QMS to realize the product. You do not yet need to know your products fully to already be able to point out those processes where a malfunction could lead to more issues down the road in other processes and in the eventual product itself. This is an important distinction between the risk-based approach and risk management in general, and a question I have occasionally received from my peers in the industry. You can, of course, later refine your understanding of process risks as you gain experience running them.

I would advocate for taking your user as the point of study in identifying your top-priority processes, the core processes where a smooth, correct, and error-free outcome is of the highest importance. By working backward from your user, you will be able to identify the tasks and deliverables that will make the biggest impact once your device leaves your doors. This way, you will be able to identify the processes that play the biggest role in keeping everything humming along nicely.

In Figure 5.3, I already gave you a sneak peek at what I might typically view as the core processes: product realization (SOP-10); communication, marketing, and sales (SOP-7); and post-market surveillance (SOP-12). Each and every SOP in your QMS should be important, and all the processes should run as intended, but out of all the SOPs, these three are the ones where I see errors as having the best and most immediate chance of affecting the product that ships so that it no longer meets all its requirements, including the expectations of the customer. If the operations of your organization are different or if your architecture of processes is somehow different, you may, of course, have other prime suspects among your SOPs.

In comparison, an error in any of the other SOPs may cause issues that trickle downstream, but many of them should be caught by various reviews and vigilance before any nonconforming product leaves your factory floor. For example, an issue in the management of human resources or even suppliers may be serious, but the error should be caught before any effects are observed on the outside.

I suppose you could label all your SOPs as "core SOPs", but this would mean that you are missing out on the opportunity to target your resources strategically and make sure you identify serious issues first. Treating all your SOPs the same would mean wasting resources, having inadequate concentration of resources where it matters, and not meeting the standard and what it expects to see in terms of the risk-based approach. If you like reading books on military strategy—for example, tank warfare—that is how you should perhaps approach the deployment of your resources: don't spread it all thin and hope all the bases are covered, but instead, identify the risks and ambush them on your own terms. To take a less conflict-oriented view, you can think of errors as the virus mutations that will occur in vivo and apply the risk-based approach to how you seek these out before they become pandemics.

Colorful language aside, once you know your process breakdown and have identified your core processes, you have the backbone of your QMS done. Now all that remains is to flesh out the processes themselves. That is what we will do next.

If you take objection to my 12-SOP model earlier, feel free to rearrange them as you see fit. The following discussion is structured around key topics inside the SOPs with the exact purpose of allowing you to rearrange the topics should you want to. Be careful about not leaving any topic out, though. You must always have a good rationale for claiming something doesn't apply to your operations, and while you can perhaps come up with other equally good solutions to mine, you should not just dismiss any topic in the following without compensating for it adequately. Some topics in the following are recommendations and not requirements, but the discussion will make this clear.

6.4 Pen to Paper

Here we go again. After working on the quality manual, you are well-set for writing the SOPs you need. The work ahead is mostly about taking a deeper dive into the subsequent details after the flyover we did with the manual. The type of text you will be writing is really the same, only now with a little less artistic flare and more detail on the processes themselves.

Writing the SOPs one at a time will let you focus on one area of your QMS at a time, think about how you want to structure the activity around that area in the context of your organization, and write the instructions you feel are necessary to ensure the activity unfolds like you have prescribed. Less is more here, so don't go into micromanagement or superfluous detail unless you strongly feel it is warranted.

As you write the first SOP, look for the right balance of details to write into your SOPs. You will want to make them detailed enough so that the processes can unfold according to the general steps you define but not so detailed that reading and following the SOPs will become an unnecessarily big task. You can leave many of the low-level details—such as what exact settings to use or what buttons to click in some software or piece of equipment—to be included in the working instructions and, in some cases, even to be figured out while conducting work according to the process for the first time. The latter does, of course, not translate well to processes in product realization, such as running the actual production line.

I might sketch the SOPs on a relatively high level, perhaps at the height of treetops as compared to a space station or an airplane, and then add as much detail below that for you to feel confident that your staff will be able to implement the processes safely. When you get scraped by branches you will know that you might be better off leaving that amount of detail to the working instructions. There is no definitive line to draw here, though. I have seen SOPs that read like working instructions, and in case these have then also been poorly constructed or illogically sequenced, it has been exceedingly difficult to discern the overall process. After a few quick iterations, you will be able to describe your process in both more and less detail, and thus, move up and down between a level appropriate for the quality manual and that of a micromanaging working instructions. The altitude you pick in the end will depend on your operations and what you feel is appropriate for carrying out those operations.

Following my 12-SOP model introduced earlier, or your own carefully curated adaptation of that, will ensure that the SOPs will slot together nicely at the end. You will, of course, be revisiting each SOP once you are finished with your first pass of all the SOPs so that you don't have unnecessary overlap and feel that you have adequate resources in place for the whole of your activities, but for now, let's concentrate on one SOP at a time.

When writing your quality manual, you used the template from Appendix 2. That same template would work for writing SOPs, but there are a few additional sections I would recommend you add to the template to make the most out of the nature of SOPs. Those are, however, optional and can be added to the documents during a second pass if you like. You can, therefore, dive straight into the core of the SOPs and worry about the extras later. If instead you want to get a feel for all the bells and whistles straight away, you may want to look at Section 20 for their discussion and refer to Appendix 3 for the ready-to-use structure.

With that, let's begin working on SOP-1. After you are done with your first pass of writing the SOP, you will find my checklist at the end of the section. The checklist for SOP-1, as indeed all the subsequent checklists for the other SOPs to come, should help you in getting the SOPs ready, but they will also be useful to you in the future as you are revising the SOPs through the document review.

Chapter 7

QMS Documentation (SOP-1)

This is where you start to give your QMS the form and structure it needs. Think of setting up an archival system for that endless warehouse in the Indiana Jones *films, how you will slot in any new crate to that collection, and how you will be able to efficiently find any specific crate afterward. Only realize that the archive you are now creating will be a living thing, a network of documents and records that your organization needs to access and maintain on a daily basis.*

If the quality manual was the entry point into your QMS, SOP-1 is the document that basically sets the coordinate system for navigating within that QMS. The SOP builds on the manual to go into more detail on your documents and records, how you manage these, and how you attend to maintaining the documents, the records, and the QMS itself.

The topics to cover here are as follows:

- Types of documents and records
- ID scheme
- Metadata
- Templates
- Access controls
- Change control for documents/records
- QMS planning

The good news to realize right off the bat is that we already covered many of the requirements related to the previous topics while writing the quality manual. We should not repeat the same information here, and we absolutely

DOI: 10.4324/9781003202868-7

should not write in description that conflicts with what we wrote in the manual. The quality manual already achieved much of the work involved in establishing the foundations of your QMS by describing your role, describing your documentation hierarchy, and even sketching out the overall network of processes you intend to have. We even promised that you will assign some form of identification to your documents and records.

The next logical step is to now go one level deeper and describe how you will create, maintain, and control both documents and records in your QMS, as well as the whole that is your QMS. Most of the topics we will address here stem from Clauses 4 and 5 of the standard, and are profound in nature, affecting just about everything in your QMS later. This will be the cornerstone of your SOPs.

7.1 Types of Documents and Records

The quality manual already introduced your stack of documentation quite nicely, but it is worth elaborating here that you intend to have both documents and records, and that you intend to control them both. These are both requirements from the standard, and they will not change over time so that much repetition will not be a headache during future maintenance of the SOP. You will remember from earlier that documents, such as your quality manual and SOPs, are where you instruct your processes, and records are the records retained from running those processes. Templates, forms, and working instructions used in your processes are, unless you argue otherwise, also documents that should be revised along with the SOPs.

If you wish to introduce your document types in more detail than you already did in the quality manual, the place for that is here in SOP-1. I would not go into too much detail, but I would flesh out the wireframe model a little here and say a few well-chosen words introducing each type of document and their function. The documentation types, grouped by class of documentation, I would cover are given in Table 7.1.

The documents were introduced in Sections 4.4.1, 4.4.2, and 4.4.3. You can jog your memory by referring back to those sections and then including a few lines on each type of document or record here as you feel is relevant. Doing so will allow you to keep guiding your reader into your QMS and help you to prevent the same types of documents from being called by more than one name in your subsequent SOPs. Remember that the primary

Table 7.1   Documentation to Cover in the Instruction

Group	Documents
Essential documents	Quality manual Standard operating procedures Templates (including forms)
Auxiliary documents	Working instructions Official copies (including standards, regulations, and manuals)
Records	Records Registries Medical device file(s)

audience here is not your auditor but your staff—particularly any new members joining that staff.

Note also that Clause 4.2.1e leaves the door open for other documentation required by regulations to be included in your QMS. The previous items should be quite sufficient if your medical device file then answers all the requirements placed on it (including clinical evaluation, declaration of conformity, and instructions for use).

This is a good time to make a reference to your document management system, although you will be introducing that in a little bit more detail in SOP-3. Here, it is beneficial to know that you are using electronic documents and some system or, if that is not the case, how you manage the paper-based documents.

7.2 ID Scheme

Just like the GPS system in the real world, or the latitudes and longitudes behind it, it is practically unavoidable to set up a good document ID scheme for navigating your QMS. You will be referring to a lot of documents from a lot of documents, especially to other SOPs from any given SOP and many records, so make sure your setup makes sense and can be used easily and safely. You do not want to quote long document names repeatedly when IDs will accomplish the same in a much more reader-friendly, efficient, and safe way. You do not want to have to describe a shelf, a box, and a folder when a robust document ID will do just the same. And it would be just silly to constantly use long URLs and web addresses inside the text.

My tips here are as follows:

- Make the IDs immediately identifiable as clearly delimited IDs within any text. Searching for them in documents should be easy. Make the IDs stand out from text in some practical way and include some common elements that can be used in text queries to bring up a list of all IDs from a text (e.g., "DOC-SOP-1" instead of "sop 1").
- Include classification information on the IDs as you see fit your operations; for example, use IDs like "QM-1" (for a quality manual) and "SOP-1" (for an SOP), instead of "ID1" and "ID2". But don't go overboard with this, and think twice before including information that may be prone to change (e.g., SOP classification of some sort).
- Make the IDs as short as possible.
- Identify the language or the product line in IDs if you need to.
- Differentiate between documents and records in the IDs (e.g., use "REC-1" with a running number to refer to records).

The design of your ID scheme is entirely up to you and probably also to the constraints of your document management software. If your software includes support for some generic IDs, I might use those for records and only assign custom-made IDs to key documents. I would, however, assign my own custom-made IDs to key documents so that it is easier to spot the references in texts and immediately figure out if the references make sense or not by the type of document. If you must refer to a lookup table to know what some document "#65825" actually is, that is not going to be optimal for documents instructing work even if it could work for records kept of that work. This may also make maintaining the list of documents (i.e., a document registry) easier as document IDs are not constantly evolving, as might be the case with document versions in some document management systems.

7.3 Metadata

The typical metadata you will want to have is discussed in Section 20, but here is a good place to introduce your reader to how you mark the important information in your documents: who issued the document and when, and who else was involved.

If your document management system includes metadata that conflicts with metadata shown in the fields of your documents and records, you should explain here what information takes precedence even if the information should generally be in sync. This is worth commenting on even if your QMS platform of choice is smart enough to have the ability to insert metadata, such as approval dates, into the files themselves. Things may go wrong, and thus, setting up a clear interpretation order for metadata in your QMS is generally a wise precaution.

7.4 Templates

Earlier, we already introduced the concept of templates, but in SOP-1, you may also want to comment on the overall practice and introduce your specific template for the SOPs and the quality manual. The point here is that when someone will be introducing a new SOP to your QMS later, they will immediately know how to format it correctly. I would not go much further in instructing the use of the template than to just state that you have a template for SOPs. The template itself is covered in detail in Section 20, and an example template is available in Appendix 3. The use of other templates can be left to the individual SOPs making use of them.

You may also want to introduce a generic record template for convenience and consistency, but whatever you do, don't force all your records to use that template as that would not be sustainable going forward. It would in fact be tantamount to a death by a thousand paper cuts. In essence, the generic record template will be your basic template for plans and reports, but you will have many other types of logs, receipts, memos, and notes that will not benefit from an imposed template. Your approach to archiving and identifying these records should be uniform, but it would make little sense to impose a uniform look and feel to the records. I doubt anyone would seriously consider it, but be careful you don't accidentally write it in here.

A further important note I would make here is that an issuance date (i.e., when a document has been approved and issued) makes sense for SOPs and quality manuals, but to also use that for records will, in many cases, be going overboard headfirst and hitting the rocky shores surrounding your QMS shipyard. Don't do it. For records, use a creation date instead of an issuance date unless you have a good reason for doing otherwise. Even then, use the creation date instead—to recall the emphatic recommendation to walk when I asked my hotel concierge how I could buy a bus ticket in Rome.

7.5 Access Controls

In addition to instructing how your documents are created and how they are revised, which will be covered next, you should also carefully consider who needs access to what documents and records. Using an electronic document management system will help you greatly in applying access controls as you need and in making sure the correct document versions are available where they need to be. The standard requires you to do the latter and implies a need to also do the former.

Figuring out what documents or records should be accessible by whom is probably quite easy, but also make sure people don't unnecessarily see unissued working drafts of future documents and records, and don't mistakenly use obsolete or unapproved versions of documents.

My advice here in this SOP is to create a table where each row is a type of document or a set of records, and then has columns after it to cover all the different access control types you have identified. The types of controls you may have include, for example, a) version control, b) access control, and c) periodic rereview (e.g., via the document review mechanism). Visualizing this information as a simple table will let you, and your reader, get a good feel of the documents and records your QMS consists of. Don't go overboard and include every single document (e.g., plan and report) you expect to have. Instead, work on the groups of documents you expect to have along the lines you set up earlier in this section.

7.6 Change Control for Documents

A "document", in layman's terms, is any document-like object, but ISO 13485 really uses the term to refer to your essential instructions in the QMS (i.e., what ISO 9000 addresses as "documented information"). These documents are your quality manual, SOPs, forms, templates, and possibly, working instructions.

The standard requires you to have a process for controlling documents (Clause 4.2.4). This involves reviewing and approving documents for adequacy prior to issue and also revising them later as needed. You will want to define a process for creating new documents via a write-review-approve model or similar. How this works exactly is up to you, but make sure you pull in the most knowledgeable people in your organization to develop the document and you also have appropriate checks in place to both review and approve the document for adequacy before it is issued. Don't forget that the writer can't be the reviewer or the approver of the document, but in most cases, the reviewer and the approver can be the same person and can even be in the same step.

Furthermore, the later revisions of the document should not just be left to chance, but instead, you should have a mechanism for reviewing and ensuring the adequacy of the documents over time. In this book, I call this mechanism the "document review" (see SOP-2). When making changes to issued documents, either via a scheduled document review or when a need is identified, you must ensure that the changes are reviewed and approved either by the original approving function or another designated function that has adequate competency and access to the necessary background information. The changes themselves must be identified, which does not just mean retaining all versions in an archive but, instead, identifying and qualifying the changes through, for example, a written description in a version history table (see Section 20.3.10). It must also be clear whether a document is a draft or a final issued version and, in the latter case, also who issued it and when. An electronic document management system will help you with all this.

Also note that according to Clause 4.1.4, changes to processes must be controlled and evaluated for effect on the QMS and products. Depending on the risk associated with the document, you may link the performing of this assessment to be a part of the document review process, but for at least the core SOPs, I would recommend running a separate Process Change Activity assessment (see SOP-2).

Your document control must also ensure the identifiability of the documents, prevent their deterioration or loss, and ensure that the correct documents are available where they need to be. Make sure your setup supports these requirements and give any instructions you need here. The requirements for identification and controlled distribution also apply to documents of external origin that have been determined by you to be necessary for the planning and operation of the QMS (Clause 4.2.4f). In writing your SOP here, it is enough that you know your document management does all this and that your actions defined here honor these features.

Finally, you must also define the document retention period so that you meet regulatory requirements and documents are available for at least the lifetime of any records made based on the documents. The good news here is that you already defined both document and record retention times in the quality manual, so you don't need to do it again here. By "need to", I really mean you shouldn't, as duplicating information will lead to confusion sooner or later as you revise the content over time. By defining the retention periods in the quality manual, you have a convenient source you can quote here and in every other SOP needing that information, and you also concentrate any edits of the instructions to one place.

You may want to create a register of your documents. My advice here is to define the term "document", as I have done earlier, to refer to your quality manual, SOPs, templates, and forms. You may also want to enter your working instructions (if any) to this registry. This way, your register will stay nice and tidy while also giving a concise overview of your key instruction documents. For discussion of registers, refer back to Section 4.4.3.

7.7 Change Control for Records

Records, as opposed to documents, are evidence of activity according to the instructions given in your documents. The standard requires you to have a process for controlling records (4.2.5). What records you keep is up to you and should be defined in the SOPs themselves while they instruct any given process. The records you keep should thus help you meet, and allow you to prove that you meet, the requirements set out in the standard and in any applicable regulations regarding your product or your organization in general. The standard also makes the effective operation of your QMS one of these requirements.

Having no records is not acceptable, but having everything recorded is not feasible. The balance here is something you will probably be fine-tuning over time, but for now, in this SOP, it is enough to state how you handle records. The exact types of records and how those are created will then be addressed in each SOP as relevant but always in accordance with your description here.

Once you have a record, Clause 4.2.5 of the standard requires you to have controls on its secure identification, storage, and use. You must ensure that the records remain legible, identifiable, and usable. In a departure from the control of documents, though, you are to ensure changes to records remain identifiable, but they need not be identified in advance. The difference here is profound: instead of writing an itemized overview of changes, it is enough to later use some comparison tool to compare any versions of the record. But don't think that you can just use Tipp-Ex on older records and write over the previous entries either.

The standard also makes a point of requiring that you handle patient data in accordance with applicable regulations. This is not elaborated on in the standard, so look toward your local regulations on the matter. In this SOP, it may be enough to note that you plan to observe such requirements and refer to SOP-9 on clinical evidence and any use of data you want to instruct in there.

Finally, you must also define the record retention period so that you meet regulatory requirements and records are available for at least the lifetime of any product addressed by the record. The good news here, too, is that you already defined the record retention time in the quality manual, so don't do it again here.

I would advise against creating a manual register of all your records unless you are really going old school, need to work with stacks of physical documents, and are planning for a *Planet of the Apes*–type apocalypse. Your electronic document management system will help you keep your records intact and in good order.

You will, however, need to create an index of your key product documents and records when you are developing the technical file of your product, but here, too, a general all-encompassing registry of records would be more trouble than its worth if you are maintaining that register by hand. It may, however, be a good idea to keep track of the documents and records going into your various technical files in one way or another. Ideally, your QMS supports this via convenient document collections. For now, if you are setting up your QMS, I would not worry too much about this special type of use, though, and only return to the question once you have put together your first technical file. If you, on the other hand, are working on improving an existing QMS, the topic of creating and maintaining document (including record) manifests, such as technical files, is a good topic to look at. Ideally, your QMS software supports pulling together technical files for various jurisdictions and enables you to address any changes in the requirements and/or the underlying documents in a convenient way. If it does, I would count my blessings if I were you, but if not, I would not despair. You may want to refer to SOP-11 here for more on the medical device file.

7.8 QMS Planning

Setting up your QMS in a planned way is what you are now in the process of doing. Keeping your QMS well-oiled and serviced also after it is online is a key requirement in the standard. In fact, the QMS not only needs to be maintained but also improved over time. To this end, you must make sure that the documentation, the documents, and the records you have defined allow you to ensure this via effective planning, operation, and control of processes. The requirement to keep up such documentation is in Clause 4.2.1d. The related requirement to control changes to such documentation is in Clause 5.4.2.

In SOP-1, I would introduce my write-review-approve model for revising documents (as we have done earlier) and perhaps refer to SOP-4 for briefing and training needed after any changes made to the documents. Also remember that some bigger changes may need reporting to certification bodies.

Additionally, it is important to set up a schedule for revising your documents for any needed changes periodically. This is done via the document review mechanism instructed in SOP-2, but as for the overall schedule or annual cycle, I would set that up here. Section 25 offers more discussion of the document review cycle. Similarly, you should set a schedule for auditing your actual, real-world operations on how they match with your instructed processes, the standard, and any applicable regulations. How this is implemented will be instructed in SOP-6 while discussing the different types of audits and the management review, but you might want to address the schedule here. In practice, I would design a template for your annual QMS cycle here and ensure that the template considers the periodic review of each SOP and the types of audits you envisage having on a rough month-by-month basis. The result will be a calendar-like record that tells you which SOPs are up for review this month and when the next audit or management review is roughly expected. In addition to this schedule, you will also have a more detailed audit plan to structure your auditing activities over the next one to three years (see SOP-6).

I would also refer to SOP-7 on internal communication, especially in terms of the periodic Quality Management Team and Management Team meetings that form a key activity for monitoring the status of the QMS. SOP-7 is also the source for instruction on customer communication, and it, along with SOP-12 on post-market surveillance and SOP-11 on regulatory affairs, will provide you good sources of ideas on QMS improvement. One further reference I might make here is to SOP-2 on process monitoring to ensure that monitoring information is linked to QMS planning. Anything you measure and analyze should, after all, lead to improvements either immediately or down the road if urgent action is not warranted. Again, leave any deeper discussion of how the monitoring is performed and acted on to SOP-2.

7.9 Checklist

Providing a complete set of checklists for the SOP you wrote earlier or the SOPs you will write in the following sections would be a magic trick worthy of the Great Houdini—or of the kind performed in Christopher Nolan's *The Prestige*. A sleight of the hand or a trick of the eye is not what we want here, though. No single set of checklists can make sure you have in fact interpreted the standard and all applicable regulations as is appropriate to your business. For that, you should be braced for learning from both the everyday practical experience gained by running your processes in the wild and the occasional trial that will come in the form of annual internal or external audit.

The following checklist (Table 7.2) is provided, as are all the checklists contained in this book, for your convenience. The checklists will help you ensure that you have covered most of the essential elements of the standard in your SOPs, but the nature of your operations will, in the end, determine if the SOPs you have written will be judged appropriate to your organization.

Table 7.2 Checklist for SOP-1

Checklist
☐ **You control the issuance of documents and records**   You review and approve documents for adequacy prior to issue.
☐ **You control access to, distribution of, and changes to documents**   You have a process for creating, revising, and approving documentation. You ensure legibility and identification (including any changes). You prevent deterioration, loss, and erroneous use.
☐ **You control access to, distribution of, and changes to records**   You control, for example, identification, storage, and security. You ensure records remain legible, identifiable, and retrievable, and any changes to records remain identifiable.
☐ **Your documentation addresses QMS planning and improvement**   You ensure QMS planning takes place according to your quality policy and any requirements.
☐ **Your documentation meets regulatory requirements**   You have addressed, for example, documentation retention times.
☐ **You have addressed how this SOP is to be applied at your organization**   And the correct versions of documents will be available at the correct places.
☐ **You know what quality indicators match with this SOP**   Record a few measurable indicators for this SOP in the appendix of the quality manual.
Once you feel confident you have ticked every box, it's time to move on.

Chapter 8

CAPA, Monitoring, and Improvement (SOP-2)

This is where you start to think about how you will want to keep an eye over your QMS. Worth emphasizing here is that CAPA (i.e., your corrective and preventive action management) will be the single most tried activity in your QMS, so it pays to make sure you like running it. It's like naming your baby son "Bond, James Bond" instead of "Mapother, Thomas Cruise Mapother IV". There is nothing wrong with either name; I am a fan of both men. But choosing the former will have you sipping your cocktails sooner.

SOP-2 is all about monitoring your processes and handling needs for change in them. This involves keeping your eye on the health of the processes via, for example, quality indicators and reacting to any nonconformities, observations, and other suggestions for improvement in them. The top-level requirements for the SOP are given in Clause 8.1, where the need to demonstrate conformity of product and the QMS, and to maintain the effectiveness of the QMS are stated as the chief motivations for monitoring and measurement. The requirement to maintain an effective QMS is also already stated in Clause 4.1.1 as something you must observe.

The topics covered here are as follows:

- Monitoring of processes and product (including quality indicators)
- Handling of nonconforming product
- Improvement (including CAPA)
- Document review
- Process change

DOI: 10.4324/9781003202868-8

Here in SOP-2, you may also come across requirements stemming out of Clauses 6, 7, or 8 of the standard that you may be able to exclude based on your type of activities or the nature of your product. You will have defined such exclusions and their rationale in the quality manual.

8.1 Monitoring of Processes and Product (Including Quality Indicators)

Clause 4.1.3 requires you to define criteria and methods to ensure your processes run effectively. This includes ensuring adequate resources and information are available. You must also have records proving that you monitor and analyze all your processes so that they continue to run effectively. Additionally, Clause 4.1.5 stipulates that your controls for any outsourced processes are proportionate to the risk involved and the ability of the supplier to meet requirements. Similarly, Clause 8.1 requires that you plan and implement monitoring and improvement of both product and the QMS, and Clauses 8.2.5 and 8.2.6 place further requirements on monitoring. All these requirements may be addressed here in SOP-2.

You may go about answering these requirements in several ways, but on the top level, you should consider how your use of the quality policy, the quality objectives, and most of all, the quality indicators begin to meet these needs. Your quality indicators are the readily measurable and trackable extension of the quality policy and quality objectives you set out in the quality manual. You may have already taken a stab at the indicators while writing the manual. When setting up the manual, I also already advocated for listing the indicators as an appendix the manual, instead of in this SOP. If you took this advice, here, it is enough to position the indicators as part of your solution to monitoring your product and processes. For this purpose, it is important that your quality indicators both match your policy and objectives, and cover the spectrum of your processes and products. If this is not the case, make sure you know why. In addition to quality indicators, you will have more detailed monitoring records, but for giving your management a concise overview of the lay of the land, the indicators serve a distinct purpose. The indicators should be continuously monitored at Management Team meetings, so make sure that any indicators you define throughout working with this book provide a concise and actionable overview of your activities. Any anomalies in the indicators will then lead to a more detailed investigation as warranted.

Your approach to measuring processes will be affected by the type of your operations. For some processes, it may be enough to obtain a proof-of-life type of a measure on the running process (e.g., personal non-QMS training records are accumulating), but for higher-risk processes (e.g., a running sterilization subprocess), you will want to apply rigor in obtaining early warning signs that something may be heading awry. Naturally, you will also measure such high-risk processes on a lower level and ensure that appropriate checks are in place.

Your approach to measuring product will be affected by the type of that product. For a software product, it may be trivial to confirm that the product is exactly identical to an earlier production batch. For a complex physical product, this will not be possible, but the production batch may nonetheless be measured to be within some tolerance. Your SOP should explain your approach here and make sure the process is running and records are kept (including conformity with acceptance criteria, identity of authorization personnel, and testing equipment). For exact product-specific acceptance criteria, you may want to establish where these are to be found but perhaps not repeat the criteria here in the SOP. On a top level, this measurement data should also feed your quality indicators and be tracked by the top management on some meaningful level. For more discussion of monitoring as it relates to product realization, I would refer to SOP-10.

In general, you should be economical and to the point with your quality indicators. Don't expect your management to go through massive amounts of numbers and deduce trends from the raw data. This will not happen as part of the already busy Management Team meetings. On the other hand, don't require unnecessary and time-consuming processing of raw data to produce indicators that aren't actually useful. Ask yourself what information the management should see to work effectively, and work out a streamlined path to feeding them that information as safely and efficiently as possible.

Additionally, I would refer to SOP-6 on internal audits, SOP-7 on feedback and complaint handling, and SOP-11 on reporting to regulatory authorities. All these are brought up in Clause 8 of the standard as part of monitoring, but I would address the monitoring functions of these activities in the individual SOPs concerned with the topics themselves. Here, it is nonetheless wise to make a mention of these types of sources of information as fitting into your monitoring activity but then refer to the previous SOPs for more discussion.

The analysis of data has its own clause, Clause 8.4, in the standard. Coming from a science background, I would argue that there is little point to monitoring without analysis and no possibility of improvement without analysis preceding it. As a result, I feel that this clause is somewhat superfluous, but it does drive home the fact that it is not enough to record but that you also need to analyze that which you recorded. The clause also gives you a base set of items to analyze: feedback, conformity to product requirements, suppliers, audits, and service reports (if available). Your monitoring activities should thus cover these topics. The clause also instructs that any signs of issues in the suitability, adequacy, or effectiveness of the QMS will lead to improvement.

8.2 Handling of Nonconforming Product

Handling of nonconforming product could be addressed in SOP-10, along with product realization, but as that SOP is already loaded to the brim and as handling of faulty product is very much akin to monitoring and the handling of nonconformities in the QMS, and the two are often linked with one another, I would place the topic here in SOP-2.

Clause 8.3 of the standard sets requirements for actions to monitor product and handle any nonconforming product detected before or after delivery. You must identify such products and prevent their intended use and delivery. This also includes requirements on any rework done or concessions made to release such product. Part of the provisions is the identification of authorities and responsibilities involved in the detection, isolation, and disposal of faulty product. You must have a process for this. It is naturally preferable to detect faulty product as soon as possible and prevent its use or delivery as cleared product.

When nonconforming product is detected before delivery, the nonconformity is eliminated, the original intended use or application is precluded, and/or a concession is made with an approved justification whereby the product still meets regulatory requirements. Records will include the identification of the person authorizing the concession. Rework, if performed, takes place in accordance with documented procedures that consider any potential adverse effects and involve the same review and approval as before. Only product meeting applicable acceptance criteria and regulations will be released. When nonconforming product is detected after delivery, actions must be appropriate to the potential effects of the issue. A process for issuing advisory notices in accordance with regulations must exist and be invocable at any time (see SOP-7).

It is important to consider whether the detected faulty product may give rise to an investigation or notifications to external parties. The goal is always to remove both harm done by the fault and the cause of the fault. Note also in this context that Clause 7.5.4 requires that servicing activities are monitored as a potential source of a customer complaints and input for improvement, which, although not necessarily a sign of nonconforming product, may be a sign of faults in the design.

8.3 Improvement (Including CAPA)

Clause 8.25 of the standard requires you to monitor your processes and to take quick corrections (if warranted) and long-term corrective action when planned results are not reached. Clause 8.5 goes into more detail on improvement and discusses the two most important actions in all quality management: corrective actions and preventive actions. These two compose the activity behind the CAPA acronym, which you will have come across earlier in this book.

The base of all improvement activity is given in Clause 8.5.1, where you are tasked with identifying and implementing changes to ensure the continued suitability, adequacy, and effectiveness of your QMS, and the safety and performance of your products. In so doing, you are expected to make use of the quality policy, quality objectives, audit results, management review, and any information from your post-market surveillance, analysis of data, and CAPA. All these items can be considered as major components of your QMS. The crux of the matter regarding improvement is that you monitor all the important information sources, pay attention to identified areas of improvement, and act accordingly. Expect to run CAPA after every audit, occasionally in between, and expect post-market surveillance to be a hot topic in any audit for at least the next few years.

Requirements for corrective actions (the "CA" of CAPA) are given in Clause 8.5.2. In response to a nonconformity (NC), you are required to take corrective action that is proportionate to the effects of the NC without undue delay. You need to document a process for the following:

■ Review NCs (including complaints).
■ Determine the causes of the NCs.
■ Evaluate the need for action to eliminate the cause of the NC (thereby also preventing the recurrence of the NC).
■ Plan, document, and implement such action (including updating documentation, as appropriate).

- ◼ Verify such action does not adversely affect meeting requirements (including regulatory, safety, and performance).
- ◼ Review the effectiveness of action taken (this may include a review as part of the management review).

You may also need to take immediate corrections that are implemented immediately to fix or contain issues that have already occurred.

Requirements for preventive actions (the "PA" of CAPA) are given in Clause 8.5.3. You need to determine preventive action that is proportionate to the effects of the problem (note that delay is not mentioned). Document a process for the following:

- ◼ Determine potential NCs and their causes.
- ◼ Evaluate the need for action to prevent the reoccurrence of NCs.
- ◼ Plan, document, and implement such action (including updating documentation, as appropriate).
- ◼ Verify such action does not adversely affect meeting requirements (including regulatory, safety, and performance).
- ◼ Review the effectiveness of action taken.

As always in QMS, keeping records is required for CAPA, but as CAPA activity will be a topic in every single audit you will have and as we are talking about actual, real-world issues that occurred in your system—and not just some theoretical chance of something going wrong—keeping easily usable records is just common sense. You will be looking at these records repeatedly over the first 3–12 months as you work to address any issue and also from time to time thereafter as you return to analyze patterns and prevent reoccurrence.

CAPA is a favorite topic among auditors and for good reason: in addition to revealing issues and their corrections, it also shows your QMS in action from the bottom to the top of your organization. If your CAPA process is found to be broken in any nontrivial way, you can bet that there are also other issues in your QMS.

8.4 Document Review

In SOP-1, we set up your stack of documentation, including the essential documents that instruct your processes: your quality manual, SOPs and the templates, forms, and working instructions that may go with the SOPs. We also discussed the need to maintain those key documents.

The later revisions of such controlled documents should not just be left to chance, but instead, you should have a mechanism for reviewing and ensuring the adequacy of such documents over time. In this book, I call this mechanism the "document review", as introduced in Section 4.4.7 and elaborated on from the point of view of running the activity in Section 25. Setting the schedule for the document review was already addressed in SOP-1 as part of QMS planning, so here, the focus is on instructing the process itself.

To write your description of the processes here in this SOP, I suggest that you review Sections 4.4.7 and 25. The document review is quite a simple process where the key features are the following:

- You go through your essential documentation periodically according to a predefined schedule. You should, of course, also react to any sudden needs to review documents in addition to this schedule, but such ad hoc needs should not prevent the periodic review.
- You employ the best knowledge and expertise from both within and without your organization to review and revise the documents. You build on standards and best practices whenever possible.
- You have a controlled mechanism for reviewing the effect of any changes on any other processes and your ability to meet requirements for your QMS or product.

In addition, SOP-1 already ensured the following important requirements for controlling documents as regards the document review.

- You have a controlled mechanism in place for reviewing and approving any changes to the documents prior to their issuance.
- You maintain all previous versions of the documents, distribute the issued documents as appropriate, and ensure no mistakes in the identity of unapproved or approved documents may occur.

In writing your instructions for the document review here, beware of going over into micromanagement. It is quite easy to write in superfluous detail about what review steps must be done when, what external references consulted, and what functions within your organization to involve in which order. If these are important to maintaining your QMS in an optimal state, include the details, of course; but most likely, you are just adding hoops to jump through every month over the next *N* years. Focus on what matters and stick to that. That will lead to the safest, most efficient, and most reliable process.

Remember to instruct the updating of any general introduction of the SOP in your quality manual and any document register you may have. Here, make sure the document control requirements from SOP-1 are met, including, for example, an updated document history table at the end of the document. I would hand over the responsibility over the last steps of document issuance to the quality manager or a small document control group to ensure consistency of actions across all documents.

8.5 Change Control (Including PCA)

"Change control" refers to your controlled mechanism for reviewing the effect of any changes made in one process on any other processes and your ability to meet the requirements for your QMS or product. I have dubbed this process simply as Process Change Activity (PCA). The mechanism should be invoked whenever you are considering making changes to your processes before you make those changes. Following a risk-based approach, you may decide to address your core processes more stringently than your other processes if this enables you to then allocate your resources better.

In practice, I would design an assessment form utilizing checklists and textboxes to ensure I have considered how any changes in the SOP affect my conformity to regulations, and product and QMS requirements. A practical way into QMS requirements is to consider the other SOPs the given SOP links to and any changes on the interface between the two SOPs. Similarly, changes in the SOP may necessitate changes into the quality manual, but if these go beyond a trivial update of the description relating to the SOP, I would analyze the circumstances carefully.

It will be quite easy to tie PCA into the document review process, but it may be less straightforward to prove which unissued draft version of the SOP was actually reviewed here and that, when approved, that was the exact version issued. Time stamps from your document management system should help you here, but if not, plan your approach carefully to preserve the integrity of your QMS.

As always in QMS, keeping records and ensuring changes propagate through your organization as intended are important. You may want to design a register of the PCA assessments (i.e., changes) you have made to act as an overview over time.

8.6 Checklist

The following checklist (Table 8.1) is provided for your convenience.

Table 8.1 Checklist for SOP-2

Checklist
☐ **You know how you want to monitor your processes and products** You determine criteria, methods, and necessary resources to ensure effective operation.
☐ **You know how you want to analyze and review monitoring and measurement data** This may include monthly Management Team meetings and the management review.
☐ **You have a process for periodic review of your documents** And you control changes to your processes effectively and ahead of time.
☐ **You have a process for handling CAPA activity** This includes immediate corrections, corrective actions, and preventive action.
☐ **You know how you want to address nonconforming product** This includes both products detected before and after delivery, and any concessions made.
☐ **You have addressed how this SOP is to be applied at your organization** And the correct versions of documents will be available at the correct places.
☐ **You know what quality indicators match with this SOP** Record a few measurable indicators for this SOP in the appendix of the quality manual.
Once you feel confident you have ticked every box, it's time to move on.

Chapter 9

Infrastructure (SOP-3)

This is where you start to define where your watercooler and fire extinguisher are, and what (if anything) those have to do with your approach to cyber-security, tool validation, and infrastructure maintenance. If you are Tom Cruise in Oblivion, *your janitorial duties will be quickly described, but if your infrastructure needs are more diverse—say your organization is terra-forming Mars—you will have more deep thinking to do here.*

Clauses 4.1 and 6.1 of the standard require you—or actually, your top management when we also consider Clause 5.1—to make sure you have supplied adequate resources, including information, to run all the processes in your QMS and meet both regulatory and customer requirements. SOP-3 is where you will address the infrastructure part of those resources: the premises, work environment, and tools—the latter of which, in this book, includes both hardware and software. Also note that the standard considers supporting services, such as transport and communication, to be a part of infrastructure, although these may also fall under supplier management (SOP-5). Remember, though, that Clause 1 may let you leave out some requirements if they stem out of Clauses 6, 7, or 8 and are not relevant to your operations.

The meat of infrastructure management is in Clause 6.3, where you are required to understand how infrastructure affects the conformity of your products and their orderly handling without any mix-up. Note that the clause does not actually require you to define a process here but instead document the requirements involved. In practice, the difference between documenting requirements and defining a process may be a slippery slope and depend on who you ask. You must also define requirements for the maintenance of

DOI: 10.4324/9781003202868-9

infrastructure, including the maintenance interval, if maintenance can affect the products produced.

The topics to cover here are as follows:

■ Work environment
■ Contamination control
■ Hardware and software
■ Monitoring and measuring equipment
■ Property owned by others

Let's look at each of these more closely in the following.

9.1 Work Environment

In this SOP, I would advise you to describe your physical work environment, which is what the standard is directly concerned with and also your software environment, if that is appropriate to you.

For describing your software environment, I would identify your essential computer systems, describe their use briefly, and assign responsibilities for maintaining those systems and granting appropriate access rights. Covering software in the SOPs like this is not explicitly required by the standard, but I would think long and hard about my reasons if I were to exclude essential software from any description of my work environment. The validation and more detailed use of these systems will be addressed in your software validation records, so it is not necessary to go into much detail here. It is not necessary to cover all your various software tools here either. Instead, I would focus on the tools you instruct in your SOPs. This would include your basic document management system and perhaps your development environment software, risk management software, version management software, and so forth. I would then have a register of all the validated and approved software separately from this SOP but referred to from here.

Workspaces are mentioned earlier in the standard, but the meat of work environment management is in Clause 6.4.1. In accordance with what was said about infrastructure management earlier in Clause 6.3, here, you are required to understand how work environments affect the conformity of your products. If the effect can be adverse, you must define requirements and, now, also procedures for their monitoring and control. In so doing, you must consider the health and cleanliness of personnel (including cleanliness of their clothing) and ensure that even temporary personnel are either competent or working under competent supervision. Note that Clause 7.5.2 says that if your product will be cleaned at a later stage, the requirements from Clause 6.4.1 may not apply until that cleaning is performed (see Section 16.4.2).

The work environment is a topic that frequently comes up in conversations with experts and auditors, especially if you are not a software-only company but have actual factory floors to inspect. Many of the horror stories you see on, for example, FDA offshore audits of pharmaceutical manufacturers also deal with work environments and occasionally have egregious nonconformities to report. Common sense should give you a good starting point here, but don't lull yourself into thinking this subclause only deals with lab coats and hardhats.

One frequent item to consider here is the availability of work instructions, including whether these are up-to-date and appropriate. This clause also appears to provide a good testing ground for comparing the theory and the practice during audits, so make sure these are in line and make sense. Also worth noting in this context is that the global COVID-19 pandemic increased the need to perform remote audits. Performing remote factory floor inspections during remote audits have apparently called for some element of MacGyverism (e.g., taping iPhones to trolleys), but these have, by and large, been a success and are here to stay, the occasional bouts of seasickness of those watching the video feed notwithstanding.

In practice, I would start off with access control, security, and fire safety, and then proceed as far toward requirements for clean rooms as is necessary. If all you need is a standard office space in any reliable business park, say that.

9.2 Contamination Control

Contamination control (Clause 6.4.2) is a topic that goes together with clean rooms, but don't make the mistake of thinking that is the only domain where it applies. As touched on in Section 3.8, contamination can also come in the form of a cybersecurity vulnerability. Contamination can, in fact, be interpreted to refer to any unwanted tampering of your product. Think carefully about what this may mean, whether concern is warranted, and act accordingly.

The standard requires you to, if appropriate, document arrangements (note that it does not say procedures) for the control of contaminated or potentially contaminated product. In so doing, you must consider your work environment, personnel, and product. The requirements for sterile medical devices are understandably even stricter, and here, it is always appropriate to document requirements also regarding microorganisms or particulate matter and cleanliness during assembly and packaging. Also take a moment to consider how such product is related to the nonconforming product discussed in SOP-2 and how your overall contamination controls fit with your product realization activities (SOP-10).

9.3 Hardware and Software

Clause 6.3 provides the basic requirements for validation and maintenance of tools, including their calibration. Machinery and hardware are naturally a part of the tools discussed, but so is the software you use. The minimum set of software you must consider is the software used in your QMS (Clause 4.1.6), the software used in production and service provision (Clause 7.5.6), and the software used for the monitoring and measurement of requirements (7.6). You must have a documented procedure for the validation of both hardware and software, as is appropriate in your case.

The software validation effort must be proportionate to the risk associated with the use of the software, and it must be performed prior to the use of the software and after changes to the software or your use of it. The risk-based approach is your key to a safe, workable process here. I would be careful not to make the update process so heavy and cumbersome that periodic security batches pile up but, at the same time, avoid making careless updates to software. It therefore makes sense to classify your software by risk (including their effect on the conformity of your product) and apply a lighter process to nonessential tools, such as word processors, and a more full-on approach to your QMS software, for example.

In practice, you will also want to set up a mechanism for tracking available software updates, analyzing the changes ahead of installing them, and then deciding on your revalidation effort based on the level of concern. I suggest you, at a minimum, retain logs of any updates installed, including the who and the when as well as a short textual assessment of why the update was installed. I would also always notify the users prior to making any updates of critical systems and ask them to apply special caution after the update has gone through as well as report any concerns they may come across with the new version. This caution is just common sense, but if you also document all this adequately, you will get to dot some i's and cross some t's. Keeping a register of the validation of your tools is a good idea.

See Section 22 for more on the validation of your QMS software itself.

9.4 Monitoring and Measuring Equipment

This topic is closely related to the hardware and software discussed earlier, but as not all hardware or software is used for monitoring and measuring, it is best addressed under its own heading. Clause 7.6 requires that you understand what monitoring and measuring is required for your operation, and that you have documented procedures for this.

The measuring equipment must be calibrated and/or verified at specified intervals, or before use, in accordance with procedures and with respect to recorded standards (preferably based on international or national standards). The equipment is to be identifiable, its calibration status is to be recorded, and the readjustment is to be performed as necessary. Safeguards must be in place to prevent tampering, damage, and deterioration. If deviation is detected, you must also assess previously recorded results and take appropriate action in regard to the affected equipment and product. Records must naturally include calibration and/or verification status, and any results, conclusions, and as always, any necessary actions decided on. The standard offers a link to ISO 10012 on measurement management systems as further reading, and many other standards, too, likely exist for your circumstances.

9.5 Property Owned by Others

Clause 7.5.10 discusses the handling of customer property, but you may also want to address other external property you have temporary possession over. Be careful not to go overboard here, but consider whether you should address, by instruction or by acknowledgment, for example, partner, distributor, and end-user property here, both in terms of physical objects and intellectual property. The standard may not require you to address intellectual property rights (IPR), but your organization will most likely want to or even must do so in order to do business.

The clause requires you to identify, verify, and protect such (customer) property, whether it is provided for use or incorporated into your product, if it is under your control or in your use. Any loss, damage, or assessment of unsuitability of use must be reported to the owner.

9.6 Checklist

The following checklist (Table 9.1) is provided for your convenience.

Table 9.1   Checklist for SOP-3

Checklist

☐	**You know your work environment requirements** This includes any requirements on premises, hardware, and software.
☐	**You know how you handle software validation** You have a process for performing validation as appropriate for each tool.
☐	**You know how you address monitoring and measuring equipment** This includes, for example, calibration intervals and prevention of tampering.
☐	**You know how you address property owned by others** This may refer to both physical and intellectual property.
☐	**You maintain registers of your infrastructure as is appropriate** This may include registers for hardware, software, and other tools.
☐	**You have addressed how this SOP is to be applied at your organization** And the correct versions of documents will be available at the correct places.
☐	**You know what quality indicators match with this SOP** Record a few measurable indicators for this SOP in the appendix of the quality manual.

Once you feel confident you have ticked every box, it's time to move on.

Chapter 10

Human Resources (SOP-4)

The sergeant from the Full Metal Jacket *and Robert Redford's* Horse Whisperer *have very different approaches to training, but both would agree with the standard that training is a key factor in success. Management of human resources should be as easy as hiring the right people, training them, giving them the right tools, and ensuring that they can do their work as efficiently and reliably as possible. You need to stay on top of things to make sure that everyone is trained for their evolving tasks, that underperforming processes are fixed, and that individual creativity does not silently thwart the processes. Change is welcome but not at random.*

The same fundamental setup in Clauses 4.1, 5.1, and 6.1—and discussed earlier with infrastructure management in SOP-3—also govern the management of human resources. That is not to say people are commodities—far from it—but you and your top management are required to ensure that also adequate human resources are in place to run your QMS as intended and manufacture the products as expected.

The specific topics to cover here are as follows:

- Qualifications, responsibilities, and authorities
- Training
- Evaluation of the effectiveness of training actions
- Planning of personal development

Also take a look at Section 24, which goes beyond the standard to discuss what forms training can actually take. The detailed discussion there may influence the instructions you write here.

DOI: 10.4324/9781003202868-10

10.1 Qualifications, Responsibilities, and Authorities

On a top level, Clause 5.5.1 requires that responsibilities and authorities are both documented and understood within your organization. The inter-relation of all personnel who are involved in the performing, managing, or verification of work affecting quality must be documented, and the independence and authority needed therein ensured. You already addressed your current definitions of these job characteristics in your quality manual, but here, you should provide the process for ensuring these characteristics are also adequately addressed and maintained in vivo.

The requirements of human resources management are principally in Clause 6.2, which requires you to ensure appropriate staff competence for any work affecting product quality based on staff education, training, skills, and experience. Your process here must address establishing that competence, providing needed training, and ensuring personnel awareness of the relevance and importance of their work and how it contributes to the achievement of quality objectives. You must, of course, run that process to ensure you determine that competence and provide the training or take some other actions to achieve and maintain the competence.

The requirement here is limited to work affecting product quality, and although it may at first seem that this means everything that gets done within or for your organization, it probably does not equate to that after you give it serious thought. For example, it would be a stretch to think that a food truck parked outside would endanger product quality, unless it also happened to block your loading bay. On the other hand, a nighttime cleaning crew that walks through your production floor could affect product quality by contaminating the environment or accidentally bumping on machinery and changing some setting. The key here is to use a risk-based approach, assess your resource needs, and assign appropriate measures.

A further item to consider here may be how the frequency of the work affects the monitoring and maintenance of staff qualifications related to the work. It may, for example, be simple to monitor some frequently performed routine operation and measure its success rate over time, but for some other tasks conducted only rarely, this may be much more difficult to achieve. Simulations, periodic test runs, and refresher training events may be a part of your solution to monitoring such qualifications, but much will depend on the risks associated with such tasks.

Keeping records demonstrating the determined, established, and maintained competence is required. In practice, you will want to write job descriptions, archive CVs, set up personal development plans, enable participation at external training events, and organize critical training in-house. You should make sure the requirements for performing any job stay in line with the competence of the personnel and vice versa. Clause 7, product realization, is naturally a high-priority domain for ensuring sustained personnel competence (Clauses 7.3.2 and 7.5.6b).

10.2 Training

You must ensure that people performing work affecting product quality are competent to perform their jobs (Clause 6.2). If you have interns or other employees who do not yet meet competency requirements, you would do well to arrange competent supervision for them. Until they are adequately trained, they are to only work under supervision—especially if they work under special environmental conditions (Clause 6.4.1b). The requirement for supervision is under Clause 6.4.1 for work environments, but it is a good measure to consider everywhere.

In terms of internal training, remember that you will probably have at least two types of training you will want to arrange: training on the QMS and its processes (e.g., following some updated SOPs from document review), and training on task-specific skills (e.g., some new skill or a paradigm that may be beneficial in some aspect of work). Also think about the different types of training events you may want to conduct; for example, simple verbal or written briefing versus a full instructor-led course with written exams. I have, for example, reached good results with briefing staff via an internal bulletin on planned and implemented QMS changes.

In practice, you will want to provide resources for implementing personal development plans, archive course certificates, maintain a registry of QMS-related training (qualifications for personnel on your SOPs), provide briefing frequently, assess needs for training periodically, organize training, and assess the success and shortcomings of it all.

Legislation, such as the General Data Protection Regulation (GDPR) in the EU, may have some effect on how you set all this up, but in general, you must be able to prove your staff members are qualified, willing, and able to do their work as instructed by your QMS. Regulations should not stop you from doing so as long as you are mindful of them.

10.3 Evaluation of the Effectiveness of Training Actions

This may be an easy thing to overlook or forget once some internal training ends and you are both happy and tired after it, but it is essential that you take the time to assess the training. The most important thing here is that you assess how your goals for the training were met and conclude that you are either happy to pass the participants or that you need to take further actions somehow.

Clause 6.2c requires you to assess the effectiveness of any training actions taken. According to a clarifying note to the clause, the methodology used should also be in line with the risk associated with the work being addressed. The common interpretation of the clause is that this evaluation is done for each individual training event you organize yourself but not necessarily for the external training events you might participate in and not for your training program as a whole (which may be a topic for the management review). The clause could, however, also be interpreted to cover the entirety of your actions taken to achieve and maintain staff competence. This could then include internal and external training, and any other actions taken.

What matters here is not that training courses are taking place but that the training is achieving the results you expect. If you achieve these results and the necessary competence through internal training, assessing that should be enough, but if you need to in addition, or instead, rely on external training to achieve the competencies required then you should absolutely address the effectiveness of those actions. In practice, and not to create artificial barriers to seeking training, I would define critical training (e.g., training on your SOPs) and see to running a tight ship on organizing that training with in-depth records and assessment. In addition, I would make it possible to take part in further external training following a lighter approach (e.g., personal attendance budgets and retained certificates). This way, I would know that the critical skills and processes are covered, but I am not, at the same time, clipping the wings of those who want to learn more on one topic or another. Even then, it would be foolish not to follow and assess external training on at least some informal level.

In its simplest form, the assessment of effectiveness for some training you organize can be based on a written or an oral exam, perhaps just a list of true-or-false statements, a work demonstration by the trainee, or the expert opinion of the instructor responsible for the training. What matters here is that you assess the outcome of the training in light of what the goals were for it and the acceptance criteria you had. You may want to define the broad strokes of the criteria here in this SOP but then leave room to adjust these if the type of training so requires.

Also consider the use of feedback forms with the training you organize, as this will give you a reading on the difficulty and appropriateness of the training. I have a habit of telling the participants at the start of an exam that the ultimate goal is not to give grades to the participants but to assess the training itself. For this reason, I also hand out a feedback form for the participants to assess how easy or difficult they found the training, what they would have done differently, or if there is anything further they would like to learn on any given topic. All this is valuable information I can then use to evaluate the training and plan any next steps.

The final assessment of the training can be recorded in many ways. A simple way to do so is to process the results in the Quality Management Team and make final decisions in the Quality Management Team minutes. In addition to the assessment, I would also retain copies of the training material, all filled-in forms, and the results somewhere in my QMS. A training register will also be a practical tool here to maintain an overview of the organized training and achieved competencies, and link between any records.

10.4 Planning of Personal Development

The standard does not call for personal development plans, but it does expect you to take action in order to both establish and maintain staff competence. You should, therefore, develop personal development plans for your staff, with the staff.

The plan can be revisited at development discussions, where also the body of training actions for any individual staff member can be discussed and adjusted as needed. Aside from any assessment of the effectiveness of the training, which might speak to Clause 6.2c requirements (see Section 10.3), the only QMS-specific topic to pay attention to here may be the QMS-specific training each employee has either had or would like to have in the future. Otherwise, planning and monitoring personal development unfolds the same way it would in other fields of industry.

Personal development meetings are also a good occasion to ensure everyone has handed in any new certificates and degrees they may have obtained recently. You may need to have these available to provide evidence on staff qualifications. The objective here is, quite obviously, to improve yourself as well as your processes.

10.5 Checklist

The following checklist (Table 10.1) is provided for your convenience.

Table 10.1   Checklist for SOP-4

Checklist

☐ **You have defined responsibilities, authorities, and qualification related to jobs**
This may, for example, be done in the appendix to the quality manual.

☐ **You have a process for training staff**
This may include simple briefing but also address both internal and external training.

☐ **You ensure that personnel are qualified and trained to work**
For example, any personnel in training or otherwise unqualified will work under qualified supervision.

☐ **You assess the effectiveness of any training you organize**
This may be based on, for example, exams, interviews, and work demonstrations.

☐ **You monitor training needs**
And act accordingly. This should also address continuing training as needs evolve.

☐ **You have addressed how this SOP is to be applied at your organization**
And the correct versions of documents will be available at the correct places.

☐ **You know what quality indicators match with this SOP**
Record a few measurable indicators for this SOP in the appendix of the quality manual.

Once you feel confident you have ticked every box, it's time to move on.

Chapter 11

Suppliers and Distributors (SOP-5)

The standard is adamant that you can never outsource responsibility. This is reason enough to take supplier management seriously, but also from the point of view of creating a smooth-running business that is resilient to any sudden upsets, it pays to consider who you take on as a supplier and how you monitor them over time.

The need to control suppliers stems from Clause 4.1.5 on outsourcing a process required by the standard and Clause 7.4, purchasing, in product realization. The effect is that you must control suppliers who take over requirements of the standard from you (although you will always retain the ultimate responsibility yourself) or provide something going into the finished product. You do not, however, need to place as much attention on controlling the supplier that washes the car park outside your offices for you or brings in the lunch sandwiches for your employees. The focus is on maintaining conformity despite any notion of outsourced responsibility and deviation in received deliverables going into the product that you ship.

Note also that according to EU guidance, distributors may be considered as suppliers. Clause 7.5.9.2 of the standard hints at this by demanding that the manufacturers of implantable medical devices require their "suppliers of distribution services and distributors" to maintain distribution records for traceability. This is no doubt a sound approach and one which also manufacturers of non-implantable devices should consider when drafting their supplier contracts and quality agreements. In principle, though, I see

DOI: 10.4324/9781003202868-11

suppliers and distributors as frequenting opposite doors of the factory, but if this is not your situation, this may be something you want to address here.

Topics to cover here are as follows:

- Outsourcing a process
- Supplier selection and evaluation
- Supplier personnel competence
- Purchasing
- Verification of purchased product

11.1 Outsourcing a Process

Clause 1 of the standard is very clear on the fact that you are responsible for any process required by the standard regardless of whether you perform it yourself or not. Note that the responsibility of such processes also extends to monitoring, maintaining, and controlling these processes. The exceptions to this are those processes that you exclude as not applicable to you under Clauses 6, 7, or 8.

Having someone else perform the processes or outsourcing the processes is discussed in Clause 4.1.5. Here, your responsibility to monitor and ensure control over the processes is reiterated, and your responsibility over conformity with the standard and regulatory requirements is firmly stated. The controls you impose are required to be proportionate to the risk involved and the ability of the outsourcing provider to meet requirements. When outsourcing a required process, you must have a written quality agreement with the supplier.

11.2 Supplier Selection and Evaluation

Clause 7.4 addresses supplier selection and evaluation as part of its discussion on the purchasing process. The context here is firmly in product realization (Clause 7), but remember that even earlier in Clause 1, the standard drove home the fact that you can never outsource the responsibility for some process that is required or has an impact on the conformity of your product. You must, therefore, show judgment in the selection and continued use of a third party, and while this is important everywhere in your QMS, it is vital in product realization activities. You would be hard-pressed to demonstrate a process of taking responsibility over any outsourced activity if you just chose the first company from the yellow pages or Google result list, and then trusted them to provide what you wanted without oversight or control.

Clause 7.4.1 of the standard requires you to have established criteria for evaluating and selecting suppliers. These must consider any effects on your product and the supplier's ability to meet your requirements (including the supplier's performance in the long run). As always, the criteria must be proportionate to risks imposed to your product and its use. The same clause also points out that you must monitor and reevaluate the suppliers. How and when you do this is up to you, but you must monitor the supplier's performance and capability, and act on any nonfulfillment proportionately to the risk involved. As always, records must be kept of evaluation and selection, as well as monitoring, reevaluation, and any actions deemed necessary. I would be wary of continually assessing suppliers who are no longer used or were used on a project basis and appropriately assessed at that time. This is particularly the case for consultants you bring in to help you carry out some project. Whether this project is developing your QMS from the start, preparing for some future regulatory need, or tweaking the settings of your active production line may have different implications for the assessment. Think about what kinds of suppliers, subcontractors, and consultants you will have and how you want to address their selection, evaluation, and later control.

In practice, for selecting and evaluating your prospective supplier, you will want to address the following:

■ What is the deliverable you need to outsource?
■ How critical is the deliverable to your operations?
■ Does the deliverable affect your current or future product somehow?
■ What credentials do you require from the supplier?
■ How will you choose which supplier to award the contract to?
■ How will you maintain a registry of suppliers?

For monitoring and reevaluating, you may want to address the following:

■ How will you monitor and review the supplier's performance?
■ How will you act on any perceived nonfulfillment of the supplier?
■ When or in which circumstances will you update the assessment?
■ When or in which circumstances will you perform a supplier audit?

All these are questions you can answer freely, and shape your process in this SOP as best meets your own operations and goals. You may want to set up some form of supplier classification; for example, simple A/B/C classification based on how critical the supplier is to your operation. This way, you can define a few different mechanisms for handling critical and less-critical suppliers more conveniently in your SOP. In addition to product safety and strategic importance, also consider relative purchase volumes as a way to identify critical suppliers, but maybe avoid writing purchase volumes into the classification itself as these may change as a result of your business growing or contracting even temporarily.

Many of the issues involved in supplier management regard business risks and, as such, are squarely out of the scope of the standard. When instructing your process here, concentrate on the safety and conformity of your QMS and product. I would still consider some aspects from the domain of business risks here for the sake of reducing sudden interruptions or changes further along the line when they might unnecessarily burden your organization at a time when you are busy concentrating on something else. Don't go overboard here, but aim for a predictable, safe, and secure process going forward. It is also good practice to maintain a registry of suppliers and periodically review any active or recently ended supplier contracts. If possible, you should also consider identifying alternate suppliers.

In general, I would argue that consultants you hire to assist you provide you opinions and suggestions; the adoption of which is then up to you. You should make every effort to ascertain competency during purchasing, but even bad advice won't compromise the product until your product realization process has run its course and you have failed to detect any shortcomings.

The situation is somewhat different when you consider a supplier who provides some component or compound for your finished product and this feeds into your assembly line. Sudden silent changes in the supplied material may be harder to detect than continuously dubious advice during a consulting project. Using a risk-based approach, the deviation in any supplied material should be seen as much more critical to your operations than bad advice during development, even though bad advice may leave your budding startup dead in its tracks.

In writing your supplier assessment process here or in creating any assessment pathways based on supplier types, I would take advantage of the previous differentiation to direct my resources where it counts.

11.3 Supplier Personnel Competence

Technically, this is a topic to be covered along with the previous subject of supplier selection and evaluation, but here, I include it as a topic of its own for shock value.

Yes, you are also responsible for making sure that your supplier uses qualified personnel even after they have contractually agreed to do so. Occasionally, it will be impossible for you to make sure of this in any fool-proof way even if you require documentation and perform audits on the supplier, but to the extent that you can take measures to verify competence, you should do so. A good example of this is hiring a group of consultants to assist you in an internal audit, agreeing on auditor competency, and then still asking for documentation to corroborate the competency of the auditors that ultimately show up. Often, the quotes you get from suppliers will already contain the documentation necessary to assess these qualifications.

In practice, you will want to define expected supplier personnel competencies (or state that none are required, if that truly is the case), gather offers, and assess them for demonstrated competencies. The tendering and purchasing documents should help you answer questions on these topics, as should CVs or bios.

11.4 Purchasing

The standard requires supplier evaluation beforehand, and it also makes it very clear that you need to stay on top of managing your suppliers once you are using them. Clause 7.4.1 requires you to have procedures for ensuring your purchased deliverables (i.e., purchased product) conform to your specified purchasing requirements, while Clause 7.3.4b insists that your product realization activities provide appropriate information for purchasing. Note that here, too, the context of the discussion has a clear product realization slant to it.

Clause 7.4.2 on purchasing information requires that you adequately define the product you are purchasing. You may do this by writing a description or referring to appropriate information. The information you should consider capturing here includes the following:

■ Product specifications
■ Requirements for product acceptance

- Requirements for QMS, procedures, processes, and equipment
- Requirements for supplier personnel qualifications
- The possibility of verification activities at the supplier's premises, including intended activities and method of product release (see next section)

The key factor in the previous items is that you are satisfied the purchasing information contains everything that is necessary for the supplier to meet your requirements for the deliverable. You must make sure this is the case prior to communicating the information to the supplier. You must also consider whether a written agreement is needed whereby the supplier commits to notifying you of any changes in the purchased product, with respect to requirements, prior to implementing the changes. This is worded as "must include as applicable", so give this requirement careful consideration when designing your process and what impact unannounced or unnoticed changes could have on your operations with a given class of supplier.

A particularly poignant requirement in Clause 7.4.2 is that traceability must be retained. What this means in your circumstances and what information must be retained by you will vary, but retaining at least the relevant set of purchasing information from the total set you defined earlier is a good start. In the electronic world, it will be easy enough to retain it all, but do think about what information is needed and why.

11.5 Verification of Purchased Product

The standard stops short of requiring a documented process for verification of purchased product, but it does require that this activity is both established and implemented (remember that Clause 0.2 defines "documented" as meaning "established, implemented, and maintained", but it does not equate "documented" and "established", per se). The difference may be academic, as you are, in any case, required to run activities, such as inspection, to ensure the purchased product meets the specified requirements. The extent of the verification activities must be proportionate to the risks involved and must also consider past supplier evaluation results. As always, you will also want to record such verification activities.

When you become aware of any changes in the purchased product, you must determine whether the changes may affect your product realization process (see SOP-10) or product. The standard also gives you and your customer the opportunity to perform verification activities at the supplier's premises; in which case, the purchasing information must describe the intended activities and method of product release. In other words, if you plan on performing supplier audits yourself, you should say so in advance.

11.6 Checklist

The following checklist (Table 11.1) is provided for your convenience.

Table 11.1 Checklist for SOP-5

Checklist
☐ **You haven't tried to outsource responsibility** You are responsible for any outsourced processes and the competency of personnel in these.
☐ **You know how you want to handle supplier selection and evaluation** You assess suppliers before use, you monitor them, and you have quality agreements as needed.
☐ **You know how you want to handle purchasing** This includes how you specify the relevant purchasing information (including possibility of audit).
☐ **You verify purchased product** You check received deliverables against the requirements in the purchasing information.
☐ **You know when supplier audits are appropriate** You know in which circumstances such audits should be performed and to what effect.
☐ **You have addressed how this SOP is to be applied at your organization** And the correct versions of documents will be available at the correct places.
☐ **You know what quality indicators match with this SOP** Record a few measurable indicators for this SOP in the appendix of the quality manual.
Once you feel confident you have ticked every box, it's time to move on.

Chapter 12

Auditing (SOP-6)

This is where you knock on the doors of your fancy new QMS or kick the tires of the spaceship you have built (if it has tires) and try to find any cracks to fix. Audits are almost never just a walk in the park, but you should orient yourself to approaching audits as opportunities for continuous improvement. You will have one or more audits per year from here on out.

The standard is adamant in Clause 5 that your management is both committed to and provides evidence of ensuring that your organization maintains an effective QMS. The management must show this commitment via setting up and maintaining a quality policy (as we did in the quality manual) and by conducting management reviews, which are your top-level in-house audit to perform at documented intervals (essentially, every year). In addition, you will also have both internal and various types of external audits to assess your operations and maintain any certificates. These may take place in person or remotely, as has increasingly been the case since the onset of the COVID-19 pandemic. The purpose of SOP-6 is to lay out your processes for planning and executing these various audits and reviews.

Topics to cover here are as follows:

■ Internal audits
■ External audits
■ Supplier audits
■ Management reviews

Each type of audit will be briefly discussed from the point of view of the standard. Before you write this SOP, be sure to also read Section 26 on practical advice for audits and Section 27 on the management review.

12.1 Internal Audits

Clause 8.2.4 of the standard holds the meat on internal audits. The gist of this clause is that you must conduct internal audits at planned intervals to determine whether your QMS is effectively maintained and whether it continues to conform to both your own arrangements and requirements, and the requirements imposed on it by the standard and regulations. You must have a documented procedure for carrying out audits, and this process must also ensure responsibilities, as well as the planning, conducting, and reporting of the audits.

In planning the program for your internal audits, you should consider the status and importance of your relative processes and the areas to be audited, as well as the results of any previous audits. It is important to record the criteria, scope, interval, and methods for any audit before the audit takes place. These can be addressed here in the SOP on a top level, as practical, and then refined within the framework set here when planning the individual audits. Note that although the standard does not require you to have internal audits every year, this is, in fact, expected. You may, however, wish to split the auditing of your full QMS over several internal audits run in subsequent years. This way, you can better prioritize and focus on select aspects every year and cover your full QMS in, for example, two to three years. Note that you should still include some critical common elements each year (e.g., document and record control, and QMS planning).

In your process description here, when defining audit responsibilities, ensure that objectivity and impartiality are always preserved when selecting auditors and conducting the audits. The first rule here is that auditors must not audit their own work. I would also be careful not to require that an internal audit is in fact conducted fully in-house. Instead, I would acknowledge the need to utilize outside help in the form of consultants or peer companies that can provide impartial expert advice. In accepting any outside help, it is still important to retain overall responsibility for the activity, including ensuring the competence of any outside personnel used (see SOP-5). Your process description here should ensure all this.

In writing your process concerning the final reporting of the audit, make sure you retain all the particulars of what was audited, when, and by whom. This includes identification of the audited processes and areas. Once the report has been issued, the management of the relevant areas must then be notified, and they must ensure the corrections and corrective actions are performed without undue delay. Finally, you must ensure that follow-up actions include verification of actions and reporting.

Section 26.3.1 discusses internal audits in detail, and you should refer to it when finalizing your process description here. The standard also points to ISO 19011 as a further optional source to study on guidelines for auditing management systems.

12.2 External Audits

External audits are, in fact, not mentioned by the standard, but these, too, will form an integral part of the reality of your QMS. External audits are, as the name suggests, audits performed on your organization by external parties, such as the certification body, notified body, or competent authority. The audits are something that are extracurricular, not covered by the standard, but that can themselves address the entire standard, your use of the standard, and how your processes and products conform to the standard. The objective here is the same as with an internal audit: to make sure your reality matches the theory and that this also matches with any outside expectations.

Most external audits are preannounced. Your auditor will contact you and say that they want to come to inspect you on a given date. You may get weeks of advance warning or only five days (stated as a common time frame at a recent FDA event), and there may or may not be room to adjust the time. The amount of leeway may depend on how good your reason is and how big a shift you are requesting. Depending on where along your certification cycle you are, these audits may be called initial certification audits (covering your full QMS), later surveillance audits (covering some subset of your QMS), or recertification audits.

Occasionally, at least once per certification cycle, an extra external audit takes place unannounced. The standard does not give you requirements for unannounced audits but your certification body might. In practice, you will want to develop your process description here to address how auditors are appropriately identified when they show up at your door, how their authority to perform the audit is verified, and how your staff then reacts to provide access and notify the appropriate staff members who should be present. Remember that the staff member who greets the auditors at the door may also be a summer intern or a janitor. The process description here does not have to be too involved; the main points are that lawful auditors are not turned away and that they are provided access to the right materials and personnel without unnecessary delay.

In practice, you must acknowledge the possibility of external audits in your QMS, and you may attempt to sketch them into your QMS planning calendar. You may also want to address the use of remote methods for external audits here or at the least ensure that your discussion of audits is not unnecessarily incompatible with the use of remote methods (see Section 26.3.4). See Section 26.3.2 for more.

12.3 Supplier Audits

The last type of audit to cover in the SOP is the supplier audit. Clause 7.4.3 of the standard gives both you and your customer the opportunity to perform verification activities at a supplier's premises. Also note that a distributor you use may, in some cases, be considered a supplier for your organization even if this sounds fairly backward in logic. Here in SOP-6, I would be content in acknowledging this type of an audit and referring to its use as part of activities arising from, for example, verification of purchased product (SOP-5). I would also mention that any auditing activities you intend to perform are to be described in the corresponding purchasing information for the supplier in question (see SOP-5).

12.4 Management Reviews

The management reviews (see also Section 27) are your highest-level in-house audit where your top management reviews the status of your entire QMS, usually once a year. Clause 5.1d of the standard requires that you conduct management reviews, and Clause 5.6.1, that you document a process for them. In essence, the standard requires that you define a procedure for the management review. The review is to be done by your top management at planned intervals to review your QMS for continued suitability, adequacy, and effectiveness. They must review improvement opportunities, any need for changes, the quality policy, and the quality objectives. As always, records must be kept thereof.

The standard goes into an exceptional level of detail on the inputs (Clause 5.6.2) and outputs (Clause 5.6.3) of the review. The level of detail here is considerable in breadth if not depth: very few other items in the standard get as many lines for the itemization of their contents. The input for the management review must include at least the following:

- Feedback (note that this is not limited to just customer feedback)
- Complaint handling
- Reporting to regulatory authorities
- Audits
- Monitoring and measurement of both processes and product
- CAPA activities (including effectiveness of corrective actions)
- Follow-up actions from previous review
- Changes that could affect the QMS (including new or revised regulation)
- Recommendations for improvement

Similarly, the outputs of the review must be recorded, and they must identify the inputs reviewed as well as any decision or actions regarding the following:

- Improvement needed to maintain the QMS and its processes
- Improvement of product related to customer requirements
- Changes needed to respond to new or revised regulation
- Resource needs

Having an agenda and a report is a good set of documentation to have here, but you may choose to also keep minutes separately. Note that the standard does not require that your entire top management must be present at the review, but plan for having at least the management representative present along with enough other key people to cover the required areas (see also Section 27 for discussion of FDA expectations). It is a good idea to prepare for the review in advance and ensure you have collected all the necessary input material for conducting a successful review.

12.5 Checklist

The following checklist (Table 12.1) is provided for your convenience.

Table 12.1 Checklist for SOP-6

Checklist
☐ **You know how you approach internal audits** You have defined the interval and process for these.
☐ **You know how you approach management reviews** You have defined the interval and process for these (including the agenda).

(Continued)

Table 12.1   *(Continued)*

Checklist
☐ **You know how you address external audits** You have defined who can perform these, when, and how you will react.
☐ **You know how you want to approach unannounced audits** You have defined the basic response your staff should take in the event of such an audit.
☐ **You know how you want to approach supplier audits** You know in which circumstances such audits may be performed on you or by you.
☐ **You have addressed how this SOP is to be applied at your organization** And the correct versions of documents will be available at the correct places.
☐ **You know what quality indicators match with this SOP** Record a few measurable indicators for this SOP in the appendix of the quality manual.
Once you feel confident you have ticked every box, it's time to move on.

Chapter 13

Communication, Marketing, and Sales (SOP-7)

Will Smith's The Pursuit of Happyness *(the spelling is intentional) has a great series of scenes where Smith, a traveling salesman for a medical device, has a unit stolen from him, keeps seeing it around San Francisco, and ultimately ends up stealing the unit back along with some choice words, fixing it himself, and selling it as new. That is probably not how you should approach your business, but writing this SOP will have you thinking about how you approach marketing, sales, and the customer-related activities that extend beyond the sale.*

You would be mistaken to think that it is enough to make a great product and ship it to customers without also keeping an ear to the ground thereafter. Similarly, it would be a mistake to think that your whole organization is on the same page and that everyone naturally talks to one another, informing them of everything they need to know. The need to communicate and set up the appropriate active and passive channels for communication is a profound feature of your QMS.

SOP-7 is your comprehensive SOP for communications, the place where you instruct both your internal and external information exchange. I have chosen to address both internal and external communication in this one SOP to improve consistency and to ensure that information flows from end to end without any unnecessary friction or need to translate information from channel to channel.

For the same reason, I have also chosen to consolidate customer-facing activities here. This includes moving in some activities from Clause 7 to

DOI: 10.4324/9781003202868-13

ensure these live on even in the case the original product development project might end. I find this is particularly important for ensuring that sifting through any generated maintenance information as a source of complaints still takes place and having the link from this to complaint handling is maintained. Product realization work according to SOP-10 naturally affects the requirements for defining how you set up and conduct production and service provision, but for the reason stated earlier, I would be happiest placing the running of my customer-facing front desk activities here.

The topics I would cover here are as follows:

◼ Internal communication
◼ Customer communication (including feedback handling)
◼ Communication with certification bodies (including notified body)
◼ Communication with regulatory authorities

In terms of the standard itself, Clause 5.2 requires that your top management ensures customer requirements, as well as any applicable regulatory requirements, are determined and met. The responsibility to extrapolate on the needs stated by your customer to also identify silent requirements, ones that your customer might not be able to verbalize, is on you. To hear any requirements at all, you need to communicate with your customer and ensure that the necessary departments within your organization talk to one another. During early product development work, this communication may be handled via the project activities instructed in SOP-10 but especially after your product ships and leaves your premises; most, if not all, of this communication shifts over to the domain of SOP-7.

13.1 Internal Communication

Internal communication within your own organization is entirely in your own hands, so there is little excuse here for not designing it to fit your setup and later maintaining it as appropriate. The first task to accomplish in this SOP is to set out your organization structure so that you are clear on who needs to talk to whom. Conveniently, we already set up your organization structure in the quality manual so a simple reference to that is sufficient here to set up the actors.

The top-level responsibility within your organization for setting up appropriate communication channels naturally rests with your top management.

You will want to set up a periodic schedule for Management Team meetings (e.g., monthly) and define a loose standing agenda for the meetings, perhaps as a template based on the agenda for the management review (so that all the key items are continuously discussed and it also becomes easier to later cross reference or check on items when, for example, conducting the management review). See Section 21 for more discussion of agendas and minutes.

To discharge their duties, the top management will need all the appropriate information, per the agenda and as needs arise, in a timely fashion. Much of this information is sourced by the management representative, who is both the liaison between the management and any lower-level quality function at your organization (e.g., the Quality Management Team), as well as the top ambassador of quality within your organization. Clause 5.5.2b charges the management representative with the task of reporting to top management on QMS effectiveness and improvement needs, and Clause 5.5.2c adds the task of promoting awareness of regulatory and QMS requirements throughout your organization. Both tasks were already addressed when setting up the role of the management representative in the quality manual, so again, a simple acknowledgment of the role of the management representative as a liaison, and a reference to the quality manual, is enough here. Sourcing information for the management should not be a full-time job for the management representative, though, so make sure your overall architecture for internal communication readily bubbles up the necessary information from other teams and departments of your organization.

On that note, and on the next level down, you will probably have the Quality Management Team who you charge with running your QMS and keeping it all well-oiled. This, too, was discussed in the quality manual. Similar to the top management, you should consider instructing a regular periodic framework of meetings, the responsible person for organizing the meetings (e.g., the quality manager), the standing agenda, and any other important aspects you deem beneficial for the Quality Management Team to address on a regular basis.

Below the Quality Management Team, you will have several other high-level teams, such as Research and Development, and Sales and Marketing. You may want to style the communication activities of these functions in a way that is compatible with the functions described earlier, but exactly which teams you have and how you want them to interact is up to you and not defined by the standard. All the teams should communicate regarding the effectiveness of the QMS (Clause 5.5.3) as they see it.

Finally, you will have individual staff members that need to work with your QMS. Unless you have specific reasons for deciding otherwise, I would not go too deep into addressing this group in much detail here. I would, however, discuss any essential intranet forums and discussion channels, such as instant messaging, wikis, and other forums or repositories of important information. If you have discussed such channels in detail in SOP-3, it will be enough to refer to that discussion here. Also remember to control and validate these systems as instructed in SOP-3.

13.2 Customer Communication

The basic requirements for customer communication are set out by Clause 7.2.3. You must have documented arrangements for communicating with your customers regarding product information, enquiries, sales (including contracts, order handling, and any amendments to these), feedback (including complaints), and any advisory notices. The standard calls for arrangements here but not necessarily actual processes. Clause 8.3.3 does, however, go a bit further and require you to have a process for issuing advisory notices in compliance with regulations. Define this process here and link to SOP-11 for any regulatory requirements on time frames and so forth.

13.2.1 Marketing

The standard mostly appears concerned with sales and post-sales communication, but if you read between the lines—or if you talk with your certification provider and regulatory authorities—your marketing communication is very much a part of the full dialogue. These bodies are interested in making sure your marketing message is in line with the intended use of your product.

It is important to consider the regulatory approvals you have, what your approved intended purpose (intended use) and indications are, and how these all should apply to your activities here. In this SOP, you do not have to solve in advance all the possible circumstances that might come up. Instead, you should decide on the basic framework: who makes sure the marketing message aligns with the product approval, what mechanisms you want to use for making that assessment, and how you ensure your entire sales and marketing staff know to abide by these constraints. Here, I would require adherence to the limits defined by your regulatory approvals and internally approved marketing material. For more information, you may refer to SOP-9 on clinical evidence and SOP-11 on regulatory affairs.

You should also address the role of non-approved products (e.g., products that have not yet been CE marked in the EU or cleared via the FDA 510(k) process in the US). I would set up clear rules for demonstrating devices that are not yet available in some new market, perhaps allowing that to take place only after some specific internal assessment and provided that the appropriate disclaimers (e.g., "Not available in the US" and "Only available for research use") are used and sales are not attempted. You may even want to consider the use of your regional trademarks as part of this instruction, but doing so is definitely not required by the standard. The reason I might address the use of registered (®) and claimed (™) trademarks here is that they are always granted in some jurisdiction and, thus, are regional in nature, whereas your communication needs may be global.

13.2.2 Readiness to Sell and Sales

Determining the requirements for a product (Clause 7.2.1) is intuitively a part of product development, but reviewing those requirements, and any requirements or later amendments to requirements made by the customer, on at least some level could be construed as a part of a safe sales process (Clause 7.2.2)—unless you have excluded the specific requirement with a good reason (see Section 4.3.7).

I would link to SOP-10 here, but instead of requiring a repeat of the whole process of determining and reviewing requirements, I would ensure that any special requirements are observed and any now apparent disconnects between what you expect and what the customer expects are resolved. Overall, you should ensure that you have documented the requirements, that any conflicts between them and the contract or order are resolved, that all regulatory requirements are met, that any necessary user training will be available, and that your organization can actually meet the requirements. All this should have been done in SOP-10, but having some simple check here could be a smart safety check if the risk profile of your product calls for it. In terms of the determination of requirements related to product (including product delivery and postdelivery activities) and the identification of any user training needed, I would thus refer to SOP-10.

In addition, Clause 8.2.6 requires you to ensure that product delivery can't take place until your monitoring and measurement process, as it has been instructed, has been satisfactorily completed (see Section 16.4.5).

13.2.3 Installation Activities

Installation may be relevant or it may seem like a stretch to consider for the type of products you work with. Nonetheless, spend a little time considering how the user takes your products into use and how you make your product available to them. This may be a clause you can exclude, but you may also learn something surprising about your product.

Clause 7.5.3 is where the standard goes into some detail on installation activities. Instead of a process, the standard requires you to document requirements for the installation of your product and the acceptance criteria for the verification of the installation. Records of the installation and its verification must be kept. The previous requirements must also be provided to any external installer (i.e., installer other than your organization or your supplier) if the use of such an installer is allowed by the agreed customer requirements.

13.2.4 Servicing Activities

Servicing of the product in use is a topic you may be able to exclude as a clause, but you should nonetheless consider what the lifetime of your product is and what its life cycle looks like from initial use all the way to disposal. Remember that you defined the basic mechanisms for lifetimes in the quality manual.

Clause 7.5.4 instructs that if servicing is a specified requirement for your product, you must have processes for this, complete with reference materials (including reference measurements) as necessary to perform the servicing and verify its result. You must also analyze the records of this activity as a potential source of both a complaint (see next section) and an input for your improvement process (see SOP-2). Records, as always, are needed.

13.2.5 Feedback and Complaint Handling

Soliciting and handling feedback from your users, and handling any complaints implicitly or explicitly stated in the feedback, is a critical process in your QMS. Think of this process as a major part of your post-market activities and one that slices through potentially the whole of your QMS. An issue gleaned from user feedback may point to a problem in your product or processes and may bubble up all the way to the top in your organization even if it is not made as a complaint by the customer in the first place. Like a nonconformity given in an audit, feedback and complaints are a real-world test on your QMS. Also remember that you should look at your own product maintenance information as a source of possible complaints or feedback on your product and activities.

The sad consensus out there in the field seems to be that many, even a majority of, feedback received does not contain adequate information to take action. This is especially problematic if the feedback was sent to you by someone who does not provide any contact details so that you could ask clarifying questions. Not all feedback is appropriate, not all of it is even sent to the right organization, but you must have a process for receiving feedback, identifying complaints, and taking appropriate action.

Today, you are also expected to take an active role in soliciting feedback and not just wait around in your ivory tower for someone to climb to your window. The same foolhardy tricks used by other businesses (e.g., hiding their contact details on a web page or burying the contact form under several levels of drop-down menus or behind an annoying robot meant to drive away complainers) have no place in medical devices. You need solutions for sifting out spam and disregarding it, of course, otherwise your operation will be distracted from paying appropriate attention to the feedback that matters. Your aim in developing feedback channels should, however, be to help your users give feedback.

In the standard, Clauses 8.2.1 and 8.2.2 address feedback and complaint handling. Both clauses are located under the heading of Clause 8.2 for monitoring and measurement, which gives the two a distinct after-the-fact tint. The gist here is that you must gather and monitor information regarding how successfully you have met the customers' requirements.

You should consider your stakeholders carefully here (see Section 4.4.4) and ensure that you fully appreciate who your customers are, whether that is the same thing or different from your users, and that you address all such stakeholders appropriately. You must document the methods for obtaining and using this information, and you must have a process for processing the feedback. What exactly that process is, is again up to you, but you must gather data from both production and postproduction, and that information must serve the needs of risk management, product realization, and improvement. Note that additional requirements on what you should learn from these activities may be imposed on you by the regulatory requirements applicable to your organization.

As for complaints, the requirements are that you receive feedback, identify complaints in it, investigate complaints, handle any related product, and determine the need to initiate corrections, corrective actions, and any reporting to regulatory authorities as appropriate. Your process must cover all these actions and ensure that records are kept thereof. Furthermore, your handling of complaints must be timely and in accordance with regulations. If you determine that outside activities contributed to the issue, you must exchange information with the parties in question.

In the interest of later recall during the investigation of some non-conformity, I would write in my SOP that it is recommended to record a justification for all classification of feedback be it an opinion, an idea for improvement, a complaint, a report of an adverse event or an incident, or something else. If you are making the assessment now anyway, why not also record it? I would then write a sentence or two to record my assessment using my feedback handling software, and that way, have it available later for jogging my memory if needed. Also note that in the case you do not investigate some complaint, you must record the justification for this.

Finally, remember to analyze the body of feedback you get (Clause 8.4) or any trends in it over time. This means analysis in the management review but, ideally, also in some appropriate meetings before then in the Management Team, Quality Management Team, Sales and Marketing Team, and R&D Team. Remember that much of the feedback that is not classified as complaints may still be relevant to product improvement. You should, therefore, polish the interface between feedback handling and product development, both in terms of process and software.

13.2.6 Identification of Products Returned to the Organization

Clause 7.5.8 requires you to identify and distinguish product returned to you by, for example, your customers from outgoing conforming product. Here, the fundamental requirement comes from the point of view of preventing a mix-up between product nearing shipment to customers and product returned by the customers. Think about how you can prevent or reduce the risk of a mix-up, whether this be through some physical marking, the use of a separate storage space, or some other measure. Also remember to consider the returned products from the point of view of a potential complaint, although I would not require that all returns are treated as complaints.

This process could alternatively be specified in SOP-10 on product realization, and it should be part of the consideration during any product development process, but as this is something that will be a part of work according to SOP-7, for the long run, I would place it here.

The overall identification scheme for product versions was already introduced in the quality manual, and that will play a supporting role here in giving you a coordinate system for investigating any potential issues and seeing what other products could be affected.

13.3 Communication with Certification Bodies (Including Notified Body)

The standard does not specify how, when, or how often you communicate with your certification body or notified body, but expect each to have their own requirements on the matter. In principle, you should always consider whether your certification body (or the notified body) would want to be informed when you communicate with regulatory authorities—the answer here is probably always yes. Certainly, if the subject is anything serious, you can expect your certification body (notified body) to want to hear about it and preferably hear about it from you instead of the regulatory authority, such as the competent authority in the EU.

Here, I would acknowledge the need to communicate with the certification provider on serious matters (e.g., serious adverse events and major nonconformities) and respect any instructions they have given on communication (e.g., notifications on changes in personnel and premises). I would not write specific provider requirements into the SOP, unless this was requested by the provider, for the reason of keeping my SOPs tidy and up-to-date.

13.4 Communication with Regulatory Authorities

The standard mentions regulatory requirements as a source of identifying required notifications to regulatory authorities. For example, Clause 8.2.3 mentions this type of communication as part of monitoring and measurement, and Clause 7.2.3 in the context of customer-related processes. Neither of these examples is too concrete on saying when, under which circumstances, or how exactly you should initiate such communication.

However, Clause 8.2.3 does require you to set up reporting criteria—for example, classes of complaints or certain types of events (e.g., issuance of advisory notices)—that trigger notification to authorities. The intention here is that you know yourself in which cases to initiate such communication, with what authorities, and how to reach the authorities. Here, I would acknowledge such criteria and refer to SOP-11 on defining the criteria in a way that is compatible with multiple jurisdictions. In the EU, you will also want to find out about the EUDAMED database set up by the regulations, and how and when that affects your communication with the regulatory authorities and the notified body.

13.5 Checklist

The following checklist (Table 13.1) is provided for your convenience.

Table 13.1   Checklist for SOP-7

Checklist

☐ **You know the communication needs for your key internal teams**
This includes communication inside and between the teams, and up to your management.

☐ **You know the communication needs between you and your customer**
This includes, for example, marketing, sales, feedback, and product returns.

☐ **You have a process for soliciting, classifying, and handling feedback**
This includes both passive (listen) and active (ask) methods.

☐ **You know when and how to communicate with your certification provider**
This also includes your notified body in the EU, if relevant. Details may be in SOP-11.

☐ **You know when and how to communicate with your regulatory authorities**
This also includes your competent authority in the EU, if relevant. Details may be in SOP-11.

☐ **You have addressed how this SOP is to be applied at your organization**
And the correct versions of documents will be available at the correct places.

☐ **You know what quality indicators match with this SOP**
Record a few measurable indicators for this SOP in the appendix of the quality manual.

Once you feel confident you have ticked every box, it's time to move on.

Chapter 14

Risk Management (SOP-8)

The sheer volume of risk-taking in movies is overwhelming. There is Stallone biding his time taking punches while waiting for the perfect opportunity to strike back in Rocky, *Stallone hanging under a cliff to impress a girl in* Cliffhanger, *Stallone leaping of a cliff to land in the trees in* First Blood, *and Stallone diving into a flooding tunnel in* Daylight *to get to the surface. Actually, we could just call this section the Michael Sylvester Gardenzio Stallone section and be done with it, but risk management is about much more than accepting risks.*

The term "risk" is mentioned by the standard often and without shame. The term is dropped by the standard almost as often as the phrase "we need to do a gap analysis" is dropped by an aspiring quality manager or as often as I referred to Stallone earlier. The term is even baked into the definition of another widely used concept, "as appropriate", in Clause 0.2 by saying that any requirement qualified "as appropriate" will be judged appropriate if it is, among other criteria, necessary for you in managing risks. It is, however, sensible to remember that Clause 0.2 frames the term in the context of the safety and performance requirements of the product and of meeting regulatory requirements for your product and QMS. The requirement to document one or more processes for risk management is itself brought up in a clause for product realization (Clause 7.1). The focus is thus on the well-being of your users and not on the business of your organization.

The management of risks is such a critical part of the development and use of medical devices that this is addressed in a standard of its own, the ISO 14971 standard on the application of risk management to medical devices. ISO 14971 is the source used for the definition of the terms "risk",

DOI: 10.4324/9781003202868-14

"risk management", and even "lifecycle" by ISO 13485; and its use is suggested in a note to Clause 7.1. The use of ISO 14971 is voluntary, but it is the standard you should most likely plan on following in your risk management activities regarding products and processes (Clause 4.1.2b control of processes in general, Clause 4.1.5 for outsourced processes, and Clause 7.1 for the product realization process specifically).

In addition to the ISO 14971 standard itself, a related technical report, ISO/TR 24971, has also been published by ISO as guidance on the application of the ISO 14971 standard to medical devices. Both documents are required reading for delving deep into risk management, but any detailed analysis of either document is necessarily beyond the scope of this book. In the following, I will, however, cover the rough framework you will probably be dealing with here. If you are looking to only understand risk management from the outside in, the discussion here will give you a good level of understanding. If, however, you will be writing your process according to ISO 14971, I strongly recommend you follow reading this section with the previously mentioned standard and technical report.

The topics I would cover are as follows:

- Risk assessment
- Risk control
- Risk communication
- Risk monitoring
- Risk documentation

Earlier, I said that nonconformities and feedback handling are some of the most comprehensive topics in your QMS processes that cut through almost all your other processes. In terms of the most ubiquitous concept, however, that would probably be a tie between "risk" and "requirement". I would argue, and I have successfully done so, that risk means two different things in the standard: firstly, it occurs in the basic risk-based approach that is used for almost any decision in your QMS. This starts with a simple questioning of why something is done and what could happen if something went wrong in it. This is the sense meant in Clause 4.1.6 when discussing the validation of your QMS software, for example. Secondly, risk refers to the in-depth management of risks related to the products you make. This does not have to be governed by ISO 14971, but in practice, it usually is and it definitely has been so in every example I have come across.

The two interpretations stated earlier are the opposite ends of the same swimming pool. In writing your SOP, and in invoking the term "risk" elsewhere, you should be conscious of which end of the pool you mean to dive in. Instructing a heavy-duty ISO 14971 process and then requiring that your organization uses that for everything—also areas that do not affect product quality or safety—is a tough sentence on your organization and not necessarily beneficial to the end result. In the name of full disclosure, I should also remind you that the use of either standard, ISO 13485 for quality management or ISO 14971 for risk management, is optional; but these are not only international standards but also de facto solutions employed by the industry across the globe. You can be an individualist and choose something else if it makes sense for your operations, but be ready to be challenged by your auditors, your customers, and your future employees if you do so.

The concepts you will want to use in your discussion here are as follows:

■ **Hazard**, as a potential source of harm that may or may not be experienced with the use of your product
■ **Harm**, as the potential damage to people, property, or environment
■ **Risk**, as the combination of the severity and probability of the harm
■ **Benefit**, as the intended support gained using your product

The following is a breakdown of the activities you may want to instruct here. You may want to primarily address your product-related risks and make some accommodations for applying the same activities to your processes, especially to processes other than your product realization process (SOP-10). You may also want to say that activities instructed in this SOP may be adapted to the management of business-related risks, but do not require this unless you have a good reason.

14.1 Risk Assessment

Risk assessment starts with the identification of possible hazards and harms using all available information on, for example, the product, any similar products, the context of their use, their intended use, and any reasonably foreseeable misuse.

The identified hazards and harms are analyzed and developed into quantified risks that have both an estimated probability and a classification of the severity of the harm potentially caused. It is typical to use some categorized classification of both the probability and the severity separately, and then specify how an overall combined score for each risk is calculated. You might, for example, have three to five categories in both probability (ranging from rare to common) and severity (ranging from negligible to catastrophic). Representing these as numbers (e.g., 1 to 5) will allow you to define the combined risk in a mathematically straightforward manner.

The final part of risk assessment is the evaluation of the defined risks against your acceptance criteria, which you may define here in this SOP or in a separate risk management plan, but in any case, before you roll up your sleeves to perform the previous risk analysis. The criteria can, for example, address the level of the combined risk and specify that some low-level risks may be accepted as is, some medium-level risks should usually be controlled via some measures, and some high risks must always be reduced to a lower level via risk control measures. If according to your criteria the risks can be accepted as is, no further risk reduction may be necessary, but if this is not the case, you move to risk control activities.

Clauses 5 and 6 of ISO 14971:2019 address risk assessment.

14.2 Risk Control

Risk control picks up where risk analysis ended and defines a way to reduce (mitigate) the risks you have identified. This may mean a change to the way your product is designed, an automatic safety check built into your product, or a warning to the user on the use of your product. As you would expect, designing your product so that it is safe should be your first goal, and relying on a warning-content-may-be-hot type of labels on your product or in its manual should only be a distant last choice. In some cases, you may even want to do all the things stated earlier to reduce a risk.

The outcome of risk control is that by implementing those mitigations, you can reduce risks and, thus, lower the likelihood of the risks occurring and possibly even lower the severity of the risk (although this may be debatable). You must then reevaluate your mitigated risks against acceptance criteria, pay attention to any new risks introduced by the mitigation, and possibly evaluate the benefit/risk of some mitigated risks that still remain unacceptably high. Once you have the residual risk scores, you are then able to look at all your risks together and compare the overall residual risk to the overall benefit you expect for your product. It is this final comparison, and the expert assessment associated with it, that you will need to give yourself the green light to proceed with the product or return to the drawing board somehow. How exactly you want to do the things stated earlier is a matter you address in the SOP.

Clauses 7 and 8 of ISO 14971:2019 address risk control and evaluation.

14.3 Risk Communication

Risk communication is where you consider who needs to know about the outcome of your risk management work. This necessarily includes those working under your QMS on tasks related to the risks or their control. This communication should be two-way so that any potential kinks identified in the day-to-day of your product realization process, or any other process targeted by your risk management activities, also lead to improvements in your risk management.

The need for communicating risks may also refer to your customers and users when it comes to disclosing significant residual risks. The requirement for this is in Clause 8 of the ISO 14971:2019 standard and discussed in the technical report. Disclosing too much—remember that large volumes of data can bury the important information you want to convey—or not enough are continuous points of discussion among professionals in the field.

14.4 Risk Monitoring

Finally, as part of risk monitoring, you will want to develop your approach to how risks are, in fact, monitored and when or how risk management files (see Section 14.5) are revised. You may want to consider how post-market surveillance (also see Clause 10 of ISO 14971:2019) and customer feedback, for example, will feed into this later monitoring and refinement of your risk management files and activities.

14.5 Risk Documentation

The previous activities produce essential records you will use in your ongoing risk management activities and in demonstrating your conformance to the standards and regulations. These records will be contained in, or referenced by, your risk management plans and reports, perhaps maintained separately for your processes and your products. The requirement to maintain such records is in Clause 7.1 of the ISO 13485 standard. Note that the ISO 14971 places further requirements on the review of such documentation, including the competence of the review team and their previous experience with the device or similar devices.

For maintaining developed risk matrices in a more practical and analyzable format, you may consider using special risk management software that does more than a spreadsheet program to help you sort, classify, and manage your risks. If you do go down this route, remember to also validate the software.

In addition to lower-level plans and reports, the Periodic Safety Update Report (PSUR), or similar, will also touch on the topic of risk management and provide a good opportunity to review the status of risks while also considering up-to-date feedback and post-market surveillance. The PSUR, as well as the risk management software discussed earlier, should help you meet the requirements in Clause 10 of ISO 14971:2019 regarding gathering, analyzing, and taking actions based on production and postproduction information. The ISO 13485 standard itself does not mention specific risk management documents you should maintain, but the uses of risk management information it foresees will create some expectations. For example, consider the following:

- QMS process controls follow a risk-based approach (4.1.2b)
- Process controls must be proportionate to the risks involved in outsourcing a process that affects product conformity (Clause 4.1.5)
- Software validation must be proportionate to the risk associated with the use of the software (Clause 4.1.6, Clause 7.5.6, and Clause 7.6)
- Methodology of evaluating training effectiveness should be proportionate to the work discussed (note in Clause 6.2)
- Risk management outputs should be considered as input for design and development (Clause 7.3.3)
- Evaluation of inputs and outputs of risk management must be included in the review of D&D changes (Clause 7.3.9)
- Criteria for suppliers must be proportionate to the risk associated with the device, and any later nonfulfillment of purchasing requirements must be addressed with the supplier proportionate to this risk (Clause 7.4.1); the extent of verification for purchased product is based on the supplier evaluation and must be proportionate to the risk associated with the device (Clause 7.4.3)
- Feedback must be considered as a potential input for risk management activities (Clause 8.2.1)

The previous items may inform your choice of what are the connected processes in your QMS and how risk information should be addressed in each implicated SOP.

14.6 Checklist

The following checklist (Table 14.1) is provided for your convenience.w

Table 14.1 Checklist for SOP-8

Checklist
☐ **You understand the term "risk" in the context of your product and your QMS** This refers to the safety, performance, and compliance of your product and QMS.
☐ **You understand how, if at all, ISO 14971 affects your processes** This refers to the management of both your process-specific and your product-specific risks.
☐ **You understand what assessment, control, communication, and monitoring is needed** Your process defines these activities to the level you feel is sufficient.
☐ **You know where and when you must define risk acceptance criteria** For example, in this SOP or in a risk management plan, but not in the risk management report.
☐ **You know how you want to structure and maintain your risk documentation** You know what types of plans and reports you want to have and how these are to be revised.
☐ **You have addressed how this SOP is to be applied at your organization** And the correct versions of documents will be available at the correct places.
☐ **You know what quality indicators match with this SOP** Record a few measurable indicators for this SOP in the appendix of the quality manual.

Once you feel confident you have ticked every box, it's time to move on.

Chapter 15

Clinical Evidence (SOP-9)

Will Smith's Concussion, *Robert De Niro's* Awakenings, *and Robin Williams'* Patch Adams *are all great films based around storylines rooted in true medicine. All these films have affected me deeply—the first so much so that it has served as a footnote to two startups I helped to usher into life. Don't believe me? You are always free to watch the films and come up with a second opinion.*

The standard is, surprisingly enough, not too talkative on clinical evidence. In fact, it only talks about handling confidential health information as records in some appropriate but unspecified way in Clause 4.2.5. The standard does not require a process for this, but it expects that you employ appropriate methods in accordance with regulations. The ISO 14155 standard on good clinical practice for the clinical investigation of medical devices may, however, give you more of a framework to talk about your approach to building clinical evidence for your device. Exactly how deep into this standard you want dive into, or whether you actually want to include an SOP on clinical evidence in your QMS, will depend on your organization.

If clinical evidence is of relevance to you, and it may be increasingly hard to claim it is not, the regulatory authorities and, if relevant to you, also the notified bodies will be pointing a magnification glass or two on the Clinical Evaluation Report (CER) you give them as part of your medical device file. In the years to come, the EU and the FDA will both be underscoring the importance of your clinical evidence and your processes for building on the evidence over time, so it makes sense to have an SOP for clinical evidence both now and in the future.

For now, you could probably get by without a dedicated SOP on clinical affairs, but as this is a very hot topic currently and as both the regulations and the standards are likely to increasingly place requirements on how you address clinical issues, I would recommend having an SOP in place here. You can start small here, perhaps even think of this SOP as a placeholder, and then expand on it as time goes on. As thinking both within and outside of your organization then matures, you may refine your initial SOP—and since you will already have a placeholder to do so in, you can achieve this conveniently in one predictable place without having to reroute a bunch of other processes within your QMS to point to the right place.

I would wager that ISO 13485 will become an increasingly important gateway solution for regulatory approvals of medical devices in the future. The best advice I can give here is to plan ahead and figure out the likely future linkages to your other QMS processes but not to jump too much ahead and set unnecessary requirements for your organization today. Remember that even the standard itself calls for continuing improvement over time, and consider clinical evidence as a major area where that improvement and new requirements are to be expected.

15.1 CEP, CER, and PMCF

The topics you will most likely want to cover from the start are the Clinical Evaluation Plan (CEP), the Clinical Evaluation Report (CER), the Post-Market Clinical Follow-Up (PMCF) documentation, and possibly also the use of preclinical and clinical data. In this book, I will not attempt to walk through the handling of clinical evidence—that deserves books of its own—but instead, I would suggest you figure out the process you need to obtain what you believe is sufficient evidence on any claims you make or now intend to make on your products.

The intended purpose (intended use) and the indications you arrive at for your product will play a big part in this; after which, it is mostly about figuring out what requirements are imposed by the applicable regulations and the standards you decide to use. ISO 13485 does not directly impose any requirements on you, but you could claim that some requirements flow over from Clause 7 on product realization, particularly in terms of verification and validation.

15.2 Checklist

The following checklist (Table 15.1) is provided for your convenience.

Table 15.1   Checklist for SOP-9

Checklist

☐	**You want to have an SOP for clinical affairs** The topic is either already relevant to you or you expect it to be soon.
☐	**You understand how ISO 14155 applies to you** If you reference the standard here, you do so appropriately.
☐	**You understand the relevant regulations applicable to you in this SOP** You address the requirements stemming from the regulations adequately.
☐	**You understand what is expected of you in terms of the CER** If the CER is relevant, your process here addresses it adequately.
☐	**You understand what is expected of you in terms of the PMCF** If PMCF is relevant, your process here addresses it adequately.
☐	**You have addressed how this SOP is to be applied at your organization** And the correct versions of documents will be available at the correct places.
☐	**You know what quality indicators match with this SOP** Record a few measurable indicators for this SOP in the appendix of the quality manual.

Once you feel confident you have ticked every box, it's time to move on.

Chapter 16

Product Realization (SOP-10)

This is going to a big SOP that is based on the massive Clause 7, making up almost 34% of the entire standard. Think Transformers, Godzilla, Heaven's Gate, *and* Titanic. *This SOP will be the place where you instruct the core development work at the shipyard, factory, or the nuclear laboratory where you create your star attraction, your product. Luckily, though, this SOP will be about 42% lighter than Clause 7, thanks to the work done in the other SOPs of your QMS.*

Clause 7 of the standard addresses product realization and will be your overall framework for writing this SOP here. The good news is that if you decided to follow my suggested 12-SOP model for your QMS, you will have already addressed many of the requirements of Clause 7 in your other SOPs. This SOP will thereby be about 42% lighter than it could be if you tried to cover everything here.

Even when focusing on the core of product realization itself, a few other standards besides ISO 13485 will probably inform your thinking within this SOP, as briefly discussed in Section 4.3.7. Exactly which standards those are will depend heavily on your product and your operations. If your product is software or has embedded software, you will probably want to look at IEC 62304 for software life cycle management and IEC 62366 for usability. The gargantuan IEC 60601 family of standards will be interesting to you if you work on hardware, but expect to spend a pretty penny to get access to that—at around a thousand euros (about the same in dollars), it is the most expensive purchase I have come across.

The best fit between any of these standards and the overarching ISO 13485 standard deserves a book or two each, but remember that it is ISO

13485 that will be your backbone and the standard you will actually be audited and, perhaps, certified against. You may perform additional certification or external assessment to the other standards, particularly if your B2B customers require this from you, but in general, ISO 13485 is the common language and the apparatus everyone will expect of you. Use the other standards to meet the requirements of ISO 13485 in a practical way that is appropriate to your operations, and don't lose sight of the overarching goal of remaining ISO 13485 certified or ISO 13485 compliant.

Remember what we discussed back in Section 3.8, the standard is your best hope of achieving interoperability and meeting the expectations of your stakeholders and partners, but no two organizations will implement the standards in exactly the same way. The standard is really about enforcing some level of a common schema (an API, as discussed earlier) over the QMS setups of the various operators. It is more about looking at the inputs and outputs instead of the value-adding processing in between. You are somewhat free to innovate and optimize within the processes as long as you know what you are doing and you are meeting the expectations at your input and output interfaces. This knowledge will help you marry the standards you need together and write this SOP for product realization.

In writing this SOP, don't rehash everything the standards contain. Instead, look at what makes sense for your operations, shape your processes accordingly, and then once you have the SOP ready and issued, focus on following it. It should always be possible to go back to the standards and check your processes against them, but it should not be required that all your readers are also familiar with the underlying standards. If you require that, you are either in some really specialized operational space or you are just setting yourself up to fail. You should, however, stay on top of how all those standards evolve over time and what the changes mean for your organization, and update the SOP accordingly.

The topics I would cover here are as follows:

■ Planning of product realization
■ Determination and review of product requirements
■ Design and development (including planning, inputs, outputs, reviews, verification, validation, transfer, control of changes, and the file set)
■ Production and service provision

Note that we already addressed software validation (not to be confused with product validation here), customer property, and the control of monitoring and measurement equipment in SOP-3. Similarly, we discussed the bulk of your customer-facing communication activities in SOP-7 (see also SOP-12 for the related topic of post-market surveillance) and the topic of purchasing in SOP-5 along with supplier and distributor management. Some product-related features (such as identification, traceability, the medical device file, and product release) are closely related to the regulatory requirements of your various jurisdictions and will be covered in SOP-11 next. In this SOP, you can link to all these other SOPs, but refrain from providing any overlapping instruction. Remember also that you may be able to exclude some of the requirements in Clause 7, including design and development controls (Clause 0.5), with a good justification. If you do make new exclusions here, the place to record them is not in this SOP but in the quality manual.

As a final friendly reminder, the term "product" can just as easily refer to both products and services (Clause 0.2). With that said, let's look at each of the topics in more detail.

16.1 Planning of Product Realization

Clause 7.1 of the standard requires you to have a process for product realization, and that this is also consistent with the requirements of your other processes. The basic framework for the process will be set in this SOP, but you can later fill in further product-specific details of the model in subsequent planning documents.

The process here must incorporate risk management, as noted earlier with the discussion on SOP-8. Records must be kept of risk management (see SOP-8) and, as appropriate, on the processes and product to prove fulfillment of requirements.

As appropriate, you must also determine the following through your process:

- Product quality objectives and product requirements
- The need to establish processes, documents, and resources specific to the product (e.g., regarding infrastructure, work environment, and personnel competence)
- Product-specific activities (e.g., verification and validation, monitoring, inspection, logistics, and traceability) and product acceptance criteria

The documentation of the previous outputs of the process may be in a format suitable to your organization. An example of a straightforward record containing your analysis of the previous items for an individual product realization project is a typical project plan. The obvious advantage of relying on a project plan here is that everyone (and their mother) will know to refer to it for this type of information. Revision of the plan should then take place if your plans change, but be careful not to interpret any language in Clause 7.3.2 or IEC 62304 to mean empty revisions for the sake of updated time stamps.

16.2 Determination and Review of Product Requirements

Determination of product requirements is the first step after embarking on a product realization project. In the standard, the determination and review of product requirements are addressed in Clauses 7.2.1 and 7.2.2, respectively.

Clause 7.2.1 places the burden of obtaining requirements from your customer squarely on your organization. This is not surprising, but it does mean that the standard doesn't want you to later claim that the customer didn't bring up this or that relevant requirement. The requirements may, for example, address the intended use of the product, its delivery activities, any postdelivery activities, and any user training needed for safe use of the device. The burden on your organization also extends to identifying regulatory requirements and any requirements left unstated by the customer but reasonably expected to be necessary based on the intended purpose (intended use) of the product. The adequacy or completeness of the list of requirements is up to you, although the standard phrases this as "any additional requirements" being up to you. You will ultimately also need to ensure that the requirements are not in conflict with each other, although this is not expressly stated by the standard until Clause 7.3.3 when discussing the review of D&D inputs.

The review of the requirements must be done prior to, and should be up-to-date, when you commit to supply product to the customer. Even if the customer does not readily provide a statement on requirements, it is still up to you to confirm the existence and contents of any requirements. If requirements are later changed, this must be reflected in your documents and the appropriate personnel must be notified (and your change control process otherwise satisfied). In essence, you must ensure that you have documented the requirements, that any changes to previous requirements are resolved, that any conflicts between the requirements and the contract/order are resolved, that regulatory requirements are met, that any necessary user training will be available, and that your organization can meet the requirements. As always, the review must be recorded.

My advice is to set up your process for developing, reviewing, and revising the requirements as a part of the project plan, or equivalent, here. If you anticipate the requirements to evolve greatly over time, you may want to develop your approach so that you do not need to revise the whole project plan every time, but even then, ensure that you stay on top of any changes to needs discussed in the plan.

16.3 Design and Development

In the world of business, and especially in the early days of getting a startup funded, DD refers to "due diligence", the process of letting your potential partner diligently go through your records to ensure that some investment or business agreement makes sense to them. In this standard, D&D refers to applying the same sort of diligence in-house to how you design and develop your products.

Under Clause 7, the fairly substantive subclause 7.3—which comprises a whopping 10% of the whole standard—is dedicated to the central topic of D&D activities. These consist of activities around planning, inputs, outputs, reviews, verification, validation, transfer, control of changes, and the set of files to use. Each activity has its own subclause, as discussed in the following. Meanwhile, the succinct message of the only general clause, Clause 7.3.1, is that you must have a process for design and development—unless, that is, you have excluded the D&D clauses altogether by perhaps employing alternate solutions (see Section 4.3.2).

16.3.1 D&D Planning

You must plan and control the design and development of your product (Clause 7.3.2). This involves the creation of the planning documents that are appropriate to you and the revision of these, as needed, throughout your progress. Your plans must address your D&D stages (including the review, verification, validation, and design transfer activities needed therein) and the overall D&D responsibilities (including authorities), methods for traceability between outputs and inputs, and any relevant resource needs (e.g., personnel competence).

All the items stated earlier can conveniently be addressed in the project plan. When defining resource needs and responsibilities on a high level, utilize the personnel roles identified in your quality manual and SOP-3 first, and only go deeper into assigning individual staff members as is needed to ensure responsibilities. This way, minor staff changes where the personnel group remains the same won't necessitate revisions.

16.3.2 D&D Inputs

You must identify and maintain records of the inputs relating to the requirements of your product (Clause 7.3.3). The inputs must include the intended purpose/use (including the functional, performance, usability, and safety requirements based on it), the applicable regulatory requirements, the used standards, the output of risk management activities, the experience from previous similar devices, and any other requirements for the product or processes that you deem essential.

You must review the inputs for adequacy and approve them after ensuring the requirements are complete, unambiguous, not in conflict with each other, and amenable to verification and validation. The standard also suggests the use of the IEC 62366 standard on usability as a further aid to consult here.

In practice, coming up with a solid list of input requirements here is both a science and an art. It may also be an iterative process where you approach and refine requirements multiple times from different points of view as your understanding grows throughout the project. The previously listed inputs are all ones you should consider, and eliciting ready-to-use requirements from your customer is usually no small feat, but a lot of your success in developing solid, complete requirements that do not require unnecessary changes later will come down to experience in your particular business. Whether you have a real or an imaginary customer—a talkative human being or a concept of a potential customer—to interview will also make a difference here. Here in the SOP, you don't need to go into too much detail, but make sure your process covers the basics set out earlier and works for your organization.

16.3.3 Actual D&D Work

Surprise. This a topic that does not appear in the standard but, instead, silently sits between its Clauses 7.3.3 (inputs) and 7.3.4 (outputs). Remember how I said earlier that the standard mainly focuses on the input and output interfaces of process and lets you innovate in between? This is a case in point. The standard does not instruct how you proceed from D&D inputs to the outputs; it only wants to make sure the output makes sense considering the input and that your reviews (including those based on your testing, verification, and validation activities) confer this regardless of whether this is a single review or a series of smaller reviews or assessments.

Here is where you can pull in the experience from your past development work, maybe even from business areas other than medical devices, and build a subprocess that you know works for your organization. If you don't like the waterfall model of development, you can design your process here according to agile or whatever sound development model you have. Even the Magic 8-Ball method may do if it consistently gives you reviewable results worth approving. Seriously speaking, standards, such as IEC 62304, should be useful for you here, and also other emerging standards for agile (I am in an ISO committee developing these at the moment) may be practical guides to consider here.

In any case, consider your instruction for D&D inputs earlier and the D&D outputs later, and then fit the bulk of your design and development work in between. You shouldn't, of course, unnecessarily duplicate later steps covered in the following sections here, which is to say ensure that you negotiate any reviews you instruct here with what is stated later in Section 16.3.5, for example.

16.3.4 D&D Outputs

D&D outputs (Clause 7.3.4) are the flipside of the coin sketched by the D&D inputs (see Section 16.3.2). Therefore, it is hardly surprising that the outputs must fulfill the input requirements and must be in a form that lends itself to verification against the inputs. The outputs must specify the essential characteristics for safe and proper use of the product, the product acceptance criteria, and any appropriate information for your purchasing, and production and service provision activities (e.g., distribution, installation, and maintenance). Whereas inputs may be objects, such as requirements, specifications, and perhaps design drawings, the corresponding outputs may then be, for example, lists of selected parts, assembly instructions, comprehensive instructions for the production line, and user instructions. In the case of a software product, the outputs may include the software binary, the installation package, and the instructions for use, for example.

Finally, the outputs must be approved prior to their release. In practice, the approval of the outputs may take the form of a review documented in your QMS. The review may reference various documents and the reviews conducted earlier (see Section 16.3.3), but here, the objective is to ensure the outputs are fit for use by the later stages. The model of action here is that of a typical checkpoint, or of a stage gate, and is not specific to medical devices in itself.

16.3.5 D&D Review

Building on what was said earlier about your output review, you must also have systematic reviews at other suitable stages throughout your D&D work. Here in this SOP, I would ensure that the basic requirements of a review and the minimum set of review points (gates) to have are instructed, but otherwise, the project plan, or a similar planning document, may assign reviews as is fitting to the individual project. The instruction in this SOP, therefore, makes up the foundation of what the standard calls "documented arrangements" when it requires that your reviews are in accordance with your planned and documented arrangements.

The basic goal to hit with a review is to assess whether the reviewed results match your requirements for them, and if this should be improved upon, identify and propose any necessary actions to that end. The participants of the review should include any necessary specialist personnel you need for the review and also representatives of the D&D stage under review. The records of the review must retain identification of the stage, the participants, the date, and any actions proposed.

In practice, some of the reviews will be internal to your D&D Team, but others will include members from elsewhere in your organization, and some key reviews (e.g., D&D transfer review) may also be of great interest to your higher management. Not including too many people in the reviews but still including all the right people will be a tightrope to test if you are a new organization starting out. As a quality manager, I might be mostly interested in the early input review and the D&D transfer review that most likely also comments on the verification and validation activities conducted in between. As a member of the Management Team, I am probably content with knowing what products we are developing, intermittently hearing how those projects are progressing, and finally, knowing when some product is ready to launch and start selling.

16.3.6 D&D Verification

Clause 7.3.6 builds on the concept of the D&D review introduced earlier to require that you also perform verification—in accordance with your SOP, plans, and other documented arrangements—of the D&D outputs meeting their input requirements. The standard does not require that you develop and describe a process for this in an SOP, only that you do verification appropriately. You must, however, have a plan for verification that addresses the methods, acceptance criteria, and (if appropriate) statistical techniques, including a rationale for sample size. A special consideration here is that if your product is intended to be connected with another device or interface, this must also be covered in your verification. As always, records will be kept, and these will include any conclusions made and necessary actions identified.

In practice, verification is largely an internal activity ensuring that what you obtained via the D&D process matches with what you set out to create. The end result of verification may conveniently be documented as a review or a report summarizing the results and approving the outcome. You will have additional records created during the verification activity that you can make use of in the final review/report, but again, the overarching goal is to ensure you are content with the output so far to proceed to the next stage. If you are not, you should return to a previous step as is appropriate.

16.3.7 D&D Validation

Validation is usually the first step where you bring in sizable user involvement from outside of your organization—at least since after the initial user requirement elicitation process. During this stage, matching Clause 7.3.7, you will check that the product you have created is capable of meeting the requirements of its intended purpose (intended use) or specified application. You must have a validation plan that, like a verification plan, addresses methods, acceptance criteria, and (if appropriate) statistical techniques, including a rationale for sample size. This must all be in accordance with your overall planned and documented arrangements.

The special consideration here is that validation must be performed using representative product. This can, for example, mean units from initial production batches. The implication here is clear but often the subject of some thought: you can't use some early prototype that does not match with what you are actually going to manufacture. You can't do validation using a paper prototype. The rationale for choosing the product to use must also be recorded here. The requirement from verification (see Section 16.3.6) to observe connections to other devices or interfaces implicated in the intended purpose (intended use) also applies here.

As part of the validation activity, you must perform clinical evaluation (see SOP-9) or performance evaluation as dictated by your applicable regulatory requirements. The standard also requires you to complete validation prior to the release of the product. Note that, importantly, a device used in the context of validation is not considered as released for use to the customer.

As always, records of the results, conclusions, and any necessary actions must be kept. In practice, a validation review or a report is a deliverable you may want to instruct in your SOP here. For help in the validation and to ensure appropriate involvement of representative end users, you may want to consider turning to the various test beds run by hospitals and other medical centers in your area.

16.3.8 D&D Transfer

Once, after going through the previous steps, you are happy with how your product meets the needs of your customer and all the other requirements, too, all that technically remains is to kick off the manufacturing of that product. You may, of course, need to obtain one form of regulatory approval or another for your device before you want to switch on the production line or before you can ship the products.

To perform transfer efficiently and safely, Clause 7.3.8 requires you to have a process for transferring the D&D outputs to manufacturing. Here, it is not enough to just do it, but instead, you must define a subprocess for transfer in this SOP. As part of the process, you must verify that the outputs are indeed suitable for manufacturing, and only after this, treat them as final production specifications. You must also verify that your production capability can meet the product requirements. Once again, the results and conclusions of the transfer must be recorded (e.g., as a review). The transfer decision will be an important checkpoint, and one where I would consider including appropriate personnel from not only manufacturing but also your management. The record of the decision, and its basis, will be a key document you may end up pulling out with a varying frequency in the future.

16.3.9 Control of D&D Changes

The best D&D process is undone if changes can be made with a brush of some Tipp-Ex (correction fluid, for those of you outside the UK) and no real record is retained of who, when, and why the record was altered. Or what the record previously said. Therefore, Clause 7.3.9 requires you to have a process controlling D&D changes.

In the subprocess you instruct here, make sure that you determine the significance of any change you are contemplating in relation to your product (including its intended use/purpose, applicable regulatory requirements, function, performance, usability, and safety). In other words, before you make the change, you must review it, verify it, validate it (if appropriate), and approve it. The review must evaluate the effects of the changes on constituent parts, product currently in manufacturing or already delivered, and both the inputs and outputs of risk management and product realization processes. The changes must be identified and recorded (including their review and any necessary actions).

In practice, you will have different types of calls for changes to the product. Some will be minor, and some will be major. Figuring out streamlined pathways for these types of changes may make your overall process much more efficient. To keep the processes tidy, and not moving backward and forward unnecessarily, I would leave the handling of any ideas that do not yet lead to actual changes on your product to the feedback handling process (SOP-7) or write in a separate internal ideation and road map handling subprocess to this SOP. Some seeds of new ideas will probably also always develop under the radar, as part of informal conversation around the coffee table or the watercooler, and it makes little sense to impose forms and processes for that infant environment, but you should have a model for harvesting the best of the ideas and developing them further when the time comes. Similarly, changes to the SOP itself should be handled by your document editing process (SOP-1) and the process change activity (SOP-2).

The choice of how to address recording of ongoing development work on an upcoming release of the next version of your product is, first and foremost, up to you. Personally, if possible, I would avoid scrutinizing every little increment of development (such as a new line of code) as a D&D change when those changes a) are not yet guaranteed to proceed further; b) do not yet affect your released product in any way; and c) will be tested, verified, validated, reviewed, and approved before a) and b) will become true. It may, however, be smart to treat some changes in the pipeline as changes early on or to prepare for their later assessment as changes to the product when the launch of the new release is nearing. Project management tools, software development environments, and other similar software may help you here in being able to track back your work as needed even during agile development cycles and in between actual D&D changes.

Records and traceability matter everywhere and at all times. The choice is up to you on how you draw the line between changes under development and the actual changes made to something out there in the wild, but the standard is adamant that, ultimately, changes going out through the door do so in a controlled way.

16.3.10 D&D Files

Clause 7.3.10 of the standard requires you to maintain a D&D file for each type or family of medical devices you work with through your product realization process. This file does not have to be, and usually is not, a single computer file. Instead, it is a collection of records that enable you to prove your D&D activity meets the requirements set for it by you, the regulations, and the standard—even by your customer, if we really get down to it (see Section 16.2). Here, the standard specifically repeats the requirement to have records on any D&D changes.

As in the case of the medical device file (see Section 17.9), the D&D files may include these records or reference them. The D&D files are a broad collection of D&D records containing much more information on your processes than is necessary for the medical device file. The two will, however, overlap. If you now record all the key bits of information from your D&D process, and if you retain these records in a manner in keeping with the requirements of the standard (see SOP-1), you will stand the best chance of building your medical device file at the end of the D&D process, translating that later to any new jurisdictional regions as needed, and defending that file during any audit you may have. The choice of what to record and how is a major part of the instruction in this SOP and in the subsequent project plans.

16.4 Production and Service Provision

Production and service prevision is addressed in Clause 7.5 of the standard. Of the subject matter covered by this clause, we address installation and servicing activities (SOP-7), identification and traceability (SOP-11, Quality Manual), customer property (SOP-3), and control of monitoring and measuring equipment (SOP-3) in your other SOPs. Additionally, we instructed purchasing in SOP-5 along with supplier management, readiness to sell in SOP-7, and control of nonconforming product in SOP-2. These are all topics that are closely related to the discussion here.

The topics left to discuss here are as follows:

■ Control of production and service provision
■ Cleanliness of product (including sterile medical devices)
■ Validation of processes for product provision (including sterilization)
■ Preservation of product
■ Monitoring and measurement of product

In addition, I will touch on two more topics—the medical device file and the process for product release—as these are essential in product realization. Both topics are also tied to regulations, which is why they are instructed in detail in SOP-11.

Each one of the previous topics begins to move the discussion from any sphere of general quality management to a level that is increasingly specific to the type of products you work with. You will probably instantaneously recognize those topics that at least apply to your business, but remember what we discussed in Section 3.8: the standard does require interpretation even if in the end you rein in some of the wilder offshoots of that interpretation. Remember to make any exclusions of the clauses as is relevant to your product and business in the quality manual.

Let's briefly look at each of the previous topics.

16.4.1 *Control of Production and Service Provision*

Just as it was important to control changes to the immaculate design you had come up with, it is also important to control what you manufacture based on that design. Your activities in production and service provision must, therefore, be planned, executed, monitored, and controlled so that the conformity of the product is ensured (Clause 7.5.1). The easiest way to achieve this is probably to plan your process and instruct it here, but the standard does not explicitly call for a process to do this.

The controls you apply must, as appropriate, include documented procedures and methods for the control of production, the qualification of infrastructure, the monitoring and measurement of process parameters and product characteristics (including the use and availability of any equipment needed), the implementation of defined labeling and packaging operations, and the implementation of product release, delivery, and postdelivery activities.

Records must be maintained, verified, and approved for each device or batch in a way that identifies the amounts manufactured and approved for distribution. Traceability must be maintained.

16.4.2 *Cleanliness of Product*

Remember how we discussed in Section 3.8 that cleaning and contamination may not seem like it applies to software but you could still think of cybersecurity as part of product cleanliness? With that in mind, you should consider how you ensure your product ships and remains clean through product provision (Clause 7.5.2).

Note also that the point in time when you perform such cleaning on the product may mean that requirements from Clause 6.4.1 may not apply until that cleaning is performed (see Section 9.1). The prerequisite here is that the product is cleaned by your organization prior to sterilization or use, or that the product is to be supplied nonsterile by your organization and then cleaned prior to sterilization or use.

In general, if process agents are to be removed during manufacturing, or if your product is cleaned by you or it is subject to be cleaned later, or if cleanliness is of significance in its use, you must document the requirements for product cleanliness. This is expressed in a rather cumbersome way in Clauses 7.5.2 a-e, which you may want to study more closely as matches your specific product and business.

Clause 7.5.5 goes on to require that for sterile medical devices, you maintain records of the process parameters of each sterilization batch and that these are traceable to each production batch of the product.

16.4.3 *Validation of Processes for Product Provision*

Clause 7.5.6 addresses the validation of processes for production and service provision and any software used therein. We already covered the process for software validation in SOP-3, so here, the first task is to instruct that the process you defined there is used for any production and service provision software. The second task you are required to do is to validate any production and service provision processes where deficiencies become apparent only after the product is in use or the service is delivered. If you can employ monitoring and measurement to verify the output prior to this, then process validation may not be required.

The aim of process validation is to demonstrate that planned results are achieved consistently. To do so, your subprocess here must address the following:

■ Criteria for review and approval
■ Qualification of equipment and personnel
■ Use of specific methods, procedures, and acceptance criteria (including, if appropriate, statistical techniques and rationale for sample size)
■ Requirements for records (including results, conclusions, and actions)
■ Revalidation (including criteria for revalidation)
■ Approval of process changes

Clause 7.5.7 adds requirements for the validation of processes for sterilization and sterile barrier systems. Unless you have excluded this clause, you must have a validation process addressing such processes. The validation must be performed prior to the implementation of the process and following changes to the product or the process, as appropriate. Records must be kept of the results, conclusion of validation, and necessary actions. The standard offers two parts of the standard on packaging for terminally sterilized medical devices as further reading here: ISO 11607–1:2019 (Part 1: Requirements for materials, sterile barrier systems, and packaging systems) and ISO 11607–2:2019 (Part 2: Validation requirements for forming, sealing, and assembly processes). You can find both via the ISO website.

16.4.4 *Preservation of Product*

Clause 7.5.11 requires you have a process for preserving product conformity during processing, storage, handling, and distribution. The obligation for you to identify requirements for preservation and maintain records on product preservation show up in a number of locations throughout the standard (e.g., Clauses 4.2.3, 7.1, and 7.5.8), but the requirement to have a specific process to address this is given here. The process must consider the constituent parts of your product and must protect it from alteration, contamination, or damage under expected conditions and hazards.

You can protect product by suitable packaging and shipping containers and, if this is not enough, by documenting requirements for any special conditions needed. In case you resort to specifying conditions, those must be controlled and recorded.

16.4.5 *Monitoring and Measurement of Product*

Technically, this is a topic covered under Clause 8.2.6 (see Section 8.1 and 8.2), but as it is closely connected to product realization and as you may want to refine your approach to monitoring and measurement based on characteristics identified via product development, I cover it here. The standard requires that you monitor and measure the characteristics of your product to verify that it meets its requirements. This must be done at applicable stages of your product realization process and in accordance with any planned and documented arrangements. Records on the conformity with the acceptance criteria must be maintained as evidence.

The planned and documented arrangements must be satisfactorily completed before product release and service delivery are allowed to take place. The identity of the person authorizing the release of the product must be recorded. As appropriate, the records must also identify the used test measurement equipment. Note also that for implantable devices, the identity of the inspection and testing personnel involved must be recorded.

16.5 Medical Device File

The medical device file is instructed in SOP-11, along with some other topics typically discussed in a regulatory setting. This instruction should not be repeated here, but instead, I would ensure the discussion here makes this link between the two SOPs apparent. The reason is that a lot of the work taking place here is expected to lead to records that are then usable in the medical device file itself. I might, for example, make the reference when discussing the D&D files earlier or include a separate section on the medical device file, as I have done here.

16.6 Product Release

The process for product release is also affected by jurisdictional regulatory requirements and is, thus, discussed in SOP-11. Here, I would refer to SOP-11 on both the approval of a new product for sales and the release of an individual device from production. These may be the same process or two different processes, depending on your circumstances. Also, if there are any special actions you want performed at the end of product development to make sure all the ducks are in a row for a subsequent market launch, you may do so here, although your D&D transfer review most likely already achieved everything you wanted to instruct.

16.7 Checklist

The following checklist (Table 16.1) is provided for your convenience.

Table 16.1 Checklist for SOP-10

Checklist

☐	**You understand what to cover in planning of product realization** You have specified your key activities and documentation for planning.
☐	**You understand what is required of product requirements** This includes both how you determine and how you review such requirements.
☐	**You understand what to cover in your D&D subprocesses** You have specified your key activities and documentation for each D&D stage.
☐	**You understand how you want to address production and service provision** For example, process validation and control, and cleanliness, preservation, and monitoring of product.
☐	**You have defined the relationship of this SOP to SOP-11** For example, medical device file and release of product.
☐	**You have addressed how this SOP is to be applied at your organization** And the correct versions of documents will be available at the correct places.
☐	**You know what quality indicators match with this SOP** Record a few measurable indicators for this SOP in the appendix of the quality manual.

Once you feel confident you have ticked every box, it's time to move on.

Chapter 17

Regulatory Affairs (SOP-11)

Regulations affect everything in your QMS. The standard itself acknowledges this and places the burden of understanding how any applicable regulations cast the interpretation of its clauses squarely on your shoulders. It's not possible to address the impact of all regulations in just one SOP, but it is possible to lay out the foundations of your approach to regulations as well as address some common elements in an SOP. If you are dealing with multiple jurisdictions at the same time, this may also be a good way of keeping your QMS documentation tidy.

The concept of applicable regulatory requirements gets thrown around a lot in the standard. I counted at least 48 instances of this in the text. The reason is, quite naturally, that the standard can't address all possible regulatory jurisdictions around the world, stay current, and end up as anything approaching a readable, actionable standard. Instead, the standard points out the areas where you are most likely to come across regulatory requirements affecting your QMS. Further points of difference between the standard and the regulations may also exist in some jurisdictions, and conformity with the standard can't give you any free pass regarding any of these.

The use of the ISO 13485 standard is optional, but it is already well and truly the norm in Europe, and seems to be expanding its circle of friends around the globe, as discussed earlier in Section 4.2. In the EU, you should look to harmonized standards and their Z annexes for more details on how meeting the requirements of the standard also help you meet the needs of the regulations. In the US, you should look for long-awaited guidance from the FDA on how the Quality System Regulation and the standard work together.

DOI: 10.4324/9781003202868-17

The inclusion of an SOP on regulatory affairs, too, is optional. Having the SOP will not save you from working on all the different ways regulations affect your work inside your other SOPs. It may, however, make it more practical to expand your reach across several parts of the globe and marry together several regulations in a meaningful, efficient way.

The topics I suggest you cover here are as follows:

■ Understanding of applicable jurisdictions
■ Monitoring of regulatory changes
■ Monitoring of changes in standards
■ QMS certification
■ Product requirements
■ Product classification
■ Product identification and traceability
■ Product labeling
■ Medical device file
■ Product release
■ Regulatory notifications
■ Contact details for regulatory authorities

As a friendly reminder from Section 4.3.1, the interpretation of the term "regulatory requirement" is limited to the context of the QMS and the safety and performance of the medical device. Other regulatory requirements will, no doubt, also be in effect, but their power over you is not exercised through the standard.

17.1 Understanding Applicable Jurisdictions

At the very beginning of the standard, Clause 0.1 points out the fact that several jurisdictions may place regulatory requirements on your QMS if you operate within those jurisdictions in some specific role. We addressed the matter, including your role within medical devices, in the quality manual. It is up to you to identify and incorporate the requirements that then apply to you. This also means understanding how the ISO 13485 standard itself is interpreted in those jurisdictions.

Consider here how you want to address different jurisdictions in your QMS. You won't want to write in all the regional peculiarities across all the different SOPs in your QMS, as maintaining that can of worms would become a nightmare. You probably won't want to write all the regional nuances into the body of this SOP either if you can avoid it. Instead, consider using appendices to address, for example, EU and FDA requirements individually in a way that lends itself to easier, more uniform referencing. That is still a tall order, but taking a modular approach and having this dedicated SOP should help you considerably in achieving it.

It will be impossible to write all the requirements in, but you may benefit from grouping certain fundamental requirements in some smart way. For example, grouping information on document retainment periods, device lifetimes, and time frames for responding to certain types of events, such as received complaints, may yield you benefits via such a consolidated approach. At the very least, you will appreciate the differences in these requirements. A small glossary mapping together the key terms used across your jurisdictions may also prove useful when first figuring things out and, later, when training new personnel. You can write this into your SOP as definitions of terms or you may reference a separate document. Be careful, though, not to squeeze all your operations on account of some regional anomaly affecting only a subset of your products and operations.

Ultimately, meeting such requirements will be a significant factor in how you develop your technical file. Maintaining some practical mapping between your EU technical file and the medical device file the FDA expects to see may prove useful also in the long run—especially as some document in the pack has changed and the release date for a new version is approaching. You will probably want to implement this in your document management software sooner or later, but instructing it can then be done here in this SOP.

17.2 Monitoring Regulatory Changes

Figuring out your relevant jurisdictions and regulatory requirements at one point in time is not enough. You must then stay on top of those requirements, even as the regulations change and as you expand to new geographies or markets. I would advocate for defining active jurisdictions in the quality manual (while still insisting on the definition of these on a product-specific level), maintaining both a registry and copies of the applicable guidance (these are usually available for free), and having a process here for developing periodic reports with assessment of any relevant changes in regulations across the jurisdictions. Such a process is not required by the standard, but the understanding you will get from it is.

The regulatory follow-up report could, for example, be issued every quarter or twice a year. It is a lot of work, but there is no real alternative to it if you want to stay on top of things. Tools such as QAiRA (https://kasve.com/qaira/) and BSI's Compliance Navigator (https://compliancenavigator.bsigroup.com/) will help you distill the information you need. In the EU, the Medical Device Coordination Group of the European Commission is a fountain of new guidance-like information, and also the regional competent authorities retain a role in providing information and oversight. In the US, the FDA is extremely good about providing in-depth guidance and training on just about every imaginable topic. You should take a look at these even if the US is not part of your present sphere of interest.

Finally, consider how you want to disseminate the information created here and how it can be useful in, for example, your internal teams (see SOP-7), product realization activities (SOP-10), and the big kahuna of the management review.

17.3 Monitoring Changes in Standards

Mirroring regulatory monitoring, you will want to set up a mechanism for tracking the development and status of standards. At a minimum, this should cover the standards you already use in your QMS and products, but also consider casting a wider net to learn of new standards you could use. The nice thing about monitoring standards, as opposed to jurisdictional regulations, is that the standards are usually international in nature and, thus, immediately cover larger swaths of the globe. Standards may, however, have interpretational differences across the globe and across different domains of applications (e.g., approach to risk in financial markets and risk in medical devices).

Again, there are several ways you could go about this, ranging from manual work to a tool to an almost outsourced service. Both tools mentioned in the previous section will help you stay on top of standardization. You may also be surprised by the level of raw information on offer at the website of ISO itself.

As with regulations, I would advocate defining active standards in the quality manual, maintaining both a registry and copies of the standards (available for a fee from ISO and your local standardization offices), and having a process here for developing periodic reports of relevant changes in standardization. I might combine the process and the report here with what was discussed earlier for monitoring changes in jurisdictions. I would monitor, at least, ISO and IEC standards, but also other regional standards as may be appropriate to you.

Finally, consider how you want to disseminate the information created here and how it can be useful in, for example, your internal teams (see SOP-7), product realization activities (SOP-10), and the big kahuna of the management review.

17.4 QMS Certification

The standard does not directly speak of the certification of your QMS according to ISO 13485. It does drive home the fact that you are always responsible for any claims of conformity you make to the standard (see Clause 0.5) and that you must justify any exclusions you make therein, but otherwise, the auditing and certification of your QMS is between you and your certification body or notified body.

Here in this SOP, I might address my overall arrangements for QMS certification and ensure that the quality manual also records the coverage of the certification. In terms of the schedule of the certification and its renewal, I might, at most, comment on the general cycle and point to where in my records I store the actual QMS certificates, audit documents, and the QMS auditing schedules. Also see Section 28 for more on certification.

17.5 Product Requirements

The impact of regulations to the determination and review of product requirements (Clauses 7.2.1c and 7.2.2c, respectively) and the use of applicable regulations and standards as part of the inputs for design and development activities (Clause 7.3.3b) are topics chiefly addressed in SOP-10. To ensure the links between regulations and these product development activities are maintained as is appropriate and that these links are also observed when expanding to new jurisdictions, I would include a brief link here to SOP-10. Further instruction can be added here later if needed.

17.6 Product Classification

Product classification under the various regulations that apply to you may be something to instruct here on a top level. I omitted this from the "Products" section in the quality manual as this is too much information to throw at your customer and any new employee at first. Here, though, you can provide any general instruction on the topic you feel necessary to ensure product classification can proceed smoothly and in a timely progression. Chief among the aspects I would discuss here is when to first consider product classification during the development of some product (sooner is better), when this must be locked down (before certification), and what should be available for the classification to take place.

17.7 Product Identification and Traceability

We addressed product identification in the quality manual on a top level. I would refer to the instruction in the quality manual here and explain how my IDs are connected to Unique Device Identifiers (UDIs), if at all. If your product portfolio or your ID scheme is complicated, you may want to go into more detail here.

In the standard, the requirement for identification is in Clause 7.5.8. The requirement is to have a process in place throughout product realization. The process must identify the status of products also with respect to any monitoring and measurement requirements. This status information must be maintained throughout production, storage, installation, and servicing. The extension of the ID scheme to the fine-grained identification of development versions still in the product development phase may be left to SOP-10, but it is, of course, important that these IDs are not mistaken for any releasable product versions. The identification of products returned to your organization is a related topic we addressed in SOP-7.

The standard also demands that if your applicable regulations so require, you must document a system to assign unique device identification to your products. You may have already explained how your product versioning is connected to the Unique Device Identifier (UDI) scheme, or similar, but if not, doing so in your QMS will soon be required. In the EU, the rollout of UDI under the new medical device regulations is taking place now. Defining or naming the different identification schemes you use in one location and explaining any jurisdictional differences in the schemes should be a practical approach to take here.

The requirements for traceability are in Clause 7.5.9. Your process must define traceability in accordance with any applicable regulatory requirements. In the case of implantable medical devices, the requirements are elaborated on in Clause 7.5.9.2. For implantable devices, you must maintain records of the name and address of the shipping package consignee, and consider whether records of components, materials, and work environment conditions are needed (records are generally needed if these matters can cause the product not to meet its safety and performance requirements). Similarly, for implantable devices, you must require your suppliers to maintain distribution records for traceability.

17.8 Product Labeling

Product labeling is not addressed by the standard to any great degree. At most, the standard requires you to consider and describe product labeling when you create the medical device file and that your production controls cover labeling operations as appropriate (Clause 7.5.1, see SOP-10). There are, however, other standards you could refer to here should you so wish. Two key documents developed by ISO are ISO 20417 on information to be supplied by the manufacturer of a medical device and ISO 15223–1 on the symbols to be used with that information. Note that the graphic files for the symbols themselves are available for purchase from ISO too.

The choice of what you include in your product labeling is affected by the regulations. The crucial bit to understand here is that labeling is a broad term that applies to more than just the label stickers on your device; it refers to all labels and manuals you expect your user to see. In particular, this means the shield label and the instructions for use (IFU) but also the user interface labels in your product. Thus, also standards like IEC 62366–1 on the application of usability engineering to medical devices and the IEC 60601 series of standards on medical electrical equipment may come into play and may affect your product realization and risk management activities.

17.9 Medical Device File

The requirements for the medical device file are in Clause 4.2.3, but as it is something needed in all regulatory contexts and as jurisdiction may have differing requirements on it, I cover it here. The clause gives you the following minimum list of contents for the file:

- A general description of the device
- The intended purpose (intended use) of the device
- The labeling of the device (including any instructions for use)
- The specifications of the device
- The specifications or procedures for manufacturing, packaging, storage, handling, and distribution of the device
- The procedures for measuring and monitoring

And as appropriate, the following are also contents for the file:

- Requirements for installation
- Requirements for servicing

In practice, you will want to look for the requirements placed on the medical device file by the regulations applicable to you. In the EU, this means, first and foremost, looking to Annex II of the Medical Device Regulations (MDR) for a very practical approach to compiling your technical file. In the US, look to the FDA for similar guidance. I would not instruct the medical device file too tightly here to avoid micromanagement and any self-inflicted issues in negotiating together jurisdictional differences.

17.10 Product Release

I see two distinct contexts where product release may be thought to occur. The first is when a new product is first cleared for production, and the second when produced products are cleared to be shipped to customers.

The first context is not instructed by the standard. If you choose to comment on the process of giving a greenlight to produce a product, make it as simple as you can. Ensure that all regulatory requirements are met and that a declaration of conformity, or similar, is only signed once your organization has reviewed and approved the product and its documentation for production. This also signifies that your regulatory approvals (e.g., the EC conformity assessment in the EU) have been obtained as relevant. The point here is in making sure you are satisfied with the product launch going forward.

The second context, releasing already manufactured products, is discussed in detail by the standard. Clause 8.1 requires you to set up measurement, analysis, and improvement processes needed to demonstrate conformity of product (see SOP-2). According to Clause 7.5.8, only product that has been correctly released (i.e., passed all required inspections or given an appropriate authorized concession) may be dispatched, used, or installed. Furthermore, Clause 8.3.2 requires that release by concession only takes place if justification is provided, approved, and in line with regulatory requirements.

Note that the previous case also involves the satisfactory completion of any arrangements for monitoring and measurement you have planned and documented (see Section 16.4.5). For such activity, the identity of the person authorizing the release of the product must be recorded, and as appropriate, the records must identify the test measurement equipment used. Furthermore, for implantable devices, the records must also contain the identity of the inspection and testing personnel involved.

17.11 Regulatory Notifications

You must understand how you are to communicate with the regulatory authorities applicable to your organization and under which circumstances (following or preceding which specific events) you should be in touch with them. SOP-7 already discussed such communication needs, but here, you can further define the circumstances and jurisdiction-specific notification and communication needs.

As noted earlier, the regulatory requirements on when to notify the authorities show up in processes throughout your QMS. The triggers for this communication are not listed by the standard, but instead, you are expected to understand the regulatory requirements that set up such triggers. You are required, as instructed in Clause 8.2.3, to set up reporting criteria—e.g., classes of complaints or certain types of events (e.g., issuance of advisory notices)—that trigger notifications to authorities. Here is where I would define those criteria in a way compatible with multiple jurisdictions, and then refer here from other SOPs as needed. Remember to retain records of the reporting in your QMS. In the EU, the Periodic Safety Update Report (PSUR) is the major topic to mention here even if you choose to instruct it in SOP-12 addressing post-market surveillance, as I have done.

17.12 Contact Details for Regulatory Authorities

Maintaining an up-to-date list of contact details on regulatory authorities (including your notified bodies) is not just good hygiene, it is step one to reliable communication with such authorities. Maintaining the list may be conveniently facilitated as an appendix or a series of appendices to this SOP.

I would always include general top-level contact information for the authorities (including their website address) in addition to, or even in place of, any more specific personal or departmental contact information. The reason for this is obvious: to act as a fail-safe and to guard against unnecessarily locking into the use of antiquated contact details as faulty or changed contact details are discovered. This is information you should remember to revise at least through your document review process.

17.13 Checklist

The following checklist (Table 17.1) is provided for your convenience.

Table 17.1 Checklist for SOP-11

Checklist
☐ **You understand what jurisdictions apply to you and what requirements these impose**   This also includes understanding how the standard is interpreted under each jurisdiction.
☐ **You have a process for monitoring changes in regulation and standardization**   This process also provides information that you can disseminate and use elsewhere.
☐ **You know when and how to communicate with your certification provider**   This also includes knowing how to contact your certification body or notified body.
☐ **You know when and how to communicate with your regulatory authorities**   This also includes knowing how to contact your regulatory authorities.
☐ **You have a process for maintaining the contact information of your regulatory authorities**   This may be incorporated into another process, for example, the document review.
☐ **You have addressed how this SOP is to be applied at your organization**   And the correct versions of documents will be available at the correct places.
☐ **You know what quality indicators match with this SOP**   Record a few measurable indicators for this SOP in the appendix of the quality manual.
Once you feel confident you have ticked every box, it's time to move on.

Chapter 18

Post-Market Surveillance (SOP-12)

Post-market surveillance is the new kid on the block—the Josh Brolin step-ping into John Wayne's boots or the Daniel Craig trying on Sean Connery's swagger—and expected to do something new and, well, unexpected. It is the one topic that no one has fully figured out yet and that may show us the future of regulating medical devices.

You could insert post-market surveillance into SOP-7, along with much of your communication and client-facing activity. In fact, for a long time, I did just that. As post-market surveillance is, first and foremost, about your customers and your products, you could address it in SOP-7 as an integral part of your communication needs. This would also be in line with how the present version of the standard talks about the post-market: in passing and mostly as something faint and in the future.

Recently though, I have opted to develop post-market surveillance (PMS) activities into an SOP of their own. Why? Because I see a lot of activity in the field, and to a great extent, the thinking out there displayed by certification providers and regulatory authorities is only now maturing. Or maybe it would be fair to say that we will know the best practices around post-market surveillance only in the years to come. Having a separate SOP for PMS will let you react to, and maybe even occasionally predict, changes to PMS requirements in one convenient self-contained location of your QMS. Much like having a separate SOP for clinical affairs or regulatory affairs, it will enable you to better address jurisdictional and future regulatory differences should you need to.

DOI: 10.4324/9781003202868-18

18.1 Information Sources

The standard requires you to gather both production and postproduction information. Post-market activities fit into the latter. Post-market surveillance starts with following up on your own customers and their experiences with your product, but it also calls for a wealth of other available information to be gleaned from, for example, current scientific publications, news, and competitor activities.

The body of the standard only mentions post-market surveillance once in Clause 8.5.1 as part of your measurement, analysis, and improvement activities; and twice more in the terms and definitions section. The term is thus listed in the standard, and it is defined as a systematic process, but nowhere does it actually say that you must have a documented process for it. In practice, you should develop your model for PMS thoroughly and include at least the broad strokes here. I would also recommend creating a more detailed PMS plan, which should define what information sources you monitor and how you analyze these. The plan should also reference your Post-Market Clinical Follow-Up (PMCF) plan (see SOP-9).

In practice, I would ensure my planned and documented PMS process covers all the bases of information suggested by my stakeholder analysis, my competitor landscape, my products, their risk management files, their feedback, and any clinical evidence (including current scientific publications). These are all topics previously discussed in this book. The sources I would at least consider here are as follows:

■ Information from R&D
■ Any CAPA and immediate corrections made
■ Customer feedback and complaints, including any identified trends, results of customer surveys, and maintenance information
■ Feedback from marketing and sales, including trade show appearances
■ Experience reported on similar devices
■ Clinical evidence, including scientific literature surveys and surveys of adverse event databases (e.g., FDA's MAUDE database)
■ New or revised regulatory requirements and standards

The standard also speaks of "post-production" in the context of feedback (Clause 8.2.1) and "post-delivery" in the context of production and service provision (Clause 7.5.1). Both terms may be implicated in post-market surveillance, and the related processes may feed into the surveillance here—as indeed is already the case for the previous list.

Finally, the ISO has also published a very practical technical report, ISO/TR 20416 on post-market surveillance for manufacturers of medical devices. This report is easy to read and matches with common sense on the topic, but at the same time, it is very much a practical document to refer to in setting up your post-market activities. In this SOP, I would acknowledge its existence and make sure any process instructions I provide here align with the report. The use of the report is optional.

18.2 Periodic Safety Update Report (PSUR)

Much of the previous information is summarized in the Periodic Safety Update Reports (PSUR), or similar, compiled on a periodic basis. These reports are developed on a per-device or a per-device-family basis and form a major milestone in your post-market surveillance. Like management reviews, the PSURs should offer information on the status of each of the previous inputs and any subsequent analysis and action based on them. Here, I would acknowledge the existence of the PSUR and provide any instruction on their development I saw fit.

The structure of a PSUR could mimic the structure of your management review report to improve compatibility between the two. Note also that regulatory guidance may affect the structure you need to use by providing templates and requirements. For maximum efficiency, I would attempt to ensure that the PSURs are created prior to the management review, and the management review can then benefit from the analysis done in the PSURs. The topics to cover in the PSURs won't match with your management review exactly, but there should be definite synergy between the two, especially in the case of a small organization with a focused range of products.

18.3 Checklist

The following checklist (Table 18.1) is provided for your convenience.

Table 18.1   Checklist for SOP-12

Checklist

☐ **I know my regulatory requirements regarding PMS**
This includes knowing how the jurisdictions applicable to you are addressing PMS.

☐ **I know the state-of-the-art standards in terms of PMS**
This includes familiarizing yourself with ISO/TR 20416, if you may want to use it.

☐ **I have defined my approach to conducting PMS**
You may do so in this SOP or instruct that this is done in your PMS plan.

☐ **I have defined my use of the PMS plan**
You have instructed the creation and use of the PMS plan.

☐ **I have instructed the creation and use of the PSUR**
This includes my process for ensuring that the necessary inputs are available for the PSUR.

☐ **You have addressed how this SOP is to be applied at your organization**
And the correct versions of documents will be available at the correct places.

☐ **You know what quality indicators match with this SOP**
Record a few measurable indicators for this SOP in the appendix of the quality manual.

Once you feel confident you have ticked every box, it's time to move on.

Chapter 19

Finalizing All the SOPs

All the heavy lifting is just about done now. You have all the QMS documents you need almost done, and only the final checks remain before they are ready for use. This section will help you wrap up the SOPs, make any remaining tweaks to accommodate them in the quality manual, and have your whole stack of documents ready to go. If you are not building your QMS documents here, you may want to skip through to the next section.

19.1 Read the Standard–At Least Once

Okay, you knew this day would come. You secretly prayed you wouldn't have to, but you sort of knew you might have to, sooner or later. I am talking about buying the standard and sitting down to read it at least once. The brilliant news here is that since you have made it this far into this book, the standard likely won't hold any surprises for you. Reading the standard now should be a breeze for you, and all you really must do is to read it and see if anything pops out at you. If anything comes up that has you chocking on what you wrote in the SOPs earlier, you can still return and revise your processes without too much effort.

In writing this book, I have gone to great effort to distill the essence of the standard and zip the requirements into succinct common sense explanations. I have attempted to stay as generic as possible in doing this to avoid explanations that would only be applicable to some specific field of medical devices. Not knowing your specific business and product, I can't really have taken the interpretation to its ultimate goal for you. But you do know both your business and product. Now is the perfect time to read through the

DOI: 10.4324/9781003202868-19

standard as you have finished work on writing all the SOPs and have their content fresh in your mind. After you have read the standard, you can then take one final look at each SOP if you wish, polish the formatting if it needs polishing, and move on toward launching your QMS.

So go to the ISO website at www.iso.org/, find the ISO 13485 standard, buy it, and get comfortable on the sofa for a few hours. Alternatively, you could buy the companion guide to the standard, *ISO 13485:2016—Medical devices—A practical guide*, which is also published by ISO. I would, however, go for the standard itself, as only that contains all the parts of the standard, and you would probably not benefit that much from reading all the additional commentary in the companion guide. The guidebook is a good one, though, so may want to read it later if you want to dig a little deeper into one topic or another.

19.2 Observe the Template

The next step is to make sure your files all look correct and contain all the bells and whistles you want in an SOP. If you haven't already, check out Section 20 for the SOP template and the few additional items of housekeeping it suggests for your SOPs. You may already have done this at the start, or you may do it now. In any case, this is just an exercise in text formatting and possibly a chance for spotting some last remaining typos.

19.3 Clear Any Unnecessary Formatting

If you use the Track Changes feature in MS Word, or some similar tool, you may have leftover annotation in the file from the editing, formatting, and commenting you have done. Make sure any remaining comments are resolved as appropriate and clean out any unnecessary annotation before you lock the file. Note that in Word, you may not be seeing all the annotations made by the Track Changes feature unless you select the correct view. These hidden annotations may mess up the documents if you, for example, need to print them out later.

19.4 Update the Quality Manual

After you have all the SOPs shipshape, it is time to make sure also the quality manual is abreast of any changes you have made. Firstly, make sure the discussion under your section on processes (Section F in the manual) is up-to-date. If you have not made changes to my 12-SOP model, this should be the case already. Secondly, make sure you update the quality manual appendix on inter-process relationships to contain all the links between your SOPs. Remember that you can compile the table in the appendix with ease based on the lists of associated SOPs you have written in each SOP (see Section 20.3.4). Thirdly, make sure that the quality manual appendix on quality indicators is up-to-date and covers all your SOPs adequately. If you would like help on the indicators return to Section 5.2.3.

19.5 Checklist for SOPs

Subsequently, you will find a short second-pass checklist (Table 19.1) for your SOPs that takes you through the previous steps, and a few more, to ensure your SOPs don't sink on the launchpad. You should go through the checklist for each SOP separately.

Table 19.1 Checklist for Polishing Each SOP

Checklist

☐ Every topic suggested in the corresponding section of this book is addressed

☐ Any exclusions I made in this SOP are explained in the quality manual

☐ I have read the ISO 13485 standard, and I am still happy with this SOP

☐ I feel I know the regulatory requirements applicable to this SOP

☐ The format is according to the template inAppendix 3(see Section 20)

☐ All comments and automatic Track Changes annotations have been resolved

☐ Any forms, templates, and registries I call for in the SOP have been created

☐ All used forms, templates, and registers are listed in "Instructed documents"

☐ Any other SOPs referenced here are listed in "Associated documents"

☐ The writer, reviewer, and approver of the SOP all consider it ready as is

☐ The quality manual appendix on quality indicators is up-to-date

☐ The quality manual appendix on inter-process relationships is up-to-date

Once you feel confident you have ticked every box, it's time to move on.

19.6 That's It

You can now justifiably feel like you have accomplished something big. Finishing your work on the quality manual and the SOPs, along with all the appendices, forms, templates, and registries these may entail, you have done more than just finish the blueprint for your space station—you have, in fact, built all the parts you will need to survive out there.

Now all that remains is to prepare for the grand opening of that space station, launch it, and attend to running it every day from here on out. There is still work ahead, but the heavy lifting has now been done, and the remaining sections of this book will help you with all the rest. The next section, Section 20, addresses the templates you used earlier and some other template items, but as you have already looked at that either at the beginning or end of your work on the SOPs, here, the next section to look at now will be Section 21 on the topic of meetings and their minutes.

But before then, take a deep breath, sip some celebratory coffee, or maybe throw a few darts at a printout of my face for all the hoops I made you jump through in the previous sections. It will be smooth sailing from here.

Chapter 20

Writing Templates, Forms, Records, and Registries

Templates are a necessary part of your QMS even though the ISO 13485 standard says absolutely nothing about them. Without the use of templates, you would be hard-pressed to explain why your records look different for every employee evaluation, nonconformity, or SOP in your QMS. In practice, you must have templates and forms, but the way you go about creating them is what makes the difference.

20.1 What Is Expected

The unstated expectation in a QMS is that for reoccurring records, you have an understanding of what those documents need to include and look like. Your SOP will instruct what needs to happen in a process and how that is recorded as part of the output from a given process. The SOP could instruct all the sections or fields that go into the record, but this would be cumbersome when you could relay the same information more efficiently as reusable templates or forms. Worse still, without reusable templates, you would need to translate the instructions in the SOP to the records each time you create those. It makes a lot of sense to instead have a ready-to-use template to aid your record creation efforts.

The use of templates serves another important goal: as the representation of the information is more consistent from one instance to the next, it then becomes easier to compare records and observe any trends in their data.

DOI: 10.4324/9781003202868-20

This will seem self-evident, but consistency, traceability, and the ability to move back and forth in records while preserving some level of compatibility between the records created at different points in time is important in QMS. This is not always trivial to facilitate either.

The number one goal in creating records is to know what information to record but also consider how you change the templates and forms over time and why. You will never have the opportunity to go back and update all your earlier records to a new template, barring some existential threat to your organization, so it is important to think about how detailed you want to make the templates, how you build in necessary flexibility, and later also, why you would want to change that template you designed earlier.

Templates and forms are not rocket science, unless rocket science is what you happen to be recording using them. But it is very difficult to anticipate every little bit of information you will want to record on the form for use both now and later. Many of the practical considerations will only be revealed through real use of the template or the form. For this reason, I advocate trying to keep the templates and forms as simple as possible and allow flexibility in how additional information may then be added when using the form. This way, you won't spin your wheels trying to anticipate all aspects of using the template or the form from here to eternity, you won't be making it harder to use by requiring nice-to-have extra information, and you won't be losing out on unanticipated valuable information that it doesn't yet happen to accommodate. The forms and templates will get better over time and meet their goals in increasingly user-friendly ways, so this is one aspect of QMS I would not try to polish too far before the launch and actual use.

20.2 A General Template for QMS Documents

The first template you will want to create really has nothing to do with your QMS in the first place: it is the letterhead or basic document template for your organization. This template sets the fonts and font sizes for all your document-based communications and will probably also display your logo and brand colors in some way. The basic template is, in essence, your look, however you define that.

The QMS adds information on top of the basic company template. You will want to make use of the document header and the footer to display key identification information, like the ID, version, and name. Having page numbers is also generally a good idea in case you need to refer to a particular page of the document or just accidentally drop the stack of papers on the floor and need to recompose it and yourself quickly. Line numbers may be practical for some documents (code printouts, draft documents under revision, etc.), but for most documents, you would not include those.

Any standard word editor, Microsoft Word included, will let you tweak these properties of your document. Selecting fonts and colors is not alchemy, but it is quite important for the look you want to project and also for the amount of printer toner and paper you want to use in the coming years. Some years ago, a 14-year-old kid by the name of Suvir Mirchandani figured out that changing the font used on documents by the whole US government could lead to real savings in toner expenses. He calculated the savings as 370 million USD per year, without changing any of the content. The calculations have since been challenged on account of governments buying toner in bulk and perhaps having to use a larger font size for a slimmer, more economical font, but intuitively, the boy was completely right: choosing a font and a font size will influence your resource use and not just how pretty or professional your documents look. Choose the balance between squinting your eyes and flipping through pages and pages of content that best works for you. Also, make sure to print out a test sample of documents created using your template—things will look slightly different on the screen and in printed form. Choosing Times New Roman 10pt or Verdana 10pt should be good starting points for most documents; choosing 20pt Webdings or Comic Sans will earn you some raised eyebrows and quite rightly so.

Designing your general document template is not a high-stakes job, but it can be fun and rewarding, so take an hour or so and design an efficient, clean template if you can. If your organization already has one, take that as the basis and make sure it includes the necessary document and version IDs.

In addition to the header and the footer, you will also want to design a document issuance record to go on, for example, the top of the first page. This record can be styled like a table and should contain easily readable entries for the name of the document, its ID, the intended audience for the document, and a date for the issuance and/or completion of the document. You may want some of this information here or you may want to leave it to the metadata in your document archival system. Some more advanced document archival systems may even be able to stamp such information onto the documents and records themselves. Table 20.1 shows an example.

For most documents, it is enough to make a record of the what (document name and ID), who (responsible person), and when (date). For some special documents, such as SOPs, you may want to also include the

Table 20.1 Example Document Information Record

Document Information

Document name	**Sheltering during the Monsoon**
Document ID	123456789
Responsible person	Raymond Babbitt
Date:	YYYY-MM-DD
Audience:	Quality management and R&D

audience as a partial answer to the requirement of identifying who should be interested in or affected by the document. My one tip here is that you should think twice before using the date field for the issuance date: this may be doable for paper-based documentation systems, but for electronic documents with electronic signatures, it may become an extra hurdle to edit the date into the document before you sign it on the same date—particularly if some signatories are then delayed while others have already signed. This is an example of an avoidable mess. Some document management systems may be able to embed the date for you, but check on this beforehand. A simple solution here would be to use a completion date instead of an issuance date in all cases not involving your quality manual, SOPs, and working instructions.

20.3 Template for the Quality Manual and SOPs

The first purpose-specific templates you will want to create based on your general document template are the templates for your quality manual and SOPs. The same basic requirements from the standard apply to both of these controlled documents (see SOP-1 on the control of documents), and except for some differences in the actual content, the same template could be used for both. The look and feel, too, from your general document template will be directly applicable here. The header, footer, and document issuance record are usable as is. You may have neglected to consider some levels of headings in defining the styles for your general document template, but that is an easy fix here. I would now make sure I have heading styles defined up to level 7, and update the general document template, too, if necessary.

The structure of the two documents is presented in Table 20.2.

Looking at the table, it is apparent that most of the sections—document issuance record, authorities record, purpose of the document, references,

Table 20.2 Comparison of Document Structures

Quality Manual	SOPs
■ Document issuance record ■ Authorities record ■ Purpose of the document	■ Document issuance record ■ Authorities record ■ Purpose of the document
■ Organization overview ■ QMS overview ■ Key roles ■ Products ■ Processes	■ Associated SOPs ■ Instructed documents ■ The process ■ Responsibilities
■ References (if any) ■ Appendices (if any) ■ Version history	■ References (if any) ■ Appendices (if any) ■ Version history

appendices, and version history—are shared by both documents. Each document then has a few more sections in between that are specific to each and carry the core of their contents. Most of the items for the quality manual were already discussed in great detail in Section 5.2. The only two sections not covered in that earlier discussion are the document issuance record and the authorities record, which will be discussed here next. These two fields were left out of the previous discussion so that we could, at the time, dive into the meat of the manual and the SOPs more quickly without yet worrying about the technicalities. The time to put in the templates is now.

Let's look at the new sections one at a time. The discussion here is structured around the outline of the SOP. After the discussion here, you will find my example templates in Appendix 2 (Quality Manual) and Appendix 3 (SOP).

20.3.1 Document Issuance Record

The document issuance record was introduced in Section 20.2. Here, the use of the audience field of the record provides the first point of distinction from the general document template. In response to Clause 4.1.2a, which requires you to determine how your processes are applied throughout your organization, I would now make sure both templates make use of the audience field in the document issuance record table discussed earlier. In assigning the audiences, use the functions you defined in the organization overview (Section B of your quality manual).

20.3.2 Authorities Record

For your SOPs and quality manual, it is crucial to know that your instructed process has been followed in writing, reviewing, and issuing those documents. Make sure the necessary roles are now represented as signatures in the document itself per the process you wrote in SOP-1 previously. If you didn't make any drastic edits in SOP-1, the roles you will want to show up here are: writer, reviewer, and approver. Each role should come with the name of the person, their function within your organization, and the date of signing.

If you are going to use some digital signature system that does not alter the look of the page when printed, I might add a note of this. Note that, especially in the US, you should consult your regulatory expert to make sure your chosen electronic signature solution meets the applicable regulatory requirements (e.g., US CFR 21 Part 11).

An example authorities table might look like the example in Table 20.3:

The Authorities record is not required by the standard, but the information on who wrote/approved/issued the document and when is, in practice, required. Note that you could also have multiple people as writers and reviewers, but that the writer should not approve or issue the document they themselves wrote. In general, having documents or records created and issued by a single person are a red flag, which may be acceptable for some records but will almost always raise questions.

20.3.3 Purpose of the Document

As already discussed in Section 5.2 for the manual, this is a short, to-the-point statement on the goal of the document. When you then produce this record during an audit, or when an employee is browsing through SOPs to find the instructions they were looking for, reading this description will say

Table 20.3 Example Authorities Record

Authorities	Written by	Reviewed by	Approved by
Authority Name Signature	Quality manager Raymond Babbitt	Management representative Charles Babbitt	Management representative Charles Babbitt
	Note: In place of handwritten signatures, this document may be signed electronically by each signee within the QMS software.		
Date	YYYY-MM-DD	YYYY-MM-DD	YYYY-MM-DD

if this is indeed the document needed. This field is not required by the standard, but you will get good use out of this field.

20.3.4 Associated SOPs

For me, this is the most interesting element to include in an SOP in addition to the instruction for the process itself. The associated SOPs can be represented as a table neatly listing together all the other processes referenced by the particular SOP. This information is compiled from the actual process instruction later in the same document, but I have wanted to display the table here at the top of the document because it provides a convenient list of prerequisites to implement all aspects of this particular SOP. The table is particularly useful when figuring out SOP linkages as part of document review.

This table not only shows you where to go for more information regarding some interface of the SOP, but it also provides a practical overview of the links this process has with any other processes. My tip here is to compile this table after you have finished the instructions for the process in the SOP and then use all these tables from all the SOPs to compile your matrix of inter-process relationships for the appendix to the quality manual (see Section 20.3.6). Knowing the network of your processes is required by the standard, and this table gives you the keys to that knowledge via one easily maintained mechanism. When you later make changes to this table, you can then easily update the appendix of the quality manual.

The table should be simple but contain the document IDs of the SOPs. I would just include the document name and the ID in a list form. Any other information you might add will be extra, and if that extra information only adds maintenance overhead and not utility, just leave it out. I would be especially weary of adding SOP version information as keeping that up-to-date will get to be a hassle.

20.3.5 Instructed Documents

The SOP may make use of templates, forms, registers, and working instructions. Those documents, too, must be part of the consideration during any revision of the SOP, say, as part of your periodic document review. For this reason, it makes sense to maintain a list of documents instructed by this SOP. The main function of this table is to provide you a clear overview of what documents to also revise when you are revising this particular SOP.

20.3.6 The Process

This section contains the actual meat of the SOP. This is what you were working on in the previous sections of this book when writing each SOP. You can divide the discussion here into any further subsections you want to organize your instruction for the process. The standard does not impose any structure here.

In the process instruction, it may be beneficial to use some text markup to make the sea of text more readily approachable, both during real-world use and audits. I have a habit of italicizing document IDs used in the text and underlining expressions of time limits and deadlines in the text. I also capitalize key roles to make them stand out from the text more easily. If you want to get fancy with formatting your text, you may consider using wider margins to provide index words and other relevant bookmarks for faster access. Before you get too fancy, though, also think about what it will take to maintain your snazzy design during the upcoming document review. Remember also that you will probably be using text search a lot in any case, so it may not be worth your while to make too much of an effort in creating keywords or visual bookmarking within the SOPs.

I would recommend focusing on the actual content of your SOPs first, and then once you are happy with the content, work more on the presentation of that content. For now, it is enough to have these layout and highlighting options at the back of your mind, and then return to them later if needed.

20.3.7 Responsibilities

The responsibilities table is intended as a convenient way of looking up who is responsible for what inside the process. This can be formatted as a table summing up the responsibilities instructed in the text in order of appearance in the text. Alternatively, I might consider organizing the table by roles (making it easier to see what function each role plays in the SOP) or by function (making it easier to see who are involved in preparing work items and who are responsible for approving them, for example). This type of a table is not required by the standard, and it is a bit of a hassle to maintain, so consider carefully if including it makes sense for you.

20.3.8 References (If Any)

This is a list of the external sources referenced in your SOP. This may include items like guidance papers, technical reports, and standards. You are not required to have any references, but if you do use references to inform your work on the SOP, it is a good idea to include them here for letting your reader understand where you are coming from and to ensure the references will be observed during future revisions.

The usual techniques in using references apply here, including the use of credible sources and using persistent URLs when referring to online sources (also consider saving a snapshot of such files so that the information will be available 10–20 years from now). When deciding which references to include, use judgment to assess how important they are and only include good references that add to understanding the instruction in your SOP. Don't expect all your readers to read all the references. Don't create problems for yourself by listing only peripherally relevant sources you would then need to observe for the years to come.

20.3.9 Appendices (If Any)

This is a list of the appendices you have created for your document. You may include the appendices as separate files in your document archival system or append them to the end of your document. You are not required to have appendices or that certain type of information always must go into appendices, but if using appendices makes sense for your QMS, feel free to do so. I find that maintaining appendices as separate identified files makes it easier to refer to them as needed and also makes the revision of the appendices more straightforward. Remember to also ensure that your document ID scheme covers appendices.

20.3.10 Version History

The standard requires that changes made to your documents are identified. It is a smart idea to use version management for all your documents and records, but even if your version management system saves each version of the files for later comparison, this is not enough for documents. Your auditors may want to see discussion of the changes made between document versions, and this is also a good idea for the other readers of your documents. Here this is required.

A major reason why I hate the idea of just refreshing document versions to obtain new time stamps, besides the fact that it is pointless, is that it causes extra headache for any users of such documents who all must figure out how, if at all, the document in question has changed. For this reason, including a straightforward version history table with a meaningful human-readable description of the changes makes a lot of sense. Remember also that once you start revising your SOPs and the quality manual, you will also need to brief or train your staff on the changes. There, too, having a concise description of the changes will come in handy.

An example of version history table might look like Table 20.4.

In the previous example, the version numbering should conform to the version numbers used by your document archival system, the date should match some internationally accepted format, the initials should be of the person who updated the version information (see SOP-1), and the description of the changes should be short and refer to the changed sections by their numbers.

A further option I have toyed with over the years is having a separate "What's new" description of the changes. This could be a little bit longer than the telegram-like account of changes used in the version history table, and it could provide a more easily readable description of the changes that could then be used in training or briefing the changes to your staff. Unlike the version history table, this section would not accumulate changes over time but, instead, offer commentary on the very latest round of changes only. The earlier "What's new" sections would, of course, be visible in the earlier versions of your document. Think about this option, and if it makes sense for you, implement it here.

20.4 Forms

Forms are, in essence, templates with a more controlled structure and perhaps limited scope of use. You can use any form editor you like (e.g., Microsoft Word) to create forms. When first setting out to develop a form, I would look at content over layout, build in necessary extensibility (flexibility in adding more information than strictly called for by the form fields), and then later work on polishing the layout and perhaps using some automated

Table 20.4 Example Version History

Version	Date	Initials	Description of changes (including section numbers)
1.0	YYYY-MM-DD	SR	First version of the document.
2.0	YYYY-MM-DD	JR	Updated launch codes in Section 4.2. Clarified wording in Section 4.5. New Section 4.7 on postlaunch protocols.

features to assist in the use of the form (remember that you may need to validate the use of such features).

20.5 Records

Records will be instructed by their associated SOPs, which may also dictate what fields and what information those records should carry. In the early days of QMS development, I would worry more about creating the content and getting real-world experience on gathering that content, and only then worry about creating templates for any particular record. Of course, the records you frequently use will jump ahead of the queue when deciding what records should get templates first.

20.6 Registries

Registries are optional and so are templates for them. How you create a register template will depend on the software you use for registries. If you use a program like Microsoft Excel, this will be like creating your general document template. If you use a database engine, creating a template or a schema for that may make sense.

The fields you will need in your register will be instructed by each associated SOP, but some fields may be the same, particularly for register-level metadata, such as who maintains that register and for what audience. Using a proper database engine you are familiar with will give you the most functionality, but using a popular spreadsheet program, like Excel, is a good entry-level alternative for a small business. With Excel, you have a solid platform to work off and have options for formatting, sorting, and filtering your content for any particular need—and most importantly, you also get straightforward ways of later exporting your data into, for example, XML, CSV, and some other software. Depending on your choice of QMS software, you may find that the software has a usable implementation for registers that you can validate and use to your ends comfortably. If not, Excel is a good choice for now.

Chapter 21

Writing Meeting Agendas and Minutes

There is really nothing new to writing meeting minutes in the QMS: all the usual practicalities involved are what you would expect from running any business. The agendas for the meetings also work the same, but there are a few items to cover that you would not typically cover in a non-QMS setting. This section introduces you to how you can use minutes as part of your QMS and how to get the most out of them.

21.1 What Is Expected

The standard requires you to ensure that appropriate internal communication processes are established and that communication takes place regarding the effectiveness of the QMS (Clause 5.5.3, SOP-7). This means appropriate and efficient communication is in place between the necessary functions of your organization as you defined in the organizational structure in your quality manual. At the very least, you should ensure meetings of your top management take place and the minutes are retained. You should also ensure communication within Quality, R&D, and Sales—and between these functions and the top management.

If you have a larger team than the handful of people you are likely to have in an early-stage startup or if your teams work very independently but still need to synchronize somehow, you may want to consider defining liaisons between your teams. That is how International Standardization Teams also work and for a good reason. It is important that information flows between your Management, Quality, Production, and Sales Teams. In a small team, I would think about how I could leverage instant messaging for real-time communication on different channels and consider short weekly traffic meetings for teams to keep track of the progress of important work items. I would be wary of having multiple teams sit in the same meetings hours on end just so that I could say everybody should have heard something that they likely won't have heard or understood correctly out of sheer boredom. Full-team meetings can be both a waste of your staff's time and a hidden drain on your resources. Amazon's former CEO Jeff Bezos reportedly had a rule that every internal team meeting should be small enough that it can be fed with two pizzas. Depending on your team's pizza consumption, that may be right on the money, or shoot over it, but having unnecessary meetings or leaving staff members feeling that they have to sit in unnecessary meetings does not have an upshot for quality management or the job satisfaction of your staff. Some meetings are, of course, required even if they are hated, but those should be precious few.

However many meetings you end up having, keep adequate minutes of the key meetings. In some cases, the meeting may be held to create some specific report; in which case, minutes may not be needed if the progress on the report already says everything you want. In most other situations, keeping good, to-the-point, and comprehensive-enough minutes will be invaluable to you going forward. Not only will minutes let you record the who, what, when, and why of your work, but they will help ensure you are all in agreement about where you are. The minutes may be the ship's log that is pulled out during audits, just like at that trial at the end of *The Bounty*, but more likely, they will be the closest thing to a diary you have to keep you happy and healthy on your small QMS island, just like Robinson Crusoe. That said, don't write your minutes to posterity or to win the Pulitzer. Keep it simple.

21.2 Pen to Paper

You may find that the same agenda, perhaps based on the agenda for the management review, can be adopted for many of these meetings. I have personally encouraged this with the goal of increasing compatibility between functions and ensuring that the right types of information bubble up in the organization as effortlessly as possible. If some item is not needed on some level or if some other item is needed in its place, you should, of course, modify the agenda as makes the most sense to you. Having the same item on multiple different function levels does not mean that the item is dealt with the same level of attention to detail on each level or that each function treats the item in the exact same way. Starting off with a single structure for all the team meetings gives you a good starting point for compatibility. This I have found to also work well in practice.

In practice, you may find that the Quality Management Team minutes are the most detailed for many of the items you are most interested in your QMS. The Management Team will make decisions and analyze the status of various top-level items within the most important topics, but it cannot go into the same level of detailed discussion on quality as the Quality Management Team can.

I have often found it convenient to refer back to older Quality Management Team documents to get more insight into one topic or another that has been addressed at our company over a specific period. I have used the Quality Management Team minutes as the atlas to our QMS or as the veritable captain's log on QMS matters. This has worked quite well, especially if you apply a simple ID scheme to the meetings, such as running numbering from your very first meeting onward. Your document management system may also help you greatly in searching, indexing, and navigating your electronic minutes.

Table 21.1 shows an example of how roughly the same agenda can vary between some of the key functions of your organization and what topics might be discussed. The common agenda items (e.g., the opening of the meeting) have been omitted from this table but are included in the example minutes in Appendix 4.

If you are now setting out to build your QMS, I recommend getting started with these meetings even before the launch of your QMS. This way, you have a record of your activities and decisions heading up to the launch, and a tried and tested framework of meetings to keep up once you are running the QMS.

Table 21.1   Comparison of Meeting Agendas

Item	Management	Quality	R&D	Sales and Marketing
Operational status	quality policy and objectives, QMS, and product status	QMS, document review, suppliers, and products	products, tool validation, and work allocation	products, sales, promotional material, and events

(Continued)

Table 21.1   (Continued)

Item	Management	Quality	R&D	Sales and Marketing
Monitoring and measurement	quality indicators	quality indicators	quality indicators and project management data	quality indicators and marketing data
Customer feedback	trends and complaint handling performance	feedback handling and complaint handling	maintenance activities	customer visits, and passive and active feedback
Audits	expected schedule and audit reports	upcoming internal audits and expected external audits	-	-
CAPA and observations	status and performance	nonconformity handling	bug fixes	customer communication
Risk management	risk reports for products and processes	upcoming guidance and standards, and risk control	risk control and risk identification	risk control and risk identification
Assessment of resources	funding, recruitment, staff, and premises	internal and external resources and areas of improvement	Resources and special working environments	resources, marketing budget, campaigns, and trade fairs
Reporting to authorities and notified bodies	reports needed or made	reports in progress, reports made, and PSUR	-	-

Chapter 22

QMS Software Validation

This is a little above and beyond to cover in this book, but since validating the software you use in your QMS is required by the standard, I will cover the basics here. Software validation is one of the processes you will have covered in Section 9, so do make sure you follow your own instructed process here.

22.1 What Is Expected

The standard requires you to perform validation of the software used in your QMS. What is more, Clause 4.1.6 requires that you perform the validation both prior to initial use and, as appropriate, after changes to the software or its use. In other words, software validation is required now before you launch and, later, if the software is updated or how you use the software changes. The first requirement, validation before use, is why you are reading this section here before the launch.

Having to validate the software may sound like a dull extra hurdle to cross, but if you think about how difficult it might be to change the software later when you already have records stored using the software and it is in use, it really is in your best interest here to make sure you like the software and are content using it for the foreseeable future. Changing your QMS software later will be like changing the cladding on your space station once you are already inhabiting that station: it can be done, but it will be a mission-critical activity. Here and now, before launching the QMS, things are easier, and you can still pull the emergency break without a major Houston-we-have-a-problem moment.

The standard also requires that your validation effort is proportionate to the risk associated with the use of the software and that, as always, records are maintained (Clause 4.2.5). You will have defined your approach to software validation in Section 9 when writing your SOP for infrastructure management (SOP-3, if you followed my suggestion earlier). Make sure you now follow your own instructed process here.

The needs for your QMS software are set by the entirety of the standard: the QMS activities and the QMS data you choose to use the software for. This means, for example, handling feedback, CAPA activities, and the whole life cycle of your device as covered by the standard. You may thus have one piece of software or several different programs catering to the previous needs, but realize that you should treat any software you use to accomplish these sorts of tasks, or any tasks called for by the standard, as part of your QMS software. In effect, you will want to have a process in place for assessing the need to validate any software you use, not just the main QMS software. The same is also expected of software you use in product realization (see SOP-10). This infrastructure SOP you wrote earlier is where you address these matters.

If you decide that validation of some piece of software is needed, as it is in the case of the QMS software, the critical functions to achieve with the validation are to demonstrate that a) the way that the software is used (its application) is suitable and b) the outcome meets your requirements. These are the two big questions for you to investigate in validating the QMS software here. For planning the validation project, I suggest writing a validation plan that addresses the following topics:

■ The selection of the software
■ The intended use given for the software by its manufacturer
■ The reliability of the manufacturer
■ The maintenance plan given by the manufacturer (e.g., update policy)
■ Your intended use of the software
■ The risks involved in your use of the software
■ Your requirements for the software
■ Your tests needed to check that your requirements are fulfilled

After the plan is approved, you run the tests defined in it and write a validation report. If you can convince yourself and everyone else, too, that you are using the software as intended by its manufacturer and are meeting all your requirements safely, you will have a validated software for your QMS.

22.2 What If We Already Use the Software but It's Not Validated?

If you haven't yet launched your QMS, it is now time to attend to its validation. If you have launched the QMS, the situation is more problematic, but even then, the basic idea is that not everything is lost. Life happens, right? If this is the case, you should talk with a quality management consultant and make sure you have a sound idea for getting yourself out of the creek. You then take stock of what impact this validation delay may have had, plan accordingly, and execute on your plan to get back on the road. It will not be that surprising you ended up here if you are only now building up your QMS, but the more time that has elapsed between now and when you started using the software, the more issues you may face.

22.3 When Should We Revalidate?

The standard requires you to redo the validation when the software changes or if how you use the software changes. In practice, there will be several different types of changes to the software: some changes will be security patches; others, new features; and yet others, changes to features you already use. You will have to keep an eye on how the manufacturer of the software makes these updates available. You will hopefully have already had a serious look at this when going over their update policy in creating your validation plan. The update policy hopefully makes a distinction between security updates and feature updates so that you address these both as you need to, and also explains the version numbering scheme used by the manufacturer so that you can tap into what they think are minor and major updates.

I would recommend tracking the changes as they become available, making a well-founded decision when to revalidate and revalidating for any significant updates. Hopefully, you are able to agree with the manufacturer that no major updates are installed without your prior consent. This is particularly relevant for Software-as-a-Service (SaaS) solutions. You will want to keep records of your deliberations and make sure that you don't have to run the full validation project with every possible test for every minor software update.

I recommend keeping a log of updates installed so that you can easily recall the version installed, who installed it, when it was installed, and what changed in the update. The last part includes making use of the change log provided by the manufacturer and also your organization's assessment on the impact of the changes as well as any revalidation activities or follow-up you may judge necessary.

The point here is that you will want to install the latest updates to keep the tools safe, but you don't want to let just any update go by and start affecting your work without due assessment. You will have to find a sensible, safe, and practical solution that meets the needs of your organization and is appropriate to the risks associated with any particular software you use. I also recommend keeping a separate registry of the validation status of all the tools you have in use.

Chapter 23

The Launch

Your spaceship is on the launchpad, the press is gathering, and the family members are holding tightly onto their hats on the viewing platform. But before you initiate the countdown, there are a few ducks to get in a row for a smooth launch. This section prepares you for the launch of your QMS and lets you then turn the key to finally clear the tower. QMS orbit here we come.

23.1 What Is Expected

The standard does not tell you what you need to do to launch your QMS. It only tells you what you must have in place once running the QMS. Even this is subject to debate, as some processes, you will run a little later as the needs arise, but some other processes, you must have a solid grip on from the zero hour.

The fundamental expectation is that you have, for now, a feature-complete working QMS to fire up at launch. The QMS does not yet have to be certified; in fact, it would be next to impossible to have it certified before launch, as you wouldn't yet have any records based on the processes of your QMS. The launch itself is a little more than a time stamp, a date and time of birth, but a lot goes into making sure it is a healthy birth. You need to secure consent within your organization to launch the QMS, plan for the launch, inform and train your organization to expect the launch, and know what to do after the launch. You and your organization should then be ready to receive any of the triggers you have defined in your SOPs—the feedback, notices, audits, and nonconformities, to name just some of the most prominent items—from the launch on.

DOI: 10.4324/9781003202868-23

The following subsections will walk you through the critical steps of the launch.

23.2 Planning for the Launch

All right, you have decided that you have a viable version 1.0 of your QMS ready. You should now make sure your QMS Development Team and your top management also share this view. There are no mandated reviews involved, but you should document the consensus somehow, for example, in meeting minutes. After you have secured a permission to launch and have a projected launch date, you will want to make sure your staff also knows to expect the QMS. You will want to organize staff training on the QMS before or very soon after the launch. Let's look at these steps one at a time subsequently.

23.2.1 What Reviews Need to Be Done?

This is up to your organization. Once you are satisfied that the QMS is good to go, you launch it. The standard does not establish specific reviews to perform here—it only implies that your whole organization is behind the QMS. The management of your organization and the team developing the QMS need to be content with the launch going forward, but this can be recorded in many ways, as reports, minutes, or—to play devil's advocate—even the lack of opposition as you are not yet running your QMS. You should, of course, heed what happened to Keanu Reeves at the end of his dealings with Al Pacino in that film and not leave consent hanging in the air.

Most likely, you have already set up a framework of periodic Management Team meetings, and those meetings have tracked the progress of the QMS with a keen eye. Similarly, the Quality Management Team developing the QMS may have had periodic meetings, and the minutes of those meeting will contain more detailed information on the maturing of the QMS toward the launch. Both meetings have minutes, and these are a good place for making the decision to launch.

23.2.2 Who Needs to Give Their Consent to Launch?

Unless you have specified differently in any of the arrangements you have made, the Management Team and the team developing the QMS should give their consent in one way or another. The Management Team can be represented by the management representative, but you will want the CEO also in the loop. The team developing the QMS is most likely the same as your Quality Management Team, and this could thus be represented by your quality manager.

23.2.3 Who Needs to Be Informed of the Launch?

You are not yet ISO 13485–certified, and launching your QMS doesn't make you so. As a result, there is no specific need yet to inform your future certification body or notified body of your QMS launch. It does, of course, make perfect sense to talk with these authorities to find out when they could come and audit you for certification, if you have not already done so.

If you are only aiming at using the standard and not getting certified to it, you will, of course, shout out to the world immediately after launch and announce your happy occasion. Be careful not to make it sound like certification, though.

23.3 Initial Staff-Wide Training

"Once you build it, they will come" goes the saying. This holds true, but it is not just about opening the bullpen and letting the bulls wander into the china shop. You must organize training on the big, beautiful QMS you have developed. And not just for some members of the staff but all members of the staff who are expected to work under the QMS or whose work could affect quality or product conformity. You can't expect employees to run processes they are not trained in, and the standard doesn't let you do that either.

When my Quality Management Team organized staff-wide initial training, we gave everyone access to the QMS documents (quality manual, SOPs, and templates), briefed them on accessing the documents using the electronic QMS platform, and then organized a mandatory two-day training session where we taught QMS basics and went through each SOP. The training also featured an introduction to QMS given by an external quality expert and several Q and A sessions (these also included the presence of our quality consultants), and it ended with an exam on the matters covered during the training. Questions and feedback were encouraged all through the training, and a separate anonymous feedback form was handed out and collected after the exam.

In preparation for the two-day training event, we prepared PowerPoint presentations to cover each SOP, as well as QMS fundamentals on why and how quality management is done, and how it affects everyone at the company. The PowerPoint presentations were also made available to the staff for later reference.

How you design your initial training is up to you. The standard, again, gives you no specific requirements on how you carry out this training, but you must ensure that every participant is trained on all the processes relevant to them and on the purpose and value of QMS, and that you are satisfied with the outcome of the training before the employees go off to do their work.

Section 24 discusses training in more detail.

23.4 Readiness for Contact with the Outside World

In your SOPs, you have stated your willingness to interface with the outside world and, among other things, be ready to receive customer feedback and regulatory inquiries. You will know, based on your circumstances, how likely each of these are once you launch your QMS, but be prepared to run the processes you have defined as you have defined them after you turn the key. Once you turn on the neon "Open" sign, expect some foot traffic.

23.5 Idea of Activities to Run After Launch

Make a plan for what processes to run right after the launch. Go through your SOPs and identify those processes you could get started with right away. Training is a good bet here, but you can also get started with, for example, supplier management (SOP-5), regulatory follow-up (SOP-11), infrastructure maintenance (SOP-3), and process monitoring (SOP-2). If you are a startup, product development (SOP-10) will also be a good bet, as your product was probably wanted yesterday.

The standard does not give you any launch order for processes. Instead, look to your circumstances, the interrelationships between processes, and their relative prioritizations, and make at least an informal plan on how to get going. After the launch takes place, you will want experiences and evidence on all the processes in short order. You will need that evidence for getting audited and certified.

23.6 Final Testing Before Launch

Now is the last time you can test-drive your QMS, create test records, and still delete them as you see fit. After you turn the key, all document and record management will take place as prescribed in the QMS. Be careful, though, that you don't accidentally change some setting or delete some intended document in your QMS. After you feel that you have done all the testing you need before the launch, it is time to go through your final checklist and get out the launch key.

23.7 Final Checklist for Launch

The following checklist (Table 23.1) is provided for your convenience.

Table 23.1 Final Checklist for Launch

Checklist
☐ **My quality manual and SOPs are ready** The quality manual and SOPs have been reviewed and are ready to be issued.
☐ **I know the regulatory requirements applicable to me** If you haven't already, check out the Z annexes of the standard (for the EU) or other regulatory guidance available for your jurisdiction.
☐ **My electronic QMS is set up** All my QMS documents have been loaded into the QMS software. The software is validated, and all accounts and access permissions have been set.
☐ **I know my schedule going forward** The schedule is not yet issued, but you know how you will run the document review mechanism and, at least roughly, when you plan to have your internal audit, management review, and after these, any certification audit.
☐ **I know my plan for initial QMS training to the whole staff**
☐ **The CEO and the Management Team have given their consent to launch**
☐ **I feel ready to turn the key** Ultimately, this is the most important question before you turn the key. If you feel ready, the odds are that you have turned every stone and covered every question.
Once you feel confident you have ticked every box, it's time to me on.

23.8 Start Your Engine

After you are happy that all systems are ready to go, it is time to turn the key. But what key is that? There probably isn't some plexiglass-covered switch you can flip or two sets of missile keys you can turn to mark the occasion. You may open a bottle of champagne, though, and record the time and the date your QMS went live.

Most likely, your substitute for turning the key is issuing all the QMS documents you want to launch with: the quality manual, SOPs, forms, templates, appendices, and any related working instructions these may have. You do this in your QMS software, or similar, by marking the documents as issued via the process instructed in SOP-1. After this small clickfest is over, you can take a deep breath and let the gravity of what you have done sink in. Everything you do from here on out must be in accordance with your new QMS.

Unlike the Skynet system of the *Terminator* films, the QMS does not live by itself, so now that you have turned the engine on, make sure you go somewhere using it. There is a great scene in the film *A Night at the Roxbury* where the two principal characters tear open brand-new calendars and compare dates to settle on a time for getting together even though both calendars are empty. A brand-new QMS is a bit like that: you need to start running it after the launch to actually get where you want to go and to have the records of that journey you need in the audits.

It is a good bet that the first item on your list is writing up a record, such as the meeting minutes of the Quality Management Team or the Management Team, to record the launch and some internal announcement on the happy occasion. Also, on the agenda for the same meeting, and reflected in its minutes, is organizing staff-wide training on the QMS. It is a good thing you planned ahead for that. When now organizing that training, make sure you review the results of the training adequately, record the final assessments you make, and then get on with the rest of your QMS business. Then return to the plan you made in Section 23.5. That time is now.

Chapter 24

Training

Cue the training montage from Rocky? *Training is not as easy as gluing together some close-ups of people doing push-ups and running on the beach to a pulse-raising power anthem. Organizing, running, and wrapping up training takes effort, but it can also be fun. In fact, an enjoyable training will be better at achieving its goals than a dreary by-the-numbers run-through of some processes.*

24.1 What Is Expected

Training will be a constant part of running your QMS as new employees come in, employee and employer needs evolve, and time passes. Training is probably the first activity you will need to run around the time of launching your QMS. There is no reason you couldn't do initial training on the QMS before its launch, but there is every reason to attend to training very soon after you launch your QMS. Training is covered here after the launch for just that reason.

Organizing the initial training on your QMS was briefly addressed in Section 23.3. The initial QMS training is an internal training on QMS-related matters and, thus, addressed in Sections 24.3 and 24.4 in the following. It would be odd to have external training as your initial QMS training, although if you decided to outsource your QMS and quality manager, maybe that, too, could happen, and it would be entirely unacceptable to only do briefing as the first introduction of your staff to QMS. The discussion in this section will address briefing, internal training, and external training to add

DOI: 10.4324/9781003202868-24

some meat around these concepts and to help you address all your future training needs in accordance with SOP-4.

Personally, I enjoy organizing training to my staff. It is occasionally hard to find the time needed to develop or update the training material, and it is not exactly always fun to evaluate the exams. Still, most parts of the training are great fun. I especially enjoy conversing with my staff about some specific QMS matters, hearing their thoughts, and seeing what aspects maybe cause friction and what could perhaps be improved going forward. The questions I get asked are perhaps the most valuable form of feedback that I can then use in organizing future training events and fine-tuning the QMS processes discussed. Similarly, the notes I get on SOPs because of the trainings, even if these sometimes are just about typos that have slipped into the text, show me my staff have taken the training seriously.

The point here is that trainings do not have to be a mundane run-of-the-mill chore. Instead, they can be mutually informative events and, in fact, a great indicator on the health of your QMS and organization. In many ways, training can be as insightful on your QMS as audits but much more relaxed to run and usually without actual nonconformities to handle.

The final point to make here before we dive into types of training is that as you are now running your QMS, make sure to follow your instructed process (see SOP-4) and create the necessary records. Remember to record what was taught, who taught it, and to whom—and crucially, also assess the effectiveness of the training. You will want to do all this for assessing the current status at your organization, but the reason I point out the importance of records here is that after a long development cycle of building the QMS, it may be easy to forget you are now actually running it.

24.2 Briefing

Briefing is the simplest form of training, although you could just call it communication in some cases. Briefing may be formal or informal, but you should achieve the outcome you wanted and you should be able to record the briefing.

I have personally been successful in implementing a bulletin on QMS-related news for the staff published at relevant points in time, such as after the monthly document review has concluded or when we have results from audits or other news to report. I publish the bulletin using my QMS software so that it automatically gets a document ID that can be referred to, its distribution is straightforward, and I can ask for read receipts in a systematic way. I also look for questions and comments on the bulletin so I know that it is achieving its goal.

24.3 Internal and External Training

In principle, there are two types of training: the training your organization runs itself and the training organized by other actors where your staff attend as participants.

For internal training, you need to specify carefully what the training is on, who gave it, when, and how it went compared to your requirements. This can all be addressed in, for example, the Quality Management Team meeting minutes where you plan and, later, review the training. Make sure the minutes, the training material, any exam results, and participant records can all be connected to each other as needed.

As for external training organized by other actors, if this is not a high-stakes training course for you that is crucial to achieving staff competence, you just attend and pay the participation fee. No documentation is required, but in practice, you will want to retain records and, particularly, any certificates awarded so that you can use these to track and to prove staff qualifications. Using the records in audits is, of course, secondary to allowing your staff to better themselves and to learn new things that may serve your organization well in the future. Your SOP for the management of human resources (SOP-4) may specify requirements for planning attendance and keeping or reviewing records, so make sure you follow your own process.

In general, external training courses, webinars, and even training via forums, such as Coursera and edX, can be a powerful way of getting access to new ideas and skills—and do so in a cost-effective way. I have personally attended dozens and dozens of training courses organized by, for example, universities, standardization bodies, notified bodies, consultancies, and various other expert organizations. The topics of these courses have ranged from standards and regulations to legal and reimbursement issues to broad-ranging topics, such as the assessment of clinical studies and the history of the FDA. I have completed hundreds, if not thousands, of hours of training, and most of it has been beneficial to me for understanding my work. Don't just attend trainings to get the certificates, though. There are plenty of courses and events out there, so find the ones that really interest you.

24.4 QMS Training and Non-QMS Training

You may choose to treat training on your QMS processes and other training on non-QMS needs separately, as discussed in SOP-4. QMS training will be the hard core of your training activities and focus on QMS-specific matters, such as an individual process or the initial QMS-wide training we organized in Section 23.3.

Non-QMS-specific training, on the other hand, focuses on ensuring your staff have the necessary qualifications to do their job in general; for example, they know a particular programming language and have an education in engineering or business management, per their job descriptions. Most likely, you are already satisfied that your staff meets the qualifications you set in your quality manual for each staff role; that's why you chose to hire them in the first place. Going forward, you want that to remain the case, so look to provide your staff the appropriate mechanisms and opportunities to refresh and expand these skills as time passes.

In practice, I have found that most QMS training is internal, and a large part of non-QMS training is external in nature. This makes perfect sense: the best experts on your QMS are in-house, and the best experts on some new technology or methodology come from the outside.

Chapter 25

Document Review

You now have the quality manual and the SOPs in place, and you are quite happy with their contents. To make sure they remain that way over the coming years and that any glitches are ironed out without undue delay, you will be running a periodic review process on the documents that repeats from here to eternity. It's not quite the sand getting between your butt cheeks on that beach in the movie, though, and it's hopefully not the giant wooden wheel Conan is forced to turn from a boy to a man, but it is one of the things you will be setting your clock to as your space station now orbits the ideal of a QMS.

25.1 What Is Expected

Your document review cycle is a key part of the engine you instructed in SOP-1. It is the primary process entrusted with keeping your QMS process instructions shipshape. It is not something that will run by itself, though, or something that the quality manager does alone.

The standard doesn't talk about a document review, or any other process of this sort, by name. It does require that once you have established a QMS, you also have a process to maintain that QMS. In this book, I use the term "document review" to refer to the scheduled maintenance of your quality manual, SOPs, and their related templates, forms, appendices, and working instructions. In other words, all the key documents in your QMS. You will already have set up the document review process previously in Section 7, so if it is now time to run that process, make sure you follow your own instructions in SOP-1.

DOI: 10.4324/9781003202868-25

25.2 Planning Document Review

The annual schedule for document review should be defined somewhere in your QMS. You could use a planning document for this purpose, but I would simply include the information as an appendix to SOP-1, which instructs your document review. This way, you are more likely to remember to observe the schedule when, for example, organizing training on the SOP in question.

In making the document review schedule for my company, I grouped the SOPs into meaningful topics then paid attention to parallel activities for any of the staff members or company functions involved and observed typical holiday periods and consistently busy periods in the annual cycle. As a result, I came up with something like the following conceptualized plan shown in the subsequent table.

In the previously stated plan, the quality manual and each SOP get assigned a specific month when the document review will address them. All the documents instructed in each SOP—the forms, templates, registers, and working instructions—and any appendices will also get revised during the same slot. The quality manual has a slot of its own to ensure it is revised as a whole, but the manual may be revised in a small way after each month if changes to the SOPs need to be reflected in it. All linked SOPs will also be

Table 25.1 Tentative Plan for a Document Review Schedule

SOP	JAN	FEB	MAR	APR	MAY	JUN
Quality manual	x					
SOP-1: QMS documentation	x					
SOP-2: Monitoring and improvement	x					
SOP-3: Resource management		x				
SOP-4: Suppliers and distributors		x				
SOP-5: Auditing			x			
SOP-6: Communication				x		
SOP-7: Marketing, sales, and post-market				x		
SOP-8: Risk management					x	
SOP-9: Clinical evidence					x	
SOP-10: Product realization						x
SOP-11: Regulatory affairs						x
SOP-12: Post-market surveillance						x

part of the review in the sense that any suggested changes will be assessed for impact to the linked SOPs.

Note that in the plan, I avoided the summer months of July and August, as well as Christmas, as during these months, the availability of staff might affect the running of the document review. It is also a good idea to consider how your major annual events—the management review, internal audits, and external audits—may affect the schedule. Here, I left the second half of the year for such activities. I would consider adding these to the same schedule, at least tentatively, to have a good overview of my overall annual cycle.

Similarly, I would record the writers, reviewers, and approvers in the documents themselves (i.e., in the SOPs and the quality manual) and have these people as the default reviewers for any new round of document review. If changes then need to be made on the assigned personnel, these can be addressed by the quality manager in accordance with your process in SOP-1. Later, when the SOPs perhaps become more stagnant, I might condense the previous schedule to take place over a shorter period of time and then use a part of the year to look at a few topical processes more in-depth.

25.3 Executing Document Review on Any Given SOP

During the document review for any given SOP, you will assign a team to revise the SOP and its associated documents, make suggestions on the edits, prepare a new draft, and have it approved through your instructed process. The basic idea is that those most knowledgeable on the process are involved in preparing a new draft, those almost as knowledgeable review it, and your quality manager or other approval function then accepts the updated SOP into your QMS after a final review. The review should not only take place but also improve your documents and processes, while changing these only in a measured and controlled way with analysis and approval of the changes conducted before enacting any changes.

25.4 Wrapping Up Document Review

Once your package of SOPs for the review are written, reviewed, and approved, and any necessary changes to the quality manual have also been made, it is time to update your document register (if you have one) so that you can easily see the status of your documents. Remember that the changes you made must not only be version controlled but also itemized in the version history of the SOPs themselves. Also remember to address the PCA activity instructed in SOP-2 as relevant.

To have the desired effect on work at your organization, you will also need to train or at least brief your staff on any changes. The choice between training and briefing may be made on the magnitude of the change and any impact it may have on your processes and product. At its simplest, you could brief your staff using a bulletin and say that only layout changes were made to some SOP. At the opposite end, you may have a full plan to train the relevant staff on some change to a process necessitated by new regulations or standards.

After all the previous items have been done, it is time to rinse and repeat, by which I mean take the next batch of documents under review. Remember also that you shouldn't defer any immediate updates of your SOPs just because their document review is coming up in a few months or next year. Any necessary updates, such as those identified by customer feedback or discovered nonconformities, should be made as soon as possible, regardless of the document review schedule, but mindful of your process for revising the processes in a controlled way.

Chapter 26

Audits

Audits will feel like a series of exams imposed on you. Depending on whether you are the auditor or the auditee, the prospect may seem like landing on LV-426 as one of the space marines or waiting there for the marines as one of the indigenous life-forms. It's an exciting event to be sure, just like James Cameron's sci-fi masterpiece Aliens. *Audits are the gates where your progress with your QMS is measured up, and depending on the outcome, you will get either a prod to action or a stamp of approval on your efforts. Either way, audits are both expeditions and mile markers.*

26.1 What Is Expected

Audits are your mechanism for checking that you are working as you have said you are in your QMS. The dictionary definition for an "audit" is an official inspection of an organization, typically by an independent body. You can perform audits on yourself and your suppliers, and you will be subject to audits as a manufacturer of a medical device.

The distinction between internal and external audits is a prominent feature in a QMS toolbox. As the names suggest, internal audits are what you run to check up on your own status, and external audits are what your certification provider performs to assess your status for obtaining or maintaining a QMS certificate. External audits can also be performed by regulatory authorities.

In addition, audits may be organized at supplier premises to assess supplier status and performance. Depending on your place in the food chain, you may be organizing these on your supplier or you may be receiving

DOI: 10.4324/9781003202868-26

these as a supplier to your customer. Doctors and nurses won't come to make supplier audits, so unless you are in the B2B market, you will probably only ever run supplier audits. Doctors and nurses may, of course, complain about you to your certification provider or the regulatory authorities; in which case, either of these may come for an extra external audit to see how you are doing.

Any of the previous audits may take place in person or remotely. Since the global COVID-19 pandemic, the world has been working toward taking more audits online, and remote audits have probably come to stay as part of the audit toolset.

This section will describe all the key types of audits you may have and help you prepare for any one of them. Let's begin with what the audits have in common.

26.2 A Philosophical Take on Audits

A bit later in this book, we will look at how to prepare for audits, attend them, and handle any outcomes. If you indulge me, I will first take a bit of a philosophical detour here in the hopes of setting the scene in a practical way for you.

26.2.1 The Time Between Audits

Preparation is half the effort, but when audits are concerned, the other half should be about actually running your QMS in between the audits. The most important thing you can do in preparation for any audit is to feel good about what you have been doing with the time in between audits. If you can be honest with yourself and be proud of what you have done, then you should have little worries about an audit. The audit will vindicate all your hard work and give you a sense that it has been worthwhile and that your organization is running as expected. The patients will get the benefit you intended, and there are no major flaws, only ideas for improvement.

If, on the other hand, you feel like you have been letting things run amok all year and now you hope all the skeletons stay in the closet for the duration of the audit, you may be heading in for a career change. We all have more things we wished we could have had time to get done, but that is not the same thing as knowing you have neglected to do some important task or, worse still, have made a half-hearted attempt at something and packaged it as the thing itself. Do what you do with pride, and the rest will follow. Don't fool yourself in between audits.

Surveillance audits after you have obtained a QMS certificate are, of course, one thing, but the whole prospect of an external audit can feel even more daunting when you are in it for the first time hoping to get your very first certificate and have no real understanding of what to expect. This book hopefully tells you enough about what to expect for you to alleviate any worries you may have and go into the audit with confidence. In audits, there is no single correct answer to any question, not really. The truly important part is that you have tried to address every important question and have ended up with good answers to each of the questions you have considered. And that you have landed at a QMS that covers your organization's operations adequately and is set to go in the right direction after the audit.

In the discussions I have had with people working on medical devices over the past years, I have noticed two characteristic inclinations: one is to shoot over the bar in the hope of surely clearing the bar, and the other, to make the smallest possible incremental effort to reach the bar. To be fair, there is no doubt a time and a place for either approach; the latter may be the optimal solution to some minor improvement you are not that desperate to achieve immediately, but the former is certainly the safer and more respectable solution in general. Safer also because audits needed to check on your solution take time and money to set up, and you will incur delays if you attempt to prod the fences to see what passes. If the raptors in *Jurassic Park* could have tested the fences once per each movie instead of however many times they did in the first film alone, the humans would have been saved from a lot of running around. In the film, the owner of the new dinosaur park brought in his grandchildren, two paleontologists, an accountant, and a rockstar to audit his dream and, thanks to insufficient preparation (with both the park and the audit), came up short. The aim of this section is to save you from such missteps.

26.2.2 Think About What Questions You Will Get Asked

The auditor will supply you with an audit agenda detailing what will be covered during the audit. The agenda references the sections of the standard that will be used to approach each topic, and based on that, you can deduce the sort of questions you will be asked: How do you approach supplier management? Can you show me the records for supplier X? How was this issue handled? And so on. These are topics that will be discussed, but the fundamental question behind each specific question made by the auditor is if they can trust your organization to do what they expect it to do. In other words, to do one of the many right things to achieve the right outcome.

Years ago, when I was still getting used to running job interviews, I saw an article in some online news outlet that succinctly stated the three fundamental questions each job interview is secretly about. According to the article, job interviews are basically about finding credible answers to these three questions:

■ Does the candidate know how to do this job?
■ Does the candidate want to do the job?
■ Can we get along with the candidate?

This rang true to me based on my experience. Today, I would venture a guess that audits, especially external audits, are fundamentally about the same three questions. Substitute candidate for organization, and all three questions apply. Of course, at an audit, it is not enough to get a feeling about the organization—the audit is not about hiring a summer trainee—so the battery of questions is more elaborate and the answers more finely documented. The audit process is, in general, about ensuring the following principles:

1. The organization's instructed processes cover the standard, and any exemptions are given an acceptable rationale
2. The organization's processes follow and fulfill the requirements of the standard, and any extensions therein are compatible with the standard
3. The organization's processes are being followed by the organization, and there is evidence of this in the form of reliable records

Also realize that the auditor is approaching your QMS from the point of view of the clauses of the standard. The audit agenda and the top-most questions stemming from that agenda are all built on top of the standard. The auditor may ask more impromptu questions during the audit based on how things are progressing, but the questions on his or her mind coming into the audit will be based on investigating how you follow the standard. You don't need to remember the clause numbers by heart, though.

A friend of mine tells a joke about a German society for good humor and jokes. In this society, all the jokes are numbered, as you would expect following German efficiency, so that at member gatherings, a person may simply get up at the podium and say the number of a joke to have the room roar up in laughter. The joke in the joke is that one person in the audience does not laugh at a joke, and when asked why, he simply says, "I had heard it before". The joke is a good one, but here, I tell it for the purpose of explaining that external audits should not work like that. A good auditor will not ask you how you have solved Clause 7.3.2b. A bad auditor or an inexplicably hostile auditor might, but that is not the way audits should proceed. The questions will not come in the form of clause numbers, but they may come in the form of clause headings preceded by some lead-in, like "How do you address . . .".

Question 1 from the previous list is addressed in the quality manual, and as long as the exemption rationale and the SOPs introduced in the manual are in check, there shouldn't be much room for doubt as to the answer.

Question 2 concerns the quality manual and, in particular, the individual SOPs it introduces. The answer to this question is probably your main focus during an initial certification audit and also an area where the extensive background of the auditor comes into play as they will be able to see some discrepancies between your process and the expected process easily based on their familiarity with the standard and the countless other process definitions they have seen. In this book, the sections presenting the individual SOPs (Sections 7–18) are intended to give you a glimpse into the essence of each required SOP and, thereby, let you try and catch up a little in terms of such experience.

Question 3 is what will give you the most cause for restlessness, particularly in subsequent audits when your processes have already been checked a number of times before. Question 3 is the classic "Show me" question, where an auditor wants to see real examples of the records instructed in the SOPs being used as they have been instructed and leading to further actions as expected. The answer to this type of a question invariably involves identifying a pool of records answering to any particular issue raised by the auditor, letting them choose which record to open up from within the pool, showing the record, and explaining any entry values seen therein. The auditor will always take note of the following:

■ The date the record was made
■ Who issued the record
■ Any record ID it may have

The auditor may have additional questions based on the contents of the record, and they may want to check that some aspect instructed in the SOP is, in fact, addressed in the record. Based on how content the auditor is with what they are seeing, and also if the record is part of a chain of records instructed in the SOP, the auditor may ask to see more records. You may be asked to show other records of the same sort or to follow the chain of records deeper (either downstream or up). During initial certification, there is much ground to cover as the audit addresses the entire standard, but later in the surveillance audits, the standard is sampled in some way, and more time can, thus, be spent drilling down in the records. Expect to be exhausted at the end of the audit in either case; your auditor will be too.

26.2.3 Have Your Ducks in a Row

Once you know what sort of questions you will be asked, you will also know what sort of answers you will want to give on those questions. You should know the standard, the applicable regulations, and your own processes. When it comes to the audit, feel free to focus on the last. If you have built your processes to match the standard and the regulations, you should feel secure in focusing on your own process that covers the rest.

Realize that in addition to showing the right SOP and the right section within that SOP, you will also have to show records of you following that process. This need to drill down into the records will probably increase in the surveillance audits, that is, once you progress beyond the first certification audit(s).

If you know you will not be the only person taking part in the audit from your organization's side, ensure you have the correct people showing up for the correct parts of the schedule. If it is the first time these people are taking part in the audit, also prepare them for what to expect—maybe by handing them a copy of this book? Personally, I like to include staff in our internal audits so that they can get their feet wet at the shallow end of the pool and then get into the more serious external audits. The choice of how many people and who exactly should attend the audit is yours.

At one meeting with the FDA, a representative of another company asked the FDA if the company could bring in their lawyer to the audit. The answer was that the company can bring in whoever they want, but that they should think carefully if they really want to bring in their lawyer. The implication was that it is not commonly done, and it might not be in the best interest for the company. The other extreme is that only the quality manager meets with the auditor. The thinking behind a limited attendance may be that the fewer outsiders are included, the smaller the chance of saying something off. Both of these examples, however, appear to approach audits as interrogation, which they should not be. I can imagine a bad audit feeling like an interrogation scene in some film noir thriller, but if both the organization and the auditor are up to their tasks, this should not be the case. The audits should always lead to improvements in quality—if that can be achieved via a soft touch, why would you need brass knuckles on either side of the table?

As the quality manager of our organization, I like including more people in the audits to, for example, bring in management personnel to talk on the processes they most directly work with. To me, this is a great opportunity to gauge people's attitudes toward their processes, notice areas of further improvement, and also commit management to the QMS as a whole. I realize that I get to do this because I am also a part of the Management Team and because our company is still on the startup-scale of operations, but I feel it is appropriate for us, and I would encourage you to consider bringing in key managers and even Management Team members as you see appropriate. As my organization matures, I will probably bring in more people on a rotating arrangement that depends on the agenda for each audit.

The standard requires the whole organization to be committed to following and improving the QMS from management to staff, and I can think of little better ways of ensuring and demonstrating this than broad participation at external audits. Even without such participation, the auditor does, to my understanding, have the right to request interviews with any staff member, so it makes sense to prepare the staff mindset for audits, both external and otherwise. It is also a very good way of feeding motivated staff members and showing them that their actions, as part of the QMS, well and truly matter.

My last piece of advice here is that you make sure the auditing space works for you, that you have accommodated all the people participating in the audit, and that you have enough rooms for all the different tracks the audit may have. Also ensure that you have a reliable internet connection and access to all the systems you intend to use during the audit. Lights, seats, power points for electricity, and enough coffee and water for everyone. The rest is, well, destiny.

26.3 Types of Audits

That's enough philosophy. Let's get into the practicalities. In the following, we will look at the special characteristics of each type of audit you may come across. Let's start with internal audits and then proceed to external audits and supplier audits. We will also touch on remote audits, which have increased in popularity because of the extraordinary travel restrictions brought on by the COVID-19 pandemic.

26.3.1 *Internal Audits*

Internal audits are about checking that your processes are working as you have said they are, but they are also about seeing if those processes could be improved somehow to run more safely or more efficiently. Both are important goals, but the latter particularly so because it is a unique opportunity to identify performance improvements.

External audits will often lead to suggestions of doing more and doing better, but rarely suggestions of doing something faster or easier, or not doing it at all. In this book, I consider "faster" and "easier" as synonyms for "idiot-safe" solutions—unless, of course, you are being a bit of an idiot yourself when paring back processes to find the essential steps at the core of each process. In comparison, internal audits give you more breathing space to figure out what matters and what is superfluous. For this reason, internal audits can be a real lifesaver and improve the efficiency of work at your organization and allow for better focus on the things that truly matter most when making sure you don't waste time on bureaucracy for bureaucracy's sake.

Internal audits can be run by you, or you can use an external expert to conduct the audit on your behalf. It is, however, vitally important that the auditor, whether internal or external to your organization, is not auditing their own work and is qualified to run the audit. For this reason, particularly small companies should consider using external quality consultants to run the audits. Otherwise, you may have a hard time providing evidence on the competence of the auditor and upholding segregation so that no one audits their own work. Some small companies have successfully collaborated with their peer companies to organize each other's internal audits, thereby circumventing the problem of not having independent auditors on their payrolls. This is a smart idea, and you may get to learn from each other's choices, but you will not be saving on resources if you do the audit well. Instead of focusing on your own QMS, you will spend that same effort on the other organization's system. On the first time around, you will probably spend even more time to audit a system that is new and unknown to you. You may also end up not raising all the issues an external consultant might raise, perhaps because you feel that how you perform the peer's audit will be reflected in how they perform your audit. This may still be a very good arrangement, and it may give you a great vehicle for finding mechanisms for improving and focusing your QMS.

26.3.2 External Audits

External audits are about reviewing whether your instructed process meets the requirements and whether you are then meeting your instructed process. The negative way of looking at external audits is that they are about finding out if your ship is seaworthy by trying to shoot holes into it. The positive way of looking at them is that you will get to have a conversation about your QMS with true experts sitting across from you on the other side of the table.

When I was preparing for my doctoral defense, one of the best pieces of advice I got was from someone who said that the defense is a rare opportunity to discuss my work with someone who has read all of it, is an expert on the topic, has really analyzed my work, and has prepared remarks on it. This way, the defense didn't feel like an attack by the opponent but instead an opportunity to discuss the topic and perhaps even come up with new ideas. This same advice applies to external audits. The auditors take their work seriously and want to see that you, too, are serious about meeting requirements, but at the same time, they are seasoned experts who really understand the standard, understand the applicable regulations, and have seen how hundreds of other companies have tackled the same issues you are facing. They are not your consultants, but they won't let you be foolish and endanger patients out there in the real world, either. Good auditors will also let you know when you have excelled in some solution, and this is as good as a nod from the powers that be.

26.3.3 Supplier Audits

If you are in B2B or if you use suppliers in your business, expect to either arrange them on your suppliers or take part in them to answer the questions your B2B customer may have. See SOP-6 for more on the topic.

26.3.4 Remote Audits

All types of audits, just about, can also take place online instead of in person. The worldwide COVID-19 pandemic in 2020 brought about a massive change in the use of remote connections. In many of the expert groups I am a member in, we had dabbled in the use of remote connections before the pandemic, but often, the results had been disappointing: the audio connection was poor, the shared screens blocked any video, the slides were difficult to read, the discussions were lacking or difficult to take part in, and occasionally, even the discussions were cut off for remote audiences as these were not part of the actual agenda. With the pandemic, all this changed in a matter of days.

After everyone was taking part remotely, the practical arrangements improved almost overnight: gone were the bad connection issues and up went the participant numbers as no one had to travel anymore. A meeting that used to be 20–30 people could now easily be 40–100 people. People also got better at using the remote connection software: there was still the occasional unintentional muting of the microphone, and a software update or two have occasionally brought things to a standstill, but in general, both people and software have taken a huge leap forward as a result of the pandemic lockdowns. The discussion parts of the meetings are still lacking from what they were before the pandemic when everyone was in the same room, but I suspect we will get better at that too.

Another definite silver lining to the horrible pandemic situation has been that although the world has gotten smaller as we all have been stuck within our homes, the world has also gotten smaller in the positive sense that more events have been arranged online, and it has now been logistically possible to take part in more of them. In 2020, I took part in dozens of online events where I also got to make questions to experts from several different notified bodies, the FDA, and a diverse group of other bodies worth talking to in the medical device field. I even got to take part in an exclusive small-group meeting with the Commissioner of the FDA, and I doubt that would have happened without the changes brought on by the pandemic.

Remote connections have also become a way of conducting audits. Recently, I had my first remote surveillance audit on our QMS. The experience was entirely positive, although I would still have preferred to meet face-to-face. There is a lot you can do to make remote audits more comfortable for yourself. I would recommend the following:

■ Get a quiet space to hold the meeting, just like you would with an in-person audit. Hearing people on the background will be as irritating as it is during any in-person audit.

- Ensure your software and internet connection are working. Before the audit, be early and launch the software to see if it wants to make any forced updates. If the updates are not forced, don't install them now, as your auditor may not have installed them either.
- Get at least two displays and extend your desktop across them. Don't duplicate your desktop. This way, you can share one of the screens with the auditor and have your audit preparation materials, video window, and so forth open on the other display.
- Get decent speakers and microphones. I recently upgraded my computer speakers to midline Genelec studio monitors, and I was blown away by how much of a difference those have made for online meetings. It sounds like complete overkill, but the level of presence I get with proper speakers is stunning. It is almost as good as being there.
- Get an electric desk. In long meetings, it is sometimes nice to get up and not have to sit for hours on end. A good electric table, preferably with memory slots, will let you do this. Get a good office chair, too, naturally.
- Get bottled water, coffee, or whatever you like to drink to have it available should you want it. For in-person meetings, you would have these, too, so why change the routine for a remote meeting? I can't be alone in thinking that a few cups of coffee in the morning to get you going and a bottle or two of water when your throat dries up are good remedies. Flavored drinks are apparently better than water if you don't want to take as many bathroom breaks.

I get fairly decent frequent flyer status, and I like sitting in the airport lounge in the evenings sipping wine while going over my e-mails and notes from the day's meetings, but even I will admit that there is sense in remote meetings. I don't love the early-morning wake-ups and the commutes to the airport, and I don't particularly like adding hours to my working day. The discussion, person-to-person encounters, and the overall level of interactivity in remote meetings is not equivalent to in-person meetings, but for some things, the remote is almost as good as in person. There is a certain charm and a definite efficiency to being able to sit at your home office having one meeting with your colleagues, refill your cup of tea or coffee, and have another meeting with participants from across the US, and then a third meeting with participants from all over the globe. It is always morning somewhere, and the remote methods give you new opportunities if you want to be a bit of a workaholic.

Joking aside, remote meetings and events will only get more popular, so get comfortable with them. Figure out how they can work for you and how you can enjoy them as much as possible, and do that.

26.3.5 Unannounced Audits

Your certification body (or notified body) may also show up unannounced at your door and expect to see your organization in its natural state. This begs the question, How do you prepare for a surprise audit? How can you prepare for something when you don't know when it will happen?

The answer is you shouldn't really be able to: the unannounced audit is supposed to catch your organization off guard and its most natural. You can, of course, try to ensure that you aren't caught with your pants down or in some other embarrassingly unprepared state. Think John McLane at the beginning of *Die Hard* running across shattered glass with his shoes off when the terrorists enter the Nakatomi Plaza. Think of the two flyboys sleeping in their car when *Pearl Harbor* was about to hit the fan. Think of Private Joker in Kubrick's *Full Metal Jacket* when he walks into that toilet in the middle of the night and finds another private cradling a rifle. I hope none of your, or my, surprise audits are that bad, of course.

The reality is that you can't prepare for a surprise, but you can do a number of things to try and make sure your organization is well-equipped to receive surprises. In Section 3.23, I advocated for daring to make yourself redundant as the architect and pilot of your QMS. That for me is the ideal, knowing that if I must step away for a moment for whatever reason, the show goes on. Again, I should emphasize that this does not mean that you should delegate your duties, only that you open them up so that others can understand them, help in them, and if the need arises, even substitute for you or anyone else at the organization. Having some reserve for redundancy is perhaps the highest mark of a resilient organization not easily hampered by disruptions.

Having an organization where everyone is interested in, appreciative of, and willing to improve quality is the goal. Training and dissemination of information is key in this but so is staff exposure to audits and other QMS activities. At our organization, we do our best to provide relevant information on quality and regulatory affairs to the whole staff via mechanisms, such as trainings, Q and As, bulletins, and access to reports. We encourage taking part in QMS activities, such as internal audits, so that staff members get their feet wet and are then, hopefully, more at ease with the surprise auditor that shows up at the door for them to greet.

So far, I haven't yet experienced a surprise audit, but I know it is coming. The shortest notice I have had on an audit so far has been a few weeks for an external audit. A few weeks leave you time to prepare, but for a true unannounced audit, all you can do is make sure your organization knows to expect surprise audits and is running as smoothly according to the QMS as is possible. Leaving something waiting that you know you will need to do eventually may hurt you in such audits. An attitude of let's-just-do-this-now-and-document-later will definitely hurt you. You can't be up-to-date or forward-looking in everything all the time, but it is a worthwhile goal and something to strive for.

All that said, it is good idea to have resilience built into your QMS. Even the standard requires you to know roles and responsibilities, and to have substitutes for key roles in the organization. Thinking about potential disruptions and change conditions possibly coming your way is a good way of building that resilience in, and if your resources allow, this may also include simulating some of those disruptions ahead of time.

26.4 Survival Guide to Audits

The audit, particularly your first external audit on which your whole certification rests, can be a stomach-churning experience. There are, however, many things you can do to prepare for the challenge and recover from it. The things I would recommend are subsequently described, grouped by the phase of preparations. You will think of more based on your circumstances, but these I find to be universal.

26.4.1 Preparing for an Audit

Every audit, be it internal or external in nature, will follow the same time-honored flow: you will have an audit invitation with an audit agenda, a time, and a place when the audit will take place; and once you get a report from the audit, there are probably going to be some improvements to make. The only deviation from the previous case is that unannounced audits won't come with an invitation beforehand. Let's go through the steps involved one at a time.

The Schedule

Before the audit, a schedule is drawn up by the auditor outlining what will be covered when and, after discussion with you, who is going to be present. The schedule will be based on the clauses of the standard, and each section will list subclauses or themes from that clause to go through in the audit. Hopefully, it will be easy to map each theme to SOPs in your QMS (the "Processes" section in the quality manual should help you in this). If this is not the case, you may want to create some sort of a quick reference table for use in the audit or just read your SOPs a few times over.

In finalizing the schedule, consider the flow of the audit, especially if you will have people coming in and going out based on the topics covered. Having your whole organization on standby during the whole audit may be an expensive proposition, whether they are in the actual audit room the whole time.

The People

As discussed earlier, the choice of who you bring to the audit is up to you. You can make the Audit Team as narrow or as wide as you see fit. Classically, it is the quality manager who sits in a room with the auditors and responds to their questions while providing evidence in the form of language in the SOPs and finished documents and records in the QMS. You may, however, have a larger team present, and the team members can answer questions directly.

I find it is a good idea to bring in staff members on specific topics so that they, too, learn how audits work and get experience in working with audits. This may be valuable experience in the future as they can take on bigger roles in audits and are also better equipped to deal with unannounced notified body and FDA audits. If the participants are answering on a process that they are directly involved in, this also tightens the link between the audit and any subsequent improvement of the process, and thereby, improves the likelihood of the process getting better in some way.

The Evidence

The audit schedule will come with a request for documents so that the auditor can familiarize themself with your QMS. The request won't be written on the level of the agenda items, but it will instead come as one list for the whole audit. Typical documents requested are the quality manual, SOPs, reports from the previous internal audit, and management review. You may choose to provide the documents, for example, as a password-encrypted zip archive; provide the auditor access to some online staging area you have; or use a file upload system provided by the auditor. These documents basically cover what you have said your processes are like. More evidence will then be required during the actual audit on how well you have, in fact, managed to work according to your instructions.

During the audit, you will look at various documents and records in your QMS to show that you have acted correctly and in the right sequence. The documents may be in paper form or in some electronic repository. You will have to show document issuance dates and signatures, whether in physical or electronic form. Having a solid document ID scheme in place across your whole QMS, and each document therefore assigned a unique ID, is expected and will make the whole process easier. Having the documents under a practical hierarchy and structure will be of great help in locating the correct documents.

My Preparation Document

Ever since preparing for my first audit, I have created a prep package for myself to act as a tool for making sure that I have all the ducks in a row for the audit, and should I need it during the audit, I would have some place to look for answers to the questions I am asked. In the first audit, this was just a simple version of the schedule where I had made notes on the various documents (the quality manual, SOPs, and plans) I could open up to show how we had instructed something and then also occasionally, notes on the records I could pull up to show what had been done. The most use I got out of the document was in doing the preparation; during the audits, I mostly just used the reverse side of the document for notes. I always prepared the document from scratch for each audit, so the preparation was a real learning experience.

After a few audits, this evolved to a fairly large undertaking of 20-plus pages for an audit. In this version, I added two levels to each slot in the schedule: a bulleted list of relevant points to consider in the answer and a table of the abridged requirements of the standard (something I had made myself) where I used documents (where something is instructed) and records (where the execution is recorded) to answer the requirements. This version of the preparation package was much more work to create than the previous versions, but it was fantastically useful during the audit. After the auditor asked some question on a specific clause, I could summarize our approach to that whole clause quite easily using the bullet points I had made, and then if there were additional questions, I could scroll down to the exact subclause and see my notes for it where I addressed both documents and records in detail. Table 26.1 illustrates this.

In preparing the document, I first went through my abridged requirements identified in the standard and answered each requirement in terms of both the documents instructing our approach and the records subsequently kept thereof. The SOP related to each topic is often my first note here then a reference to a relevant document, such as the minutes of the Quality or Management Team or the report for the management review. High-level reports provide great definitive reviews on the topics they address, and occasionally, documents, such as the minutes of the Quality Management Team, may provide a good overview of some pertinent topic (e.g., nonconformity handling) and contain both a practical timeline of handling and a list of relevant document IDs and dates to discuss the topic.

After identifying documents and records, I would distill my answers down to the bullet points themselves at the top of the entry on what our process was and how it was recorded. Then for the audit, I flipped around how I used these so that I first looked at the bullet points and could then drill down if the need arose. My final document thus consisted of page after page of such notes for the slots.

You don't have to go through all this effort to prepare for an audit, but I heartily recommend it. This last time around also, others in my Audit Team used the same document template, and they, too, reported back saying that the document removed unnecessary palpitations. There is no substitute for preparation—and why would you want to leave the work of coming up with the right answers to the moment you are put on the spot if you can, in fact, approximate the questions in advance? This way, you can, at the very least,

Table 26.1 Sample Prep for a Slot of the Audit

Time	Title for topic *X* addressed during this slot of the audit		
People present	– *My bullet points outlining our process and records, as well as any people present who would answer questions*		
	Abridged requirements	**Documents**	**Records**
	Requirement 1	*Document X instructs*	*Records of type A and B*
	Requirement 2	*Document Y elaborates*	*Records of type A*

review your processes to know where you could improve. As your operations grow, this, no doubt, gets harder, but by then, your experience will also have grown. For now, if you are a startup, use your size to your advantage and prepare as only someone of your size perhaps can.

26.4.2 *Last-Minute Advice*

Going into the audit, it is natural to feel a little nervous. After all, someone is going to come in and inspect your work to see if it is done well enough. You should be able to walk into the room knowing that you have done all you have promised and approach the situation as an opportunity to have a conversation with people who are as interested in quality management as you are.

The audit is not really an exam. It is a meeting of people who have poured their heart and soul into building and running a QMS, and people who are passionate about seeing quality management done correctly. The auditors have gone through the trouble of familiarizing themselves with your QMS based on the material you have provided and are now prepared to verify that it meets the requirements of the standard and regulations. Your solutions don't have to be perfect in every regard, but they do have to be good enough to be worth sustaining and perhaps improving.

If you have done your work well all along, there should not be much to do running up to the audit. I find it best to go over my preparation document and look for anything that pops out in terms of the answers and in terms of the schedule, including who needs to be on which audit track at which moment in time so that there are no surprising conflicts. Other than that, sleep well, eat your breakfast, drink your coffee, and get to the audit venue ahead of time. And most important of all, remember to breath once there.

26.4.3 *The Audit Itself*

If you are feeling confident that you have tried to do a good job and feel like you have succeeded well for the most part, you should be facing the coming questions with moderate ease. Realize that even if your heart is racing somewhat before the audit, that is only natural, and all will be all right after a while. The first question will always be the hardest one to take; after that, you will find your swing quite naturally.

In all the oral exams I have ever taken, and there have been quite a few, the most important part to remember is not all the things you think you need to remember to answer the questions but to breathe. Breathe when you listen. Breathe when you think. And breathe after you have answered— let the examiner ask the next question; don't go rambling on volunteering unnecessary information that may perhaps get you into trouble but will definitely make you feel out of breath when the auditor asks their next question. Breathe.

Once you get a question, think about what SOP in your QMS covers this particular topic or if it is a topic best addressed through the quality manual. In some cases, you may be able to bypass the process description and go straight for the document that addresses the question—a document, like the latest management review report, the handling plan of an internal audit, or some particular minutes of the Quality Management Team. In most cases, you will open up the answer from the SOP.

Having a good electronic document management system and being familiar with how to browse and search documents within it will work wonders for you in the audit. In many cases, I have been able to preempt a question or open up the next document while the auditor was still asking the question. With a paper-based solution, this would have been impossible to do. In the ranks of quality professionals, you will hear fantastical stories about big corporations and how they approach audits. One particular story, relayed to me by a firsthand account, tells of a big company who had a team of helpers outside of the audit room photocopying and providing copies of documents into the audit room as needed. I can only imagine the amount of coffee and roundabout conversation needed to smooth over the delays in seeing any particular record emerge using this approach. With a good electronic system, the same outcome can be achieved in a matter of seconds with a team less than a tenth of the one needed by the big company. If the objective is to waste away the active time of the audit, then the paper-based approach may be a good one, but I have yet to see the wisdom of wasting time.

The audits will be full-day events or perhaps even lasting a few days. MDSAP audits are legendary for their duration; the longest one I have heard of firsthand was 14 days of audits. But basic ISO 13485 surveillance audits should only be a day or two on one or two tracks. Your certification body will be able to explain the calculation formula used here, and you will know the duration in advance (based on everything going well, of course).

The audit agenda will include slots for lunch breaks and one to two coffee breaks per day, and you can bring in people and excuse them as needed. You yourself as the quality manager will be there for the entire duration, probably wishing you could take part on all the tracks, but even so, short restroom breaks and quick opportunities to refill your coffee cup and so forth may be taken by either side. Here, too, I would argue that playing for time is silly and will frustrate your auditor, leading to a more heated and impatient exchange than necessary.

The Structure of the Audit

The audit event will proceed along the agreed schedule. The agenda has some protocol items, mainly the opening where the scope of the audit and those present are stated, and the closing meeting where any found nonconformities are presented by the auditor. In between, the auditor will ask a question on how some topic is dealt with, ask for evidence in the form of documents and records showing that this is in fact how the topic has been dealt with, and make a record of the document IDs used as evidence, when these have been issued, and by whom.

Breaks

The agenda will come with defined start and stop times for each day and each slot too. If you must rush off to the restroom or if everyone wants to refill their coffees at the same time, that can be done as needed. In general, though, the times reserved for slots on various topics should be respected and any deviation from the agenda addressed while remaining respectful of the time of the other party.

Occasionally, it also happens that your presence, or that of someone else on your Audit Team, is needed on another trail at the same time. Usually, this does not cause a break to your track, but occasionally, it might cause a short pause or a momentary reshuffle of questions being discussed on that track. If these breaks don't add up and if the audit is otherwise proceeding well, such modifications will be dealt with flexibly.

A word of caution, though: you should not play for time by taking extra breaks. If you are being intentionally absent or uncooperative in some way, your auditors will pick up on this and act accordingly. At the end of the day, the auditor has to be satisfied with the results they got, and if that is not the case, you will be in more trouble than just a few nonconformities to fix. You will hear stories of taking things slow or perhaps taking the scenic route with your auditor in getting from one place to the next on the factory floor, but I personally haven't seen any point to such tricks—you would be wasting both your auditor's time and your own. And annoying both.

End of the Audit

I will admit some of the most satisfying words I have ever heard were from my opponent at the end of my doctoral defense. When he said that he had nothing further to ask and that I had answered all his questions satisfactorily, I felt a new level of calm cross my body, and I just let the defense roll on through to the end on its own inertia. The same is true of any QMS audit I have ever been in. You might not usually get an equally poignant cap on the proceedings, but that point in time after which there are no further questions on that day is a very satisfying moment.

After all the clauses under inspection have been dealt with, the auditors will politely kick you out of the room and regroup among themselves to compare notes. The time for this, too, will be on your schedule. After their meeting, the auditors will reemerge to give you their final assessment of the good, the bad, and—hopefully not—the ugly. You will hear the list of nonconformities the auditors found and that will be in the final audit report you will receive later. Note that all the nonconformities you will get are now presented and that no new nonconformities will appear in between the audit and the audit report. After that, it is time to pack it up and head home for the day. In the coming days, there will be plenty more to unpack, but for now, you can call it a day.

26.4.4 After the Audit

After the audit, it is standard practice for the auditor to provide a written report of the audit, internal or external, within a few weeks of the audit. The report will describe the nonconformities in more detail and may also contain other observations and comments, but it should not introduce any new nonconformities.

The audit report will say how quickly you are to respond to the findings and what forms you are to use in your response. The number one thing to do now is to carefully analyze each nonconformity and plan what actions to take. You will proceed to handle all the nonconformities and observations as you have instructed in your processes. Most likely, the Quality Management Team or the Audit Team will lead the work on evaluating the items and developing appropriate actions. In the case of an internal audit, the schedule for handling the items is probably more relaxed than during a certification audit, but realize that also your certification provider will later want to see your internal audit report and how you have handled it.

What to Do When You Do Get a Nonconformity?

So you feel like you have been hit by the stick, but the auditors feel like they have given you the seeds to grow carrots? Most audits will lead to some issues to address, whether these are called major or minor nonconformities, or observations, in general. You are expected to take these seriously and think hard how you can improve your QMS so that the same or similar issues don't occur in the future.

The good news is that the question of what to do next has already been solved by you in your SOP-2 detailing the handling of Corrective Actions and Preventive Actions (CAPA). In some cases, you may be able to explain why some nonconformity was incorrectly recorded or provide a missing document that was not found during the audit, and have the nonconformity effectively deactivated that way. In most cases, though, I would argue that such discussion is pointless and that you should address all these issues via your CAPA handling.

In the actual audit report, you will get a list of the nonconformities. You may also get a list of other observations. The nonconformities are classified as either major, requiring immediate correction, or minor, requiring a plan for correction. Each nonconformity should also reference the clause of the standard it is made against and provide a description citing the inflicting evidence or the lack of supporting evidence. The list will come with the timeline expected by the auditor in the handling of the nonconformities. In the case of an MDSAP audit, the classification of the nonconformities is more fine-tuned than just major/minor, but the implication is the same: there are priorities you should attach to each nonconformity.

If I were an auditor myself, I might always consider raising a nonconformity just for the purpose of seeing if the organization's CAPA handling is working as it should. Particularly, if this were my first time auditing the organization and I had no firsthand knowledge of how they would respond to raised issues. The nonconformities, thus, serve a dual purpose: they fix issues found in the processes, but they may also reveal further issues in how those issues and fixes are dealt with on any level of your organization. I know I am not the only one who has thought of this probe-like use. So expect to get nonconformities and be glad if they are easy to fix.

Chapter 27

Management Review

The management review is the pinnacle of your QMS calendar for the year. It is the one single-out occasion where your top management gathers around that oval meeting room table, like in Kubrick's Dr. Strangelove, *and pores over every facet of your QMS to figure out where you are and where you need to be going. The outcome of the review is hopefully not that you are all cowboys sitting on top of an out-of-control QMS hurling toward the ground but rather a solid overview of your activities and decisions on steps forward. You do also need the review in black and white, like the film, to show it to your auditors and interested stakeholders.*

27.1 What Is Expected

The management review is the number one periodic activity where your top management reviews your entire QMS at documented planned intervals to ensure its continuing suitability, adequacy, and effectiveness. Usually, the review takes place once a year, but technically, the standard does not require this, only that the review is done periodically. Management review reports are often reviewed in external certification or notified body audits.

I recently attended an FDA event that covered some of the differences between the standard and the US CFR title 21 part 820 requirements concerning the management review. The differences in terms of compatibility where slight, almost nonexistent for a manufacturer already operating by the standard, but the level of much greater detail in the standard was striking. The speaker remarked that in the US, the manufacturer is quite free to choose the agenda for the management review and concentrate on what is topical at that stage of their operations. This makes sense, but under the standard, the minimum requirements for inputs and outputs to the review are listed clearly in Clause 5.6 and now addressed in your SOP-6. If you are accustomed to running your reviews according to FDA guidance and not the standard, you should take a hard look at the requirements for the inputs and outputs set by the standard. Also note that the standard talks of the review as something arranged by your top management and not just the management representative, although the latter is, of course, a part of the former.

The minimum inputs and outputs of the review, when done according to the standard, are given in SOP-6. The agenda of the management review should reflect these input and output items, but it may also include further items as beneficial to your organization. I would recommend setting up a draft agenda, along with your SOP instructing audits. That way, you can easily refer to the agenda and also adopt it as the agenda for your Management Team and Quality Management Team meetings.

Worth noting here is that the report you will write of the management review should clearly differentiate between the input information and any output assessment and action plans made during the review. This is just common sense, but from what I have heard, it can often be problematic to discern from the reports what was actually decided during the review. Preventing the input and output from becoming one hard-to-read spun yarn will be easy via document formatting, but it will be greatly appreciated by both your staff when later referring back to the document and also by your auditors. Hiding the crucial information in volumes of text, or boxes and boxes of documents, is a tactic employed by legal firms in movies, but that should not be your goal here. Conciseness and to-the-point decisiveness will be virtues in developing your report here, but don't forget about providing adequate background and linking to your inputs as appropriate, either.

To keep things simple, I would prepare a draft report ahead of the review, including the input information (or referring to it as the case may be) and put in placeholders for where the management assessment and decisions go. This way, you can prepare a compact package where the inputs are clearly identified and the outputs equally clearly laid out. The preparation can be done or lead by the management representative.

In writing the report, you may find that it resembles an annual summary of your organization's activities and its outlook on the future. This is okay and probably quite beneficial for your improvement operations over time. However, beware of making the report too heavy, particularly in reviewing any tails of actions to be followed from the previous review. The report is intended to be practical and a good point of entry for anyone, such as your auditors, to take a deep dive into your organization. If you go into verbose description of all the individual trees, you won't see the forest they make up, and your management, too, will be sawing logs by the time they finish the review meeting.

27.2 Rolling Up Your Sleeves

The management review is a fairly massive undertaking. In many ways, it is the annual review and report of your organization's activities and status. It is quite easy to go too deep and to go into too much detail in preparing the input material or the final report itself. Think about what matters, and only reproduce or quote text if it makes sense. In most cases, you will be better off only summarizing the situation succinctly—what is the lay of the land and why it matters—and then referring to other reviews, surveys, and reports for more information as needed. When, for example, discussing the auditing status for that year, you should state the end result and any significant developments (e.g., what types of nonconformities were discovered and what is the overall status of nonconformity handling) but then refer to the individual reports themselves for more detail.

The structure of your report will follow your agenda, which in turn you set out in SOP-6 based on the standard. If you followed my suggestion of aligning the management review agenda and, at least, your agenda for Management Team meetings, you will already be familiar with the structure you will want to use here. These meetings, and especially the meetings taking place immediately preceding the management review, will act as a convenient source of information for your review. In case you want to refer further back on some details, you will have that luxury by rewinding the minutes of the meetings and finding the right point in time. But do not try to rewrite all this history into the management review. You will go nuts and spend a good few months hitting your head against the wall. Regurgitating information is not what the review is about, especially not in a small organization where facts are readily knowable and what matters most is coming up with a joint analysis and a plan for going forward. In many cases, too, the registers you have set up in your QMS, for example, on tracking nonconformities, incidents, training, and tool validation, should be helpful in giving you a big picture on the state of your affairs.

In addition, you can consider how the big periodic documents your organization will be creating factor into to the topics. Risk management reports will be a prominent component here, but perhaps the most convenient document to utilize here is the Periodic Safety Update Report (PSUR), or similar, you will be creating periodically and wherein you will be covering just about all aspects of relevance to your operations (see Section 18).

If you have just launched your QMS, you probably won't be running a review just now. I would familiarize myself with what type of information is needed in the review, prepare for how to best ensure that information is available at the time of review, and pencil in my date for the review. Calling the review to be arranged at a specific time is up to your management and the management representative, but having a rough idea is part of the QMS planning activities you instructed in SOP-1. You will want to run it quite soon, though, to have everything ready for any certification audits you may have your eye on.

In general, I would recommend running your internal audit before the management review so that you have all the key information and analysis to base your management decisions on. I would also make sure that the management review takes place before the expected external review and that I have time to finish the management report and get it to the certification body or the notified body a few weeks ahead of the audit they will carry out. You may also want to run two management reviews within the first year of running your QMS to ensure that everything really is heading in the right direction.

In the coming years, you will probably not return to many other periodic documents, unless there are issues and root causes to trace, but the report of the management review appears to be a document you will want to refer back to every once in a while. Make sure the review report serves its purpose now, that it acts as a good base of reference for your next management review, and that it will also remain practical as a body of records going forward.

When you are ready to execute the management review, refer to SOP-6, gather your source documents together, and get to work compiling the input material. All that is required is some perspiration in doing the grunt work in advance and then smart thinking at the review.

The review is not a performance for the benefit of your auditors but a genuine opportunity to review your operations and come up with the appropriate actions. The standard does require that you consider certain inputs and output for the reviews—and verifying that you have done so may be a topic for audits—but the number one goal here is that the review serves a distinct purpose in assessing the status of your operations and improving them. If the review does not do that, you are heading for a rethink sooner or later.

Chapter 28

Certification

The ISO 13485 certificate will seem like the Holy Grail when setting out to develop your QMS. It is definitely an achievement—something which tells you the things you have done and the processes you have drawn up are planned and executed well in your organization. Getting certified is more than just writing the QMS, though; you will need to secure a certification body to take you on as a client, learn to work with them through the audits, and perhaps even be a bit of a diplomat to control the process and manage expectations and activities at your own organization.

28.1 What Is Expected

The fundamental thing your certification body needs to check is that your QMS meets the requirements of the standard, as the standard is what you are wanting to get certified to. This means firstly making sure your QMS covers the standard adequately, any exclusions you have made therefrom are justified, the processes you have set up comply with the requirements of the standard, and the records you have show that you are complying with your own process instructions. For this reason, expect to be asked for your QMS documents and key records before the audit takes place, and then for more records during the actual audit.

The certification process may consist of both an off-site review of documents and an on-site audit at your premises. The COVID-19 pandemic has opened the door on remote audits, and while you may or may not be able to use a remote audit for initial certification in Europe, they will be an option during surveillance audits in the subsequent years. You will find out

DOI: 10.4324/9781003202868-28

if remote audits are an option in your case by talking with your potential certification providers (i.e., certification body or notified body) in your area.

After the audit, you will get a list of issues and nonconformities, which may be minor or major to fix as judged by the auditor. Minor nonconformities should not halt the certification process; you may get the certificate and then fix the issues. But major nonconformities will at least pause the process. For the nonconformities, you will get a deadline to provide either a plan on how you will fix those (minor nonconformities) or evidence that you have fixed them (major nonconformities). The evidence of planned fixes will be checked in subsequent surveillance audits.

After all issues have been handled to the providers' satisfaction, there may still be a delay in getting the actual certificate as your case travels through the internal checks needed at the certification provider. Even after the certificate is signed, it may still take a few weeks for you to get a copy in digital or physical form, and not just in the time of a worldwide pandemic.

28.2 Decisions before Diving into Certification

The conversation on certification within your organization should be quite straightforward: you will want to do it if you can afford it, and if you can't, you might be aiming at the wrong business. But there are a number of real-world factors to figure out when making the arrangements for certification.

28.2.1 What Do You Certify?

You already defined the scope of your QMS in your quality manual (see Section 5). The scope defined there, along with any exclusions you made on the clauses of the standard that apply to you, is what you will want to get certified here. A further detail to think about is the number of locations you will want the certificate to cover. Expect every location you specify to add another audit to the to-do list. Also, your device type and head count may matter here and add time to any audits you will have. Check with your certification provider on your particulars.

We had two separate locations from the start and a Class IIb medical device in our sights, so for us, certification was a plunge in at the deeper end of the pool. Some types of low-risk devices, on the other hand, may not require you to get your QMS certified at all (such as basic Class I devices in the EU), but you may still be required to maintain a QMS matching the requirements of the standard. Some certification providers may also have new services available to help you assess the status of your uncertified QMS and give you more peace of mind in case your regulatory authorities later decide to come inspect you and expect to see ISO 13485–compatible documentation.

In the very first lesson in this book, we discussed how there is no universal QMS that would apply to all types of manufacturers; similarly, the type of the manufacturer's operations also affects the amount of work necessary in, for example, looking at your risk management activities. This is as it should be, but realize that arranging the certification audits is more like going to the barbershop with your present hairdo and asking for a totally different haircut than going to a restaurant and asking for the soup of the day. The amount of work will vary for the same list item, and so will the price.

28.2.2 When Should You Have the Certification Audits?

Your schedule for when you would like the audit(s) done depends on the maturity of your operations. If you haven't yet performed your first internal audit and management review, and don't have the reports form these, you probably should wait a little before agreeing on the audit dates.

You will also need a fair bit of coin to go into certification, particularly after the steep price increases caused by the EU MDR if you are based in Europe. It is not going to be prohibitively expensive, but for a startup being asked to pay in the range of 10,000–20,000 euros (about the same in dollars) may cause gray hairs in budgeting—and this is just for year one. You will, of course, spend more time and money in setting up that QMS before any audits take place.

Also note that the timing of your audit greatly depends on the availability of your certification body, particularly if that body is also a notified body. The bottleneck in this availability was at its worst when we set out in 2018: the oncoming switch from directives to regulations in the EU and the recently revised standard itself meant that many certification providers were effectively dropping out of the race for us, and some of them couldn't yet handle the then new version of the standard. This brings us to the next topic of how to start the discussion with your potential certification bodies.

28.3 How to Open the Conversation?

Toward the end of the first six months of our QMS project, I contacted several notified bodies to inquire about obtaining a certificate for our QMS.

The transition from the Medical Device Directive (MDD) to the Medical Device Regulation (MDR) in the EU was only two years off at this point, and that caused great uncertainty regarding the availability of notified bodies. I established discussions with half-a-dozen reputable notified bodies, choosing only those I could be reasonably sure of making the transition to MDR later. A few notified bodies threw their towel in at that point regarding MDR and, thus, were out of the race. I also contacted a certification body that was not a notified body to understand how the process could work with them even though they could not help us with the EC conformity assessment for our product. A further factor was that the ISO 13485 standard had recently been updated to the 2016 version and not everyone was yet accredited to perform audits to that version of the standard.

During this process, I talked to all the big notified bodies with three-letter names and a few of them with even longer names. Overall, I was impressed by how responsive most of them were to questions and discussion. Although I did not seek and would not expect consultation on the content of the QMS from any of them, the discussion on how the audits could proceed and what documents should be available and when was both professional and courteous. The difficult part of the equation, as if the uncertain availability discussed earlier was not enough, was knowing exactly when we would ourselves be ready to be audited. At the beginning of the conversation, we had not yet launched our QMS, and after launch, we were still in the progress of creating various records, some more critical than others. Securing even an offer from the certification providers required having a very good idea of the time frame, and even then, getting a quote was a matter of months and not days.

In the end, after a great deal of diplomatic back and forth, we received offers from a number of certification providers that could perform the necessary audits and potentially provide us with a certificate on our QMS. We were extremely satisfied to get several offers, which, considering the circumstances, was a great result that went far above the worst-case scenario of zero offers. After choosing our certification provider, the conversation then continued to how and when the certification could take place. The later stages of the certification process where even delayed because of the COVID-19 pandemic, which just goes to show that you make the best of plans and then God laughs at your plans. Luckily, what matters is that you have your windshield wipers on and are looking ahead.

The answer here is to open the dialogue as soon as you can. This was true when we got started, and it is still true today, as the certification providers continue to see both increased demand for their services and increased demands on them by the regulations.

28.4 What Is Needed before Certification?

Some weeks before the actual audit, you will be asked to provide a pre-audit package containing the quality manual, the SOPs, and the internal audit report and the management review report as key records. You may be asked for additional documents and records, but the previous items are the major ones you will most likely need.

For the actual audit, you will need to have access to these documents in your QMS but also have other records available based on what the audit agenda will cover. Depending on how mature your QMS is, you may have records of every process defined in it running, but if you are just getting started, some records may still be missing. If the missing records are crucial, say subcontractor evaluations of existing subcontractors, you may be in trouble, but if they are less critical and can be expected to be created as your operations get going fully, you may be all right.

28.5 What Happens during a Certification Audit?

The certification audit is much like other external audits already covered in Section 26.3.2. An initial certification audit covers the whole standard as it applies to your organization, and therefore, it is necessarily an audit in breadth more so than in depth. The subsequent annual certification surveillance audits will then focus more on individual aspects of the standard and drill down deeper into those processes. For more discussion of audits, see Section 26.3.2.

28.6 What Do You Do after Getting a Certificate?

After you have announced the joyous occasion to the world in the form of a press release or a news story distributed through your own channels, and drunk all the champagne, it will be time to keep calm and carry on. You will now have a QMS in place that meets the requirements, but it is your job to keep it that way and head toward an ever-improved state of operation in the future. You will also see the next announced audit loom in the future, probably less than 12 months away from where you are, and there is now also the prospect of an unannounced audit.

Talk to your certification provider and ask them to explain the certification cycle to you if they haven't already. This way, you will also be able to gauge their approach to arranging new audits, informing you about any changes in their processes or pricing and about giving you advance warning of announced audits. Most likely, the offers you received on certification already detailed the three-year cycle and the costs involved in maintaining the certificate over the next few years. At the end of the cycle, you will go through a QMS-wide recertification audit to renew the certificate, but until then, you will undergo lighter annual surveillance audits (also known as maintenance audits) and at least one unannounced audit. The surveillance audits will only sample your QMS as the certification provider sees fit. You will see the processes covered in each audit in the audit agenda given to you.

Note that ISO 13485 training is also available for individuals. I have taken courses on, for example, carrying out internal audits based on the standard, and there are also full auditor training courses where passing an exam earns you a personal certificate. These trainings may be a good way of learning more about the standard and how your organization may use it to its fullest.

Chapter 29

Business as Usual

After your QMS is launched, trained, and maybe even certified, you can take a deep breath and perhaps finish that bottle of champagne you opened up at launch, but it's still no time to drop the ball and rest on your laurels. The launch is just another start, albeit a very positive one.

At the beginning of this book, Section 3 introduced you to the top 25 lessons to know before getting started with your QMS development project. Out of those lessons, one is now topical if you think you are finished with the project: namely, that your QMS will never be fully done.

At my high school graduation decades ago, our principal spoke of life-long learning and made it sound like a life sentence, and that nothing we had learned up to that point was enough. She meant it in a positive sense, and I took it that way too. At the time, the scientific world still thought that humans are born with some set of neurons in the brain and that number will only decrease thereafter. From this point of view, the idea that high school had only prepared us for more learning while our brain cells were dying all the time did sound vaguely daunting. Luckily, the scientific community has since learned of its error, and just as new neurons are born all the time so are new ideas and reflections on old ideas. This is true for QMS also: nothing in QMS is static, and every status quo can be improved upon in some way.

This is the philosophy upon which I continue to run our QMS. If a process is not broken, don't fix it, but you can maybe learn why it works and apply those lessons to other processes too. You won't want to overhaul your processes with any big strokes just to try a new idea, but you can always pilot some new idea, perhaps simulate it, and then if it still looks worth

DOI: 10.4324/9781003202868-29

implementing, go for it as part of your whole QMS. Simulating will always be easier than implementing a change and then perhaps rolling back that change. The standard, too, gives you a free pass on simulations, which it does not mention, as long as these do not affect your QMS except through the definite actions taken based on them at the end and implemented in accordance with your change controls.

After finishing version 1.0 of your QMS, it is time to graduate to running that QMS in the real world. In your QMS, you will have defined several processes that need to run without interruption and produce the instructed records too. Your engine may now be running, but it will perhaps feel like you still don't have too many records of its output. Now is the time to start changing that. You will already have records from your QMS training, management review, internal audit, and perhaps also external audits and certification. Make sure you process all these appropriately, following your own instructed processes.

It is also time to make a plan for your future audits and your next document review, if you don't yet have these. Running the document review for the first time may seem artificial as you have already poured your heart and soul into the quality manual and SOPs over the past months, but you should get the periodic cycle turning fairly soon. You may give yourself a little time to breath here before starting the cycle if you do have many other things to ramp up at the moment and if you think the documents are working nicely at the moment. The review will form a key piece or even the backbone of your QMS improvement activities for the years to come, so it is worth getting that rolling sooner rather than later.

You will also have several other processes to ramp up, not all of which you will have fully run during the development of the QMS. For example, your product realization process will probably still be heading toward the first release of your product, and subsequently, the post-market surveillance process is probably still more of a concept than a firm part of reality. All these processes you will need to get off the ground and make sure they are producing the outputs needed of them.

At the beginning, if you must err, err on the side of documenting a little too much rather than much too little. You can review your processes over time to streamline them, but it will be impossible to retroactively create missing records. That said, don't panic and cover-up if you realize a mistake was made: review the situation, find its cause (not who did it but why it happened), plan how to fix this situation and how to prevent it from happening again, and go from there. If the omission is bad enough, raise the necessary red flags and act accordingly, of course, but if it is a minor thing short of that, then just take it as a call to improve without undue delay. That's quality management, and after a while, you will hopefully discover that the mistakes get smaller and smaller, and your QMS is running along like a well-oiled machine.

29.1 Tools to Help You

In setting up your QMS, you will have at least selected a software tool to act as your platform for QMS activities. This tool should make sticking to your processes easier and greatly assist you in gathering and interacting with the necessary records. In addition to the QMS software, there is a range of other tools that should come in handy as you are turning the wheels of your QMS. Many tools will be specific to the way you plan and execute your projects, keep track of your budget and contracts, write code, or maintain machinery. Other tools are specific to the needs of quality and regulatory affairs.

Of the tools that might help you from the beginning of your QMS activities here, I would recommend DocuSign for digital signatures (they also have a US CFR 21 Part 11–compliant add-on for dealing with the FDA and the US requirements); BSI's Compliance Navigator for insight on standards and regulations; the device classification wizard by Lean Entries; and the versatile QAiRA tool by Kasve that, among other helpful tasks, helps monitor medical device standards and regulations, assess essential device requirements, and conduct internal ISO 13485 audits. In the interest of full disclosure, I have been involved in the development of the QAiRA tool, so it matches with my views and needs regarding medical device development in the context set out by the standard. Also, the various device and device experience databases maintained by the FDA have proved valuable as free resources to access, whether you would call these "tools".

In addition, I would recommend signing on to receive newsletters from the FDA, your certification body (or notified body), and your regulatory authorities (e.g., competent authority). Many of these organizations also offer training courses you can check out. Similarly, the training provided by various universities and other organizations online via initiatives, such as edX and Coursera may offer you valuable information you can make use of.

In addition to the previous items, this book will have given you several useful paper-based tools for organizing your information and workflows that will be practical as you run and gradually improve your QMS. Particularly, the multiple checklists provided should prove useful also over the long term.

Finally, as some of the previous tools are actually channels of information to keep you up-to-date, I should add that a lot of good information is flowing online, but more so on LinkedIn than on any specific webpage. To see what sources I have found worth following, feel free to check out my LinkedIn page (look for Ilkka Juuso) and even add me as a connection to liven up your feed with good tips and tidbits of news from me and the industry professionals I follow.

29.2 Constant Improvement

Once you find that everything is running as required, you can take a considered look at what to do next. Constant improvement is a part of the QMS, so don't plan on growing moss anytime soon. Constant improvement is a nice idea, but to avoid change for the sake of change, you must have a plan and an aim. So where should you focus then?

You will have a whole host of ideas on how to improve your QMS from the experience you are building by running it. You will also probably have ideas on how your organization's product portfolio may evolve over the coming years, and this may also involve new geographic expansions that come with new applicable regulatory requirements too. All this will instruct how you will want to develop your QMS further. Think about your needs now, think about what they could be in the near future, and make a road map for improvement. Draw it on a napkin or record it as a survey in your QMS—it does not have to be a hard plan until you are ready for it to become one. Even in the strictly regulated world of QMS, it is good to look ahead and make up scenarios and plans you could execute. Just because you document something in your QMS doesn't mean that you must do it but only if you document it as a survey or an option, and not as your standard operating procedure. Just like in the real world, the QMS, too, recognizes the difference between "must" and "could", just like Clause 0 of the standard pointed out.

The last piece of advice I would venture here is that a QMS is about maintaining quality, for sure, but it is also about maintaining your organization's competitive edge in doing that. Trying to do more and more things will probably mean that you do those things in ways that are not only increasingly shallow but also increasingly inefficient. Instead of always looking to add more to the processes, I would think hard about what is frivolous in them and how I could make any given process faster and safer to run without sacrificing on any critical output.

In this vein, you should also approach internal audits, external audits, and management reviews as not just occasions for discovering things you have not done but also occasions for identifying things that really were not that useful to do. Any company will look to save money on these activities, but in my view, the real cost savings come from the outcomes of the streamlining activities and not from the bill you pay for the streamlining activities themselves. For this reason, I expect I will always look to bring in new perspectives and outside voices to such activities also beyond audits.

Chapter 30

What to Know When You Are Up and Running

Now that we have covered the whole QMS and you have a grasp of every important aspect to running that QMS, it's time to look at a few last lessons to maybe consider in the present situation. This list is more philosophical and not as comprehensive as the list of lessons at the beginning of this book, but I hope you will also get some utility out of these observations.

30.1 It's a Lifestyle, but It's Not a Free-Hippie Thing

QMS is about quality. It is about safety. It is about performance. But it is also about competitive advantage in streamlining your operations so that your organization itself is a well-oiled machine. In fact, as an organization, your QMS is probably your most important strategic decision for gaining competitive advantage aside from R&D and blind luck. As a startup, the choices you make in shaping your QMS now will be among the most important design choices you will make, certainly for the first few years at least.

It is an easy mistake to think that the less time you spend on building or refining your QMS, the better you are at quality management. Don't fiddle with things constantly as this would only make it harder for your staff to learn the processes or for any uniform way of doing things to emerge. Find your course, stick to it as best you can, but realize that spending a few extra days on planning any subsequent course correction will save you from at least as many days running around after a fumbled course correction in

DOI: 10.4324/9781003202868-30

some process. Appropriate planning will not only steady the ship, but it will keep it from floundering due to an own goal.

For the impatient manager, it may seem like the few additional days could have been spent on something else, but depending on the changes you ended up making (or not making), you may have saved weeks or months of combined effort over your entire staff and the longer time span the process is run. Trust me, I am always conscious, perhaps occasionally too conscious, of wasting other people's time so that in company-wide meetings, I have a tendency to be conscious of the cost of the combined time everyone is there for and try to be very efficient in how I use that time. Occasionally, "wasting time" to build team spirit is very much needed, so you shouldn't get too uptight about the cost of time. Where this line of thinking is always warranted is in thinking about how often some process will be run at your organization and how any improvements in efficiency will be multiplied over time. You must think about quality, safety, and performance in terms of product and patient benefit first, but after that, you should also consider operational performance. This will not just lead to a safer and more efficient process that is better liked at your organization but also a genuine competitive advantage, as your organization is able to perform its tasks and achieve its goals more efficiently. Quality is not a one-way street, and it definitely is not just the cost of ticking some abstract box.

30.2 Listen to Everything, but Don't Believe Just Anything

If you are now setting out into the world of QMS, you are bound to hear a lot of stories, theories, and pitches. Some of these will offer valuable insight to you, but not all fishing tales are based on real fish. Don't try to memorize all the individual examples and exceptions you hear and then take account of these in your QMS. You will be optimizing your QMS to noise. Instead, try to discern the patterns behind those anecdotes on what matters to whom and why—particularly as it comes to how your stakeholders think and operate. Read the standards, regulations, and guidance yourself; understand what you read; and distill the information to the core aims behind the requirements as they apply to you. That is the only way you will not go crazy trying to make sense out of the signposts.

In the same vein, see the obvious, but find the flip side too. Every challenge is also an opportunity. Every competitor is also a possible customer.

When you are trying to make heads or tails out of something, it often helps to realize that the issue probably has more than one correct answer. The first answer you hear or come up with may be the best or it may just be the most banal.

30.3 Everything Is Always an Evolution, Not a Revolution

If you are in Europe, you will have heard years' worth of talk on the new Medical Device Regulations and how everything will be completely different and so much harder and more expensive after the date of application. Similarly, the uncertain regulation of artificial intelligence technology continues to be a hot topic around the world. While some pundits prophesize for a seismic shift that opens the bullpen, others have been moving the needle in that direction in some discernible increments.

There is little of revolution in anything, but evolution is the way to push the envelope. That type of change is also safer and more controllable than a seismic shift. The point is not to get debilitated by waiting for change to happen but to work toward preparing for change within the accepted space. The cliché says that most people overestimate what they will be able to do over a long period of time and underestimate what they can do over a short one. The cliché happens to be true and, for a forward-looking QMS, almost equivalent to an epiphany.

30.4 Things Will Go Wrong Occasionally; What You Then Do Makes All the Difference

No matter how hard you try to prevent it, things will occasionally go wrong. A check you wanted done is forgotten, a plan you made wasn't followed to a tee, or someone just forgot to do something they were supposed to. Don't hide this; don't gloss over it. What really matters here is that the error gets corrected, and any additional issues caused by the error also get noticed and corrected.

Figure out who will be surprised by the deficiency and discuss with them on how to proceed. The nice thing is that the QMS is built out of processes with inputs and outputs that you should be able to use in figuring out who is affected. Product traceability also exists so that it will be useful here.

Convene the group; figure out what should have been done, why it wasn't done, what was done instead, and how the outcome differs from what was intended. Assess the need to rectify things, make a plan for the rectification, and proceed from there.

In many cases, it is the Quality Management Team, or the Management Team, who will be involved in deciding what to do and how. In a large established organization, you may have specific procedures in place to fix the deficiency in question, but in a smaller organization, the most important thing is to get the right people together to analyze the situation and agree on a remedy. Don't be afraid of invoking the nonconformity handling process either; that's what it is there for.

30.5 Don't Fear Nonconformities and Negative Feedback

Nonconformities will seem like the boogeyman when you are setting out to develop your QMS, but as Section 3.18 argued, they are more like seeds for improvement. They are, of course, seeds with an expiration date; after which, they will become toxic to you if not met, but if you attend to them swiftly, the outcome for your QMS will be positive.

You will get nonconformities from one audit or another. The nonconformities will be minor or major, and you will need to address them to plan and implement the correct immediate corrections (if needed), corrective actions, and preventive actions. The good news is that you will most likely have several days to plan how you address the issues. Take this time to make a careful and considered look into what the nonconformity says and how it should be fixed. Unless something really has hit the fan, you won't get additional points for speed here.

Customer feedback, too, will probably be more negative than positive just on account of how likely users are to take the time to provide feedback on how wonderful something was versus how badly it sucks in their view. Take all the feedback seriously. Even the feedback that sounds dumb or hostile may have a nugget of truth within it and something that you can, again, choose to use in improving your product and processes.

Before my present gig, I dabbled in selling websites and online apps to a wide range of SMEs. During the 13-plus years, I received the whole spectrum of feedback from customers, ranging from jubilant words of unexpected praise to a drunken call where life itself was in the wrong. The overwhelming majority of the feedback was positive, but every once in a while,

I did receive genuine complaints. With most of the customer encounters, the most important thing was that you listened to the customer. Being able to air their grievance, however warranted or not, was already a part of the fix itself. The ability to then come up with immediate corrections and perhaps corrective actions came as an important second task.

The important thing here is that if you really try to do things correctly and are making progress along the right path, not only will you get less nonconformities and other issues, but the ones you do get will be less serious. Nonconformities and negative feedback are a part of life; don't look to get them, but expect to get them sooner or later.

30.6 Beware of Lone-Wolf Activities

No one should audit their own work. The requirement for that is written into the standard clearly, but separation of powers and a second pair of eyes are also a fundamental expectation in just about everything in the standard. Just think about how many good films you have seen that have been written, directed, produced, and starred by the same person. Vincent Gallo's *The Brown Bunny* comes to my mind, but that is not exactly a good movie. The lesson here is that something done by someone alone is a prime suspect for unnecessary and/or underperforming activity.

The outcome of such activity may not be needed, it may not be checked to hold water, and it may not lead to anything else. In a startup, it will occasionally be difficult to have other people involved, but this should never be overwhelmingly difficult: mostly, it is a question of remembering to get a second opinion, as you might do with doctors. It is possible that in trying to secure that second opinion, you notice that you can save resources by not having to do the thing in the first place.

30.7 Plan, but Plan to Be Flexible

I brought this up in Section 3.21, but it is worth repeating here: plan your schedule for maintaining your QMS, but build in flexibility with the knowledge that not all things have to happen at equally strictly defined points in time. This is especially important to realize when you are now getting going with your QMS. Trying to be unnecessarily rigid will mean you miss out on some quality benefit.

30.8 Arrange Time to Read Uninterrupted

If you are in charge of your organization's QMS, everyone is expecting you to always have an answer on everything. Regardless of whether the question is what the process is for this or that thing under the QMS, or what impact any upcoming change in regulations or standards will have on your QMS. It is good that your staff and your management come to you with their questions, but to be able to answer these far-flung questions, you will have to keep digesting a lot of new information from many different sources all the time. A lot more effort goes into this than just standing there listening to the question and opening your mouth.

To do the required background work, you will be reading a lot of information and tracking a lot of different sources all the time. Make time for this in your schedule to secure interrupted studying time every once in a while. My personal favorite before the pandemic was to catch up on my reading while traveling. It is a one-hour flight from where I live to the capital where many of the standardization and regulatory follow-up meetings I participate in take place, and that flight has been a perfect opportunity to carefully read some new guidance paper or a draft standard that has come out and could affect our company. Similarly, the time spent sitting at the airport is a good opportunity for some off-the-grid working time. At times, you are, of course, too busy to be looking at what's ahead in any great detail, but I find that having at least some time available to read and digest is necessary for both doing my work and feeling good about my work.

30.9 Think about Your Audience

By far the most important question I always ask myself on any topic is why this matters to me. That simple question is the jumping-off point for just about any question you are asked to answer. The second most important question is why it should matter to your audience, particularly if you are the one with an agenda.

Answering the why question is the subject of many a book offering business advice, and it can also become an infuriatingly debilitating prospect in the wrong hands, but for most questions, it is the key to the answer. This applies to when you are attempting to give your staff context on some aspect of their work that has requirements from your QMS and equally also when your CEO or other manager comes to ask why some activity was done a certain way or why it is taking more than 15 minutes to do. Knowing what they want to hear will help you shape your message, but you shouldn't, of course, just tell everyone the yes or no they want to hear. For this reason, I have relished the opportunity to draft our news stories from the beginning of our life as a startup company: it is both intriguing and insightful to try and step into the other guy's shoes.

The point here is that you should address your audiences on the terms that they accept and expect. Don't be an idiot and write memos to your staff because they are required to read them; instead, write the memos (and any other communication) in a way that the reader can relate to. I may not always have succeeded in this, but at least, I always try.

30.10 Be Creative in Raising Awareness for Your QMS

At my companies, we have been successful in using news to both raise outside awareness for some new thing we have achieved and to also keep our own people up-to-date on everything that is going on in a way that lets them appreciate what they, too, have achieved. The news, thus, serves a purpose of not only informing but appreciating achievements and achieved milestones. It is a welcome pat on the back as well as a raised hand saying, "Look at our organization". This internal satisfaction was not a factor I planned on beforehand, but it is a factor we noticed very early on.

The same applies to QMS as well. When you first obtain a certificate for your QMS, you will want to make a press release about the happy occasion. Your potential customers will hopefully take note of this, realize that they can now rely on you to operate based on the standard, and use that to alleviate any apprehensions they might have about working with you. Equally importantly, making a splash with the news stories will let your team take pride in the accomplishment, maybe tick something off mentally from their to-do list for good, and lower their stress levels in general. For QMS matters, the news does not always have to be published on your website or made into a distributed press release. Publishing a periodic or as-needed newsletter to your staff may be just the right tool to keep QMS on everyone's minds and raise awareness for some strategic issue or accomplishment.

30.11 The Supreme Court of Your QMS Is You, Sort Of

This lesson was much too dangerous and almost heretic in nature to include in Section 3, but now that you have gone through designing your QMS and are thinking about how to best manage it going forward, it is time to bring this up. You are subject to regulations, which you must follow. The standard, too, places requirements on you, which are exacted through the certification body or the notified body. All these actors are in a position to dictate requirements to you. However, the arbiter of those requirements is you. Even in the theoretical case that you get bad advice from your auditor, it is you who will suffer and will have to turn it around so that the benefits of your product do not suffer and the risks involved in its use don't unnecessarily increase.

You are the best authority on the entirety of your QMS and how the different requirements affect it. If you can argue to yourself honestly and without wavering that a certain design choice should be made, the decision will most likely hold water also when inspected by auditors. Use this realization to give you peace of mind and certainty in knowing your own pockets, especially when figuring out what to put into those pockets, but don't use it as a call to do as you please without concern for others. You are the director of the QMS, the auditors represent those who control the cinema chains, your distributors are the cinema chains, and your patients and users are, naturally, the patrons of the establishments. You will want to listen and understand them all.

In going through the exercise of creating your own QMS and running it for a while, you will have learned a huge amount of new information, and the information can be empowering. It should be that. But as much as you know and as many things as you have gotten right, know that the world is in constant change and new things will always come up. Don't turn a blind eye to this change just because you think you know better.

Chapter 31

Conclusion

Congratulations! You have now gone through everything you need to do to set up and maintain your quality management system according to the ISO 13485 standard. You will have sketched out the way of life for your medical device organization for the years to come and figured out what steps along the way matter the most and what areas could perhaps be streamlined to improve both safety and performance. The QMS you have built following the principles set out in this book will hopefully set you up for running your QMS efficiently and ensuring it remains suitable, adequate, and effective in the long run.

In learning all that new information during this development project, if I have written this book well enough, you will not just have learned individual pieces of information, but you have also seen a glimpse of the Matrix behind all that information. This understanding of the fabric of QMS comes with the superpower of being able to fit new things into that network and to even predict some events and reactions in the quality community and the regulatory landscape around it—or at least, the superpower of convincing yourself you can do that.

In going through the sections of this book, you will have realized that the Dunning-Kruger effect really has no place in quality management—the more you know, the more you know you know. This is no time to get arrogant, of course—there are always those Rumsfeldian unknown unknowns, for example. However, if you subscribe to the principle that doing less is in fact the surest way of doing those things better, you will eventually arrive at a lean set of base process descriptions that let your organization realize the patient benefit it set out to achieve as efficiently and reliably as possible.

DOI: 10.4324/9781003202868-31

Lean does not have to be mean—in fact, to succeed, it shouldn't be that. A mean process is one prone to cutting corners and neglect at every turn. A lean process, on the other hand, is easier to learn and easier to follow, and it provides the expected outcome more reliably and with less resources.

Probably nothing I did in developing our QMS was all that extraordinary in the end, but it did require long hours, long days, and long weeks with a lot of effort spent in focusing on what was really the objective in any specific subprocess of the QMS and streamlining or connecting dots to create a QMS that not only fulfilled the requirements but was also feasible to run with the resources I could count on us having. The QMS we have as a result meets the requirements, is certified, and is a great deal more streamlined than it could easily have been. No doubt more streamlining, improvement, and optimization will take place as we go forward—in fact, that is required by the standard—but the system we now have more than does its job.

If you have gleaned some insight from the pages of this book, or if the book has given you new questions or ideas, please let me know. Feel free to contact me via e-mail or LinkedIn and share your comments. I would love to hear from you. The biggest lesson for me over the 20-some years I spent at the university, and reinforced by my experience in regulatory and quality affairs in a medical device startup, is that if we share, we learn. I am always interested in both.

Thank you for reading my book. I hope to hear from you.

Appendices

Appendix 1

Terms and Definitions

The following list provides an overview of terms introduced in ISO 9000 and ISO 13485, and those with a changed meaning in between. The classification of terms into thematic groups is based on ISO 9000. The counts given in brackets refer to basic text string occurrence counts from ISO 13485 and are included here as an indication of the continued relevance of each term.

Some terms have a changed meaning in ISO 13485 as compared with ISO 9000 (marked with a single asterisk in case the standard makes a mention of this and a double asterisk if the change is not mentioned in the standard).

Terms from ISO 9000

Person or people: Top management (13), Quality management system consultant (-), Involvement (-), Engagement (-), Configuration authority (-), Dispute resolver (-). **Organization:** Organization (217), Context of the organization (2, in annexes), Interested party (2, in annexes), Customer (51), Provider (5, in annexes, replaced by "supplier"), External provider (5, in annexes), DRP-provider (-), Association (4), always used in the sense of the "European Free Trade Association"), Metrological function (-). **Activity:** Improvement (25), Continual improvement (3, in annexes), Management (235), Quality management (147), Quality planning (-), Quality assurance (-), Quality control (-), Quality improvement (-), Configuration management (-), Change control (-), Activity (5), Project management (-), Configuration object (-). **Process:** Process (147), Project (-), Quality management system realization (-), Competence acquisition (-), Procedure (59), Outsource (3), Contract (6), Design and development (99). **System:** System (214), Infrastructure (12), Management system (150), Quality management system (140), Work environment (17), Metrological confirmation (-), Measurement management system (2, in references), Policy (21), Quality policy (16), Vision (-), Mission (-), Strategy (-). **Requirement:** Object (-), Quality (253), Grade (-), Requirement (365), Quality requirement (-), Statutory require-ment (-), Regulatory requirement (69), Product configuration information (-), Nonconformity (7), Defect (-), Conformity (48), Capability (3), Traceability (15), Dependability (-), Innovation (-). **Results:** Objective (17), Quality objec-tive (15), Success (-), Sustained success (-), Output (35), Product* (254), Service (61), Performance (35), Risk* (95), Efficiency (-), Effectiveness (18). **Data, information and document:** Data (18), Information (56), Objective evidence (-), Information system (2), Document** (243), Documented infor-mation (6, in annexes), Specification (10), Quality manual (9), Quality plan (3, in annexes), Record (96), Project management plan (-), Verification (34), Validation (46), Configuration status accounting (-), Specific case (-). **Customer:** Feedback (14), Customer satisfaction (3, in annexes), Complaint* (20), Customer service(-), Customer satisfaction code of conduct (-), Dispute (1, not relevant). **Characteristic:** Characteristic (13), Quality characteristic (-), Human factor (-), Competence (7), Metrological characteristic (-), Configuration (-), Configuration baseline (-). **Determination:** Determination (11), Review (69), Monitoring (50), Measurement (50), Measurement process (2, in refer-ences), Measuring equipment (11), Inspection (5), Test (31), Progress evalua-tion (-). **Action:** Preventive action (9), Corrective action (29), Correction (4), Regrade (-), Concession (6), Deviation permit (-), Release (14), Rework (6), Repair (1, in a note), Scrap (-). **Audit:** Audit (48), Combined audit (-), Joint audit (-), Audit programme (-), Audit scope (-), Audit plan (-), Audit criteria (1), Audit evidence (-), Audit findings (-), Audit conclusion (-), Audit client (-), Auditee (-), Guide (-), Audit team (-), Auditor (2), Technical expert (-), Observer (-).

Terms from ISO 13485

The terms introduced by the newer standard are: "advisory notice", "autho-rized representative", "clinical evaluation", "distributor", "implantable medical device", "importer", "labelling", "life-cycle", "manufacturer", "medical device", "medical device family", "performance evaluation", "post-market surveil-lance", "purchased product", "risk management", "sterile barrier system", and "sterile medical device". If you need to refer to definition of any of these terms, you will find the definitions in the ISO 13485 standard.

Terms with Changed Meaning from ISO 9000 to ISO 13485

In addition to the new terms introduced by the ISO 13485 standard, the standard also changes the definition of a few terms originally introduced in the ISO 9000 standard. These terms are "product" (254), "risk" (254), and "complaint" (20). In addition, although not flagged up by the standard in any way, I would suggest that the definition of "document" has silently evolved in ISO 13485 from a document-like object (ISO 9000) to what is meant by "documented information" in ISO 9000. See Section 4.4.8 for discussion.

Appendix 2

Quality Manual Template

Header and footer (including document name, ID, version, and page numbers)

Document record (e.g.)

DOCUMENT INFORMATION

Document name	Quality Manual		
Document ID	123456789		
Responsible person	Raymond Babbitt		
Date	YYYY-MM-DD		
Audience	Quality management and R&D		

Authorities	Written by	Reviewed by	Approved by
Authority	Quality manager	Management representative	Management representative
Name	Raymond Babbitt	Charles Babbitt	Charles Babbitt
Signature	*Note: In place of handwritten signatures, this document may be signed electronically by each signee within the QMS software.*		
Date	YYYY-MM-DD	YYYY-MM-DD	YYYY-MM-DD

Table of Contents

A) **Purpose of the document** (including why this document exists)

B) **Organization overview** (including information about the organization, its identified role in medical devices, the type of products manufactured, and basic organizational structure of the organization)

C) **QMS overview** (including the scope of the QMS, rationale for any exclusions, quality policy, quality objectives, structure of QMS documents, and document management principles)

D) **Key roles** (including definition of top management and key roles, such as the management representative and the quality manager)

E) **Products** (including any generic definitions on device lifetime, product version numbering, etc.)

F) **Processes** (including an overview of the processes defined by the organization, their interrelationships, identification of any critical or prioritized processes, and mapping of the processes to the clauses of the standard)

G) **References** (if any)

H) **Appendices** (including staff responsibilities and qualifications by role, quality objectives, and inter-process relationships)

I) **Version history** (e.g.)

Version	Date	Initials	Description of changes (including section numbers)
1.0	YYYY-MM-DD	SR	First version of the document.

Appendix 3

Standard Operating Procedure Template

Header and footer (including document name, ID, version, and page numbers)

Document record (e.g.)

DOCUMENT INFORMATION

Document name	**SOP for Sheltering during the Monsoon**
Document ID	123456789
Responsible person	Raymond Babbitt
Date	YYYY-MM-DD
Audience	Quality management and R&D

Authorities	Written by	Reviewed by	Approved by
Authority	Quality manager	Management representative	Management representative
Name	Raymond Babbitt	Charles Babbitt	Charles Babbitt
Signature	*Note: In place of handwritten signatures this document may be signed electronically by each signee within the QMS software.*		
Date	YYYY-MM-DD	YYYY-MM-DD	YYYY-MM-DD

Table of Contents

A) Purpose of the document

This is the SOP for the appropriate behavior to take during a monsoon when you want to find shelter.

B) Associated SOPs (e.g.)

ID	Document
SOP-1	QMS documentation
SOP-2	CAPA, monitoring, and improvement

C) Instructed documents (e.g.)

ID	Document
TMP-1	Template report
TMP-2	Template assessment form

D) The process

The actual content goes here. Use subheadings as appropriate to structure the discussion here.

E) Responsibilities (e.g.)

Role	Task
Quality manager	Prepare the activity and prepare the report.
Management representative	Review and approve the report.

F) References (if any)

ID	Document
ISO 13485:2016	Medical devices—quality management systems—Requirements for regulatory purposes
ISO 14971:2019	Medical devices—application of risk management to medical devices

G) Appendices (if any)

ID	Document
Appendix 1	Factors to consider during a monsoon
Appendix 2	Assessing the severity of a monsoon

H) Version history (e.g.)

Version	Date	Initials	Description of changes (including section numbers)
1.0	YYYY-MM-DD	SR	First version of the document.

Appendix 4

Meeting Minutes

Meeting of the Quality Management Team—1
Time: DD.MM.YYYY at HH:MM—HH:MM
Place: X (or online using platform Y)
Present: Person A (quality manager and chairman), Person B (secretary), and Person C

1. Opening of the meeting
- The chairman opened the meeting at HH:MM. The whole team was noted as present and the meeting as having reached quorum.

2. Approval of the agenda
- It was noted that the agenda for the meeting had been delivered to all participants ahead of the meeting. No changes to the agenda were requested. The agenda was approved for the meeting.

3. Approval of previous minutes
- The minutes of the previous meeting were delivered to all participants after the meeting, signed, and now noted as approved here.

4. Reports
- 4.1 Operational status
- 4.2 Monitoring and measurement
- 4.3 Customer feedback
- 4.4 Audits
- 4.5 CAPA and observations
- 4.6 Risk management
- 4.7 Assessment of resources
- 4.8 Reporting to authorities and notified bodies

5. Other business / announcements
- Other content here.

6. Next meeting
- The next meeting was agreed to take place on DD.MM.YYYY at HH:MM.

7. Adjournment
- The chairman adjourned the meeting at HH:MM.

Person A   Person B   Person C

(The document is signed electronically.)

Index

Note: Page numbers in *italics* indicate a figure and page numbers in **bold** indicate a table on the corresponding page.

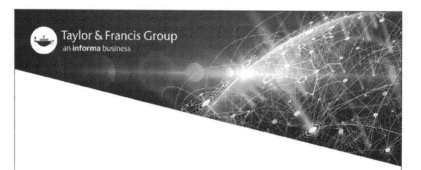

Printed in the United States
by Baker & Taylor Publisher Services